Sinda Eggerman

Personal Construct Counseling
and Psychotherapy

WILEY SERIES ON
METHODS IN PSYCHOTHERAPY

Series Editor
Boris Semeonoff
Department of Psychology
University of Edinburgh

Jungian Psychotherapy
A Study in Analytical Psychology
Michael Fordham

Lives People Live
A Textbook of Transactional Analysis
Mavis Klein

**Personal Construct Counseling
and Psychotherapy**
Franz R. Epting

Further titles in preparation

Personal Construct Counseling and Psychotherapy

FRANZ R. EPTING

University of Florida
Department of Psychology

JOHN WILEY & SONS

Chichester · New York ·Brisbane · Toronto · Singapore

Library of Congress Cataloging in Publication Data:

Epting, Franz R., 1937–
  Personal construct counseling and psychotherapy.

  (Wiley series on methods in psychotherapy)
  1. Psychotherapy.   2. Personal construct theory.
I. Title.   II. Series.   (DNLM: 1. Psychotherapy.
2. Psychological theory.   3. Counseling.   WM 420 E645p)
RC480.5.E67   1984   616.89'14   83-6913
ISBN 0 471 90169 5

British Library Cataloguing in Publication Data:

Epting, Franz R.
  Personal constsruct counseling and
  psychotherapy.—(Wiley series on methods
  in psychotherapy; 3)
  1. Personal constsruct theory
  I. Title
  144.2   BF698
  ISBN 0 471 90169 5

Phototypeset by Dobbie Typesetting Service, Plymouth Devon
Printed by The Pitman Press, Bath

To
Linda Kathleen

Contents

Editor's Preface

It is a pleasure to welcome a contribution to this series from the United States—particularly this one. Although an American by birth and early education, George Kelly had his first exposure to psychology, as his countrymen would put it, at the University of Edinburgh, and in his major work *The Psychology of Personal Constructs* he pays tribute to both James Drever, Sr., and Godfrey Thomson. Kelly's dissertation for the degree of Bachelor of Education was entitled *The Social Inheritance*, and although it contains no specific adumbration of his later teaching, one can see in it already his concern with the person and the importance he placed on the total experience of the individual. Learning is one of the time-honoured concepts of psychology that Kelly discards, viewing it rather as 'synonymous with any and all psychological processes'. Other abstractions for which Personal Construct theory has no room include ego and unconscious; nevertheless Kelly acknowledges his debt to psychoanalytic thinking, and Personal Construct psychology is dynamic in the sense that it recognizes the possibility of therapeutic change. Indeed, Kelly's major publication, already alluded to, 'started out'—to quote his own words—'as a handbook of clinical procedures'.

Personal Construct psychology, however, is primarily identified with Kelly's concept of 'Man as scientist', and this emphasis on cognition, or thinking, may perhaps reflect its author's early training in mathematics and engineering. It also finds an echo in the Transactional Analysis notion of the 'Little Professor', the aspect of the child that likes to explore, to 'get into things' and, later, ask questions. In Jung's teaching, thinking and feeling are both rational functions—opposites, but nevertheless complementary. Those who feel that contemporary concern with personal growth overemphasizes feeling may find Personal Construct Theory helpful in restoring a proper balance. That is not to say, however, that the Personal Construct therapist or counselor is indifferent to how a client feels—as Franz Epting's text amply demonstrates.

Dr Epting is fortunate to have had the opportunity to study with George Kelly at Ohio State University, and has succeeded not only in distilling the essence but also in conveying the flavour of Kelly's work and outlook. And, in common with the other contributors to this series, he has also added much that is his own.

B. SEMEONOFF

Preface

This book was undertaken to provide a relatively concise description of personal construct counseling and psychotherapy and to give an account of how personal construct therapy has been developed since its original publication by George A. Kelly in his (1955) two-volume work. Inevitably this book will reflect my own interpretation of construct theory, but I have attempted to the best of my ability to remain as close as possible to the core of Kelly's original formulation. To some extent I have condensed and rearranged the presentation of therapy issues contained in volumes one and two, as well as brought into this presentation material found in the other papers Kelly wrote on therapy between 1955 and his death in 1967. Extracts from Kelly (1955), *The Psychology of Personal Constructs, Vols. I and II*, are reprinted by permission of W. W. Norton & Co., Inc. It is hoped that the present book will interest the reader in Kelly's original formulations, inform the reader concerning more recent developments, and afford a glimpse into what the possibilities are for the further development of this way of conducting psychotherapy. It is further hoped that the book will convey, at least in part, just how useful and exciting it can be to undertake a psychotherapeutic venture from a construct therapy point of view.

The book is designed as a basic introduction for professional workers or students who may wish to involve themselves in a counseling relationship based on this theory, and for other persons who wish to inform themselves generally concerning the components of this system of therapy. The first section of the book gives a general introduction to the therapeutic enterprise and the basic theoretical terms of the theory. The middle section describes the five basic components of the therapy along with case illustrations. The last section contains a description of general techniques and special procedures dealing with construct therapy and also contains a general overview and evaluation of the total enterprise. In writing this book I have attempted to be non-sexist in the use of pronouns. My main methods were to use both he and she together in some places and in others to use either he or she in the hope of somehow balancing the frequency of use.

In writing this book I consider myself very fortunate to have had the opportunity to study with George Kelly while I was a graduate student at a stimulating and exciting graduate program at Ohio State. Without blaming this book on that graduate faculty, this book in many ways is, contextually, a product of that graduate training. More immediately and specifically, however, this book reflects the work I have done with my students here at the University of Florida over the past fifteen years. I am very grateful to Judith Isaza, Ann Howland, Jack Schaff, Betty Jenkins, Charles Hayes, Seth Krieger, Jerome Tobacyk, Evans Harrell, Katheryn Peres, Fred Eland, Larry Leitner, Carl Nickeson, Greg Neimeyer, Greg Wilkins, Peter Dingemans, Brian Lindner, Elizabeth Best, Patricia Boger, Martin Amerikaner, Louise Ousley, Carol Zempel, James Penrod, John Crum, Robert Neimeyer, Larry Rainey, Priya Neelakantan, Michael Rigdon, William Chambers, Awilda Oliver, Brian Lewis, and Charles Rubio who were as much my colleagues and teachers as I was their graduate or undergraduate advisor. We explored construct theory together. I am also very grateful to both David Suchman and Greg Neimeyer, colleagues here at the University of Florida, for their friendship and stimulating conversations about the nature of construct theory, and to Merle Meyer, for helping me to arrange and rearrange my priorities so that this book could be finished.

It must be noted further that special gratitude goes to Fay Fransella and Don Bannister who encouraged me to undertake this project, to Al Landfield for his encouragement, and to Boris Semeonoff who served as my very considerate and helpful editor. Special thanks also goes to Cecilia Bibby and Cheryl Phillips who kept asking me for the next chapter so they could get on with their typing and eventual retyping. They did a marvelous job in helping me to get the manuscript ready for publication.

Finally, I would like to thank my wife Linda for her love and support throughout this whole project and for her reminder that a book on psychology, especially therapy, is supposed to be useful and focused on the nature of everyday experiences. Her help with the manuscript and her love and support made it possible for this project to reach its completion.

Gainesville, Florida, 1982   Franz Epting

Acknowledgements

I wish to express my gratitude to the following publishers and individuals for permission to reproduce copyright material: Professor Alvin W. Landfield; Macmillan Publishers Ltd.; John Wiley and Sons, Inc., Publishers; University of Miami Press; W. W. Norton and Company, Inc.

PART I

Introduction

This first section containing Chapters One and Two is designed to 'set the stage' for the material that follows. In the first chapter a general overview and description of the therapy is undertaken. This covers the aims and objectives of the therapy, as well as a description of the role of the therapist, the role of the client and the nature of the psychotherapeutic relationship. In some respects similar to other brief accounts of personal construct construct psychotherapy (Bannister, 1975; Landfield, 1978; Patterson, 1980; Epting, 1981; Epting and Boger, 1981) the purpose of this chapter is to focus on key issues which will, it is hoped, give the reader an impression of what personal construct therapy is designed to accomplish. In the second chapter, the technical terms which form the language of a construct theory approach are presented and discussed in the context of the psychotherapeutic enterprise. This presentation covers both the terms used to describe the personality structure of clients and the terms specifically designed to help the counselor understand the nature of the psychotherapeutic process.

CHAPTER 1

General Approach to the Person and Psychotherapy

From the Personal Construct Theory point of view, psychological material is grounded in the person's own experiences. In fact this approach might be viewed as a study of personal experience. Psychotherapy is understood from the personal point of view of both the client and the therapist rather than from the viewpoint of an outsider observer of this process. Taken as a whole this book is concerned with elaborating and providing an exploration, in some detail, of psychotherapy from this point of view as George Kelly (1955) originally formulated it and as it has been modified in the clinical work and research of others. If a person, however, goes no further than this first chapter, it is hoped that there will be enough material contained within this one chapter for him to grasp the essence of what it means to take a Personal Construct approach to psychotherapy.

The Term Psychotherapy: What Does it Mean?

The term psychotherapy is used here to represent the general collection of activities that might be described as the helping relationship. This includes the professional activities of counseling and clinical psychologists, counselor educators, psychiatrists, psychiatric social workers, psychiatric nurses, rehabilitation counselors, ministerial counselors, and school counselors, to name but a few. The word psychotherapy is employed here because it is widely recognized as a term which indicates such helping relationships and not because the term itself is a particularly accurate label for the type of helping relationship presented here. In fact only the first part of this term *psychotherapy* has any real meaning for our purposes. The prefix *psycho* is meant to convey the idea that the approach taken is psychological in nature. The approach deals with the meaning the world has for an individual, which includes the way that individual transcends his or her own individuality and becomes a part of a social community. The term *therapy* refers to a concept in which less is invested than one might expect. This is because therapy often conjures up the image of a treatment that is actively administered to a rather passive recipient called the patient who, as Kelly points out, must learn to wait patiently. From the personal

3

construct point of view, psychotherapy is practically no therapy at all in that sense of the term. Instead it represents a relationship between two persons which enables the one person (referred to as the client) to actively make use of the skills and knowledge of the other person (referred to as the counselor or therapist) in order that the one person (the client) might deal more effectively and creatively with life. The purpose of this therapy is *both* understanding and effective action.

The Person in Personal Construct Therapy

Before going further into the development of Personal Construct Therapy as such, it may be wise to consider the nature of the person within this theoretical framework. A way to begin is to say that the person is a being whose nature it is to anticipate what the future holds (both long range and moment to moment) by imposing some understanding on the events of life. This understanding is represented in terms of dimensions of meaning referred to as *personal constructs*. The person is seen as operating within a system of personal construct dimensions. For any given individual there are a large number of different meaning dimensions that form various relationships with each other and carry direct implications for how the person acts, thinks, and feels.

The person in personal construct psychology is viewed as a *scientist* who builds a theory which, in fact, is his or her own personal theory. This personal theory is constantly being tested out, refined, and revised. Subsequently a decision is made, at some level of awareness, to either abandon or maintain this theory depending on the final outcome of this testing. Stating it another way is to say that every man, woman, and child, black, white, red, or yellow, is a scientist. Hypotheses are formulated about the nature of life events and these hypotheses or anticipations are tested out in the way a person goes about living his or her life.

The main job, for the professional investigator, is to understand the person in terms of these construct dimensions. This might be illustrated by the following account of a therapist attempting to understand a certain male client. Let's suppose that during several sessions the client continues to repeat the idea that one of the worst situations for him to face is having to show his appreciation to someone else after the other person has done something particularly nice for him. The therapist might begin to understand this client's construct system by grasping the idea that one of the ways his client has of managing his relationship with others is through the concept of 'showing appreciation'. At this point it should be mentioned that personal constructs are viewed as being both bi-polar and dichotomous. This means that the question is raised concerning what, for the client, is the *contrast*, in his system, of 'showing his appreciation to others'. When this is explored a bit further, it is discovered that maintaining a cool reserved stance would be his alternative in the situation and this is, for him, just the opposite of, 'showing appreciation'. One construct dimension for this fellow might then be something like 'showing your appreciation to others' versus 'remaining cool and somewhat aloof'. The question is next raised concerning what this dimension means to the client in terms of how it fits in with the rest of his construct dimensions. Upon further conversation about this topic, it is revealed that the client believes that showing your appreciation is a real sign of weakness, whereas remaining cool allows you to maintain your strength. Now the construct 'strong versus weak' has been introduced. Subsequently the client reveals that people who show their appreciation to others are weakening their position in relationship to others because it then obliges the person to return that kindness, rather than being able to maintain a freedom of manipulation and control by the other person. Yet another construct dimension of 'freedom' versus 'being obligated and manipulated by others' has been brought into the picture.

This brief description of a portion of a person's construct system illustrates just what is meant by a personal construct which is contained within an interlocking system of other constructs. A single construct gains its meaning and realizes its anticipatory values by being linked with other constructs. The counselor now beings to realize what it means for the client to show his appreciation to others. It means that he is leaving himself open to possible manipulative abuse from others and he is weakening, if not losing, his own personal freedom.

Constructs reside at various levels of abstraction. The one that we started with here, 'showing appreciation', is at a very concrete, almost behavioral level, whereas the last construct mentioned, 'being obligated versus freedom', was at a very abstract, value-oriented level. This could begin an involved discussion of the formal properties of construct systems which might be best deferred until the next chapter. For the present it is sufficient only to grasp what is being referred to when we speak of a construct system.

These constructs are the avenues down which our lives are led, or rather the avenues down which we choose to lead our own lives. There are many different things a person must deal with in life, and therefore construct meaning dimensions are designed to deal with many different things. In Personal Construct Therapy these 'things' with which we must deal are called *elements* or *events*. They can literally be anything: fur caps, garden tools, mathematical symbols, bicycle parts, interpersonal relationships, social issues, personal characteristics of one's self and others, to name but a few. Construct dimensions are employed so that the nature of these things can become known to us and the possibilities for us explored. It is quite common to find that we have somewhat different constructs for dealing with different sets of elements, nevertheless it is also a common occurrence for some constructs to be designed in such a way that they can handle a great variety of things. For example, we might find the construct 'kind–cruel' being used most commonly when dealing with interpersonal relationships or characteristics of one's self and others, but it might also be used to think about the implications of certain social issues.

In describing the nature of psychotherapy, most of our attention will be focused on constructs that are applicable to the interpersonal situation, with the elements (other people and ourselves) being collected under one of the two poles of the various construct dimensions. This is to say psychotherapy deals mainly with how a person is structuring his or her life in relationship to other people. Of course at times the array of elements becomes somewhat wider than this and might include body sensation, aspects of the physical environment and perhaps ideas about God or some ultimate Being. Throughout this discussion it is important to remember that there is a constant interplay between the elements and the construct. The one gives meaning to the other; they are like the warp and the woof of the fabric that is the personal construct approach to understanding the person.

The Aim of Personal Construct Psychotherapy

The clearest and simplest statement concerning the aim of personal construct therapy is that 'psychotherapy should make one feel that he has come alive' (Kelly, 1980, p.29). Psychotherapy, at its best, is an enlivening and awakening kind of experience; a life-giving, inspiriting enterprise. The opposite of this is to continue to live a kind of deadened or numbed life. The person through therapy has awakened the creative and spontaneous qualities that have been too long left out of everyday experience. This is illustrated in the report of a male client who said that he had started to notice just how beautiful a tree that could be seen out of the therapy room window was. It was as if, before the therapy, trees were just objects to walk around as they blocked your path, rather than a real part of nature with a value and beauty in their own right. This client further reported that the leaves seemed more separate and brighter in color and that the movement of the leaves and limbs took on a new beauty that he remembered noticing much earlier in his life but had somehow overlooked for some time.

More in terms of Personal Construct Theory, the aim of therapy is to enable the person to actively elaborate his or her own personal construct system. The manifestation of this active elaboration is the previously mentioned feeling of 'coming alive'. An active elaboration of the construct system means that the person is able to assert aggressively his or her own understanding of life events in order to deal with these events in some creative way. Failure to elaborate the system is a kind of deadening of the human spirit. Bannister (1975, p.132) goes so far as to say that *all* personal problems 'are ultimately failures to elaborate one's personal construct system'. A personal system that is not growing—progressing—developing is in trouble.

In many ways the person is no longer as alive as he or she used to be. There is just less life about a system that has lost most of its elaborative capability. The person might be in this sense experiencing an alienation; a kind of dead or numbed existence, as mentioned earlier. It is like having an existence that parallels the feeling in one's lips after being injected with novocain at the dentist—it is possible to move but all the liveliness has gone. To the problems of life no really acceptable answers are forthcoming; no answers that the person can use. The world has become, in many ways, a very difficult place in which to live. This is not always experienced as a depression but often there is a kind of sadness that accompanies this failure to elaborate the system. There is a real frustration present. The evidence that is received is at least potentially invalidating to the system without the person's being able to enter into a constructive revision and subsequent constructive elaboration of the system.

Bannister (1975) states that one of the best ways to describe the problem in psychotherapy is to see the person having become stuck or trapped. But this is not stuck in the sense of being blocked or damned up with pressure increasing, like in the psychoanalytic–psycho-hydraulic formulation. It is rather the kind of 'being stuck' experience when one's feet become fixed in a bog with a definite bottom on which to stand. While the person doesn't sink completely, movement is definitely restricted. The problem is seen as a total system involving an account of the sequence of things (the multiple connnections in the system) rather than an analysis involving single stimulus-response connections.

Kelly has often stated that it is the job of the therapist to do more than to just get the person back on his or her feet. The therapist must enable the person to really get going again in life. It is not enough to enable a person to adjust more effectively; although that is a legitimate aim. The therapy should enable the person to become creative and inventive in living. This means that the person is able to assert aggressively his or her own understanding of the world and to do it in such a way that both effective and creative action take place. There is a tone here of an active progression of things. The person begins to anticipate life events in a way that is in the direction of growth. The therapy enables the person to build a better construct system for predicting what will come next. Some anticipatory certainty is thought to be helpful. At least part of the time people find themselves in a world they expect. Additionally the person is aided in accomplishing some of his or her intentions. Clients are aided so that they are able to accomplish some of the things they intend to do. There is an investment in helping the person gain personal control over some of the events of life. The person is then better able to predict and control life events. These are things one might expect from the earlier statement about viewing the person as a scientist.

Therapy, however, only begins here. The further aim is to enable the person to gain an understanding which goes beyond simple prediction and control. This something further is an appreciation of what possibilities might be open to the person beyond those life events over which the person can at present exert some personal control and prediction. This kind of understanding is called placing events in sequence, or offering a sequential explanation. It means seeing things as a total process involving the past present and future along a common line of progression (Kelly, 1966a, p.41). This is an exploration which enables the person to use his or her own behavior, as a probe to open up the future. It enables the person to start to use behavior as a way of asking a question and of seeing life events taking on a shape that really follows from a behavioral innovation.

The aim of therapy is to help the person pour his or her creative abilities into the real world. In this way a Personal Construct Theory approach is very much concerned with what a person believes and understands about his or her world, and with what effective action might be undertaken on the basis of these understandings and beliefs. Personal Construct Theory often uses the person's behavior in order to create this kind of understanding. The emphasis then is not on trying to explain behavior or to modify behavior but to use behavior as a tool for aiding people in making something out of their lives. As was stated earlier the aim of therapy is not a simple adjustment. The aim is instead to assist the client in his or her pursuit of what possibilities may be ahead in life. It is not enough for a therapy to simply aim for the client to be able to cope effectively with the stress and strains of everyday life. It is the aim of Personal Construct Therapy to enable the person to pursue his or her own great expectations, his or her own dreams.

Personal Construct Therapy goes even further, however, and asserts that 'the long view' must be taken in dealing with psychotherapy. The therapist should be concerned with what may go on long after the formal therapy is over. The therapist is 'interested in paths for movement opening up long after his formal contacts with the client are concluded' (Kelly, 1955, p.582). Through effective therapy the person is able to plan for the future. Effective psychotherapy should aid the person in future ventures; for example as the person approaches marriage, parenthood, major crises, major success, and finally death. The person's system is to be continually capable of elaboration and continually able to anticipate life events.

A way of summarizing the main aims of Personal Construct Therapy is to say that it enables the client to become his or her own therapist. The client is able to solve life problems in such a way that the personal system will not become dysfunctioned and start a process of destruction without beginning the process of replacement of the old system with a better system. The question is 'how to system-build for the future?' One way to characterize this approach is say it is a kind of phenomenological–existential–behaviorism; however, that is confusing. Why not just say it is a personal construct approach to therapy.

The Personal Construct Therapist

In this section we will explore some of the ways in which the therapist is characterized and some of the attitudes and skills the therapist might possess. The main job of the therapist is to aid the client in embarking upon a revision of his or her own construct system. This means helping the person to change so that the person will be able to be more effective, more fully alive, more fully human, and able to realize more capabilities. This has led Bannister (1975) to conclude that the personal construct therapist might best be described as *useful*; useful to the client as he or she attempts to elaborate, thereby changing, his or her construct system.

Credulous Approach

The first characteristic of the therapist has to do with a special kind of acceptance of the client by the therapist. This particular kind of acceptance is called 'taking a credulous approach to the client'. The therapist should be prepared to accept, for the time being, the client's construct system as it stands (Kelly, 1955, p.586). This means taking the person, initially at least, on his or her own terms. This involves respecting the person and investing the person with a kind of dignity for being a real and whole person in the presence of the therapist. This acceptance, however, does not mean that the therapist is attached to this initial presentation of the person, nor does it mean that the therapist thinks that the client should become permanently attached to just this initial version of herself or himself. It only means that there is a personal human recognition, by the therapist, of what the person's outlook is presently and how the person is going about living based on this outlook. The counselor is attempting to be very concrete and literal about the highly abstract features of the client's system. For example, a therapist might attempt to understand just how it is that a particular male client begins to feel compelled to exhibit himself at the end of a day which he has spent confined to his engineer's drafting board contemplating the prospect of going home to the kind of relationship with his wife that he presently has. It is a recognition by the counselor of the type of personal constructs with which the client is presently operating that would lead such a client to feel and behave in just this way. One might think of this as a kind of controlled yet compassionate phenomenological approach to understanding the client from the client's own point of view.

Another aspect of the credulous approach concerns how the therapist goes about gaining this understanding of the client. The advice given is to start by asking clients how they see things. There is a great deal of similarity here to the advice given by Allport and other personologists that, 'if you want to know something about someone why not ask them; they just might tell you'. It is not that the counselor is gullible and believes everything the client says without question, rather the counselor just accepts what is said as a point at which to begin in order to understand the client. In the above mentioned case, the therapist would listen very intently to what the client says with his words and with his actions as he tells the therapist about himself and the difficulties that face him. As this listening proceeds, it is very important that the counselor should not try to make everything fit logically, or conform immediately to the facts as externally perceived. Instead there is a recognition that the person's 'words and his symbolic behavior possess an intrinsic truth which the clinician should not ignore' (Kelly, 1955, p.322).

The therapist should maintain his or her own perspective in this acceptance of the client and not be swallowed up in the client's world view; otherwise the therapist would reduce his or her usefulness to the client. Sometimes the therapist gains a different perspective on matters that proves to afford some advantage for the client. For the therapist, the concern is not with being taken in by the client, but rather on being left out by the client so that no real view of a personal world is ever gained. In fact it may be better to be taken in by the client, temporarily at least, long enough to find out a few things about what things are truly like for this client.

Without this the therapist is left with merely *treating* the client in some way just to see if something will happen. This credulous approach is letting the client be the therapist's guide in trying to understand just how complicated matters are. This is opposed to the situation in which the therapist starts to listen to the client already knowing that there is a 'deep structure' that 'really' underlines what the person is thinking and feeling. With the credulous approach one starts with the client's own view and modifies that only as much as will be needed for the client to start actively exploring ways to help himself or herself. This is just to say that therapists can get overly enthusiastic about their own complex exploration, which may far outreach what is called for with a specific client in a specific situation. At the same time, it is important to remember that often people's lives are very complex and the therapist often needs to be as complex as he or she is able to be in order to be useful to the client.

Yet another aspect of the credulous approach is the ability to develop the 'talents of the novelist in entering into other people's worlds' (Bannister, 1975, p.130). This requires a certain level of verbal skill to actually talk the language of the client. This is particularly important when the therapy is being carried out with persons of a different socio-economic class from the therapist or from some ethnic or religious group of which the therapist is not a member. The therapist should try to employ the terms of the client. Of course it is helpful if the therapist has some direct experience with the client's sub-culture but this is not absolutely necessary. What is necessary is for the therapist to attempt to use the client's language. In this way personal construct therapy escapes being a therapy that is only suitable for useful with one narrow band of society.

In addition, however, to the constructs of the client that the therapist strives to employ in order to see the world from the client's point of view, the therapist has his or her own set of professional constructs concerning how a construct system works. These concern the characteristics of the construct system, the content of the constructs, and the way different constructs are related to each other. Kelly (1955, 1965) points out repeatedly that the personal construct theory therapist is one who is able to subsume the construct system of the client. The therapist must have the knowledge, ability, and desire to cast an over-arching network of meaning which enables that therapist to make sense out of the client, and the nature of the therapeutic relationship. Much more will be said later about the different kinds of professional constructs, but for now it will suffice to mention that the therapist should employ constructs which are *permeable* and *propositional* in nature. By *permeable* is meant that the constructs employed should be able to let in many events in the client's life so that as much material as possible of the client's system can be understood. By *propositional* is meant that the therapist remains open to different possibilities concerning what the client might be meaning. The therapist resists the temptation to pre-empt on any one interpretation of what the client is saying until a great deal of information and a great deal of experience with the client is gained. It might be added that the therapist conveys the idea of propositionality to the client so that the client is able to start looking at alternative interpretations that can be tried just to get a feeling for them. The client obtains a sample of these alternatives without having to make a commitment to any of them prematurely.

Best Human Qualities

The Personal Construct Therapist has yet another obligation, that is the obligation for the best human qualities, of the therapist, to be brought forward for use by the client. This is the requirement that the therapist make his or her best self available to the client. The kind of validation and invalidation which takes place at the therapist's hand, within the therapy hour, should be based on the best the therapist has to offer. This stems from the position stated by Kelly that the therapist serve as a validator during the therapy hour: 'The therapist takes the best to be found in human nature and portrays it in such a way as to enable the client to validate his constructs against it' (Kelly, 1955, p.593). Another way of expressing this idea is to say that for a client it is very helpful if your therapist can be sanely creative.

Creativity

The personal construct psychotherapist should be able to be creative and original in the approach taken to the client. The therapist needs to be able to use constructs that are new (Kelly, 1955, p.600). The therapist personally may not have previously used some of the client's constructs, but must be able to quickly 'catch on' and start to use these unfamiliar constructs of the client's. In addition, the therapist has to help the client articulate some completely new constructs that may not be, as yet, clearly formulated for *either* the client *or* the therapist. This is a process of creative problem solving for both the client and the therapist.

A part of this creative quality is the ability to be open to a great number of different possibilities for the client. 'The clinician is not only tolerant of the varying points of view represented in his clients, but he is willing to devote himself to the defense and facilitation of widely differing patterns of life. Diversity and multiple experimentation are to be encouraged' (Kelly, 1955, p.608). The counselor, in fact, strives to make the constructs of the client the values the counselor has for the therapy. The person is encouraged to develop life along lines of his or her own choosing. The counselor should not over-generalize from client to client concerning what deserves to be validated or invalidated. Of course the human condition being what it is, there will be some commonality; however, the points of difference might be point for point almost as great.

There are many different ways a client might choose to elaborate his or her construct system (that is lead his or her life) that might work out equally well for all concerned. Personal construct psychotherapy turns away from the position of thinking of just one or two strategies for living that are healthy or possible and embraces a position which enables different clients to work out both goals and means to the goals that might be all quite different one from the other. This is getting ahead of our planned introduction of formal terms, but Personal Construct Theory is based on a philosophical position known as *constructive alternativism* which states that men and women are limited only by their imagination in formulating different possibilities for their life. The position further implies that in our present state of knowledge, we might expect quite a few of these different approaches to life to have some definite advantages for one person or another. In light of this diversity, one practical suggestion might be to have a simple catalog of effective life styles to be used by both therapist and client. These would be strategies of living that, have the potential to turn out rather nicely for the persons involved. Why such a catalog might be needed is because the creative imagination of both the client and the therapist needs to be sparked from time to time.

The quality of creativity is also manifested in the therapist's need to go beyond what is known cognitively. The effective counselor must go beyond what he or she can presently verbalize about a strategy in therapy. This is in contrast to the mistaken image of the personal construct therapist as a therapist who completely maps out and completely knows the terrain (the construct system of the client) and then carefully says just the right (premeditated) thing that the therapy calls for. In Kelly's (1955, p.601) terms 'The psychotherapist who dares not try anything he cannot verbally defend is likely to be sterile in a psychotherapeutic relationship.' The therapist has to develop the skill to be sensitive to an emergent quality of what needs to be said, and in other ways expressed, so that it flows from the therapist in other than a deliberate premeditated plan. It is not possible to lay out a therapy like a road map. Sometimes the counselor has to take (perhaps even fake) the turns as they come in the therapy based on the feeling that this is the right direction. At times the therapist has to launch into things based on nothing more than a feeling. As a counselor, you sometimes have to trust that eventually you will reach a place in the therapy that will give you reason to believe that where you have been was either fruitful or not.

Courage

The way of understanding this quality in therapy is for the therapist to have a 'clear understanding of his psychotherapeutic role' (Kelly, 1955, p.598). By the nature of the kind of involvement the therapist has with the client, the therapist leaves himself open to the possibility of being threatened and made to feel guilty by what goes on in the therapy. The therapist has to realize that in an effective therapy there may be things brought up that might be in an area with which the therapist personally has not yet come to grips. This could affect the therapist and the therapy very profoundly. The courage required here is involved in realizing this and persisting in such a way with the client that a constructive perspective is eventually gained by both.

In very fundamental ways personal construct psychotherapy implies change not only for the client but for the therapist as well. Again getting somewhat ahead of our schedule of introducing formal terms, it is important to state that in personal construct psychotherapy a *role relationship* is established by the therapist toward the client. By this term *role relationship* we mean that the therapist approaches the client using both personal and professional constructs which are designed to attempt both to subsume the construct system of the client, and at the same time to attribute to the client an outlook that operates on human principles which are filled with content not completely unlike the therapist's own system. The therapist lets the client matter as a fellow human being. Because of the involvement and investment by the therapist in the client as a person and the therapeutic relationship, the implications for change go both ways, i.e. the therapist is seen as changing as well as the client. It may be that the most effective psychotherapies are those in which not only the client changes, but the therapists changes as well. The change for the therapist is usually not along the same construct lines as occurs in the client, but it does not necessarily have to be different. In Personal Construct Theory the therapist is leaving him or herself open for possible change by the very nature of establishing a true role relationship with the client.

In conclusion all this discussion of characteristics and skills of the therapist needs to be kept in the larger perspective of the therapist as a person. These characteristics and skills seem quite demanding for the therapist, as indeed they are. Nevertheless the therapist is seen as human and not superhuman. There are a lot of demands on the therapist but at the same time the therapist is seen, as well as the client, as a person who has a right to make mistakes. The therapist as well as the therapy is seen as being constantly in process. The therapist is seen as being on the way to becoming, over time, a better and more skilful therapist.

The Client in Personal Construct Therapy

In Personal Construct Therapy considerable attention is paid to how to teach the client to be a client who can maximally benefit from what therapy has to offer. To this end, the client has to become generally less intense about his or her problems and allow the therapist to have access to these areas of his or her life. The client must adopt a kind of explorational and experimental attitude. The client must be willing to take a chance with his or her feelings and thoughts. The client must remain open to the possibility of entertaining alternatives to the present world view. There are some ways this can be done without having the client risk too much. More detail will be provided about this in subsequent chapters. In Kelly's (1958, p.229) terms 'the client needs to assume that something can be created that is not already known or is not already there.' The client has to have the faith or belief that at the present moment there are the possibilities of creating new alternatives, in the future, for the way he or she is now living life and attempting to solve life's more significant problems.

Another aspect of being a client pertains to the willingness to enter into a role relationship with the therapist. Bannister (1975, p.130) talking with a client describes this very concisely: 'The idea is that I should try and understand you because being understood has not been a common part of your experience. You should try and understand me because understanding someone else has also not been a common part of your experience. If we succeed it may do us both some good.' Again we see the therapist and the client entering into a relationship of mutual influence. The emphasis here, however, is on the fact that the client must be willing to try to understand another person from the point of view of the other person. In other words the client must try to fit him or herself momentarily in the shoes of the other. The client also has to be open to the therapist's approach. The client must experience the feeling of being understood by the therapist.

The Relationship between Client and Therapist

The analogy often used in Personal Construct Theory in order to describe the therapeutic relationship is the sea voyage. 'The client and . . . therapist embark together as shipmates on the very same adventure' (Kelly, 1958, p.232). The picture here is of a relationship characterized by cooperation between two people who mutually respect and are attempting to understand each other. Another part of this sea voyage analogy is that these are two people who are going to be spending a part of their lives in the presence of one another. The time together should count for something because the time is real time and a part of the lives of both people. The opposite of this type of relationship is an authoritarian relationship where the time spent with the other is not a 'real' part of the life of the other. The unproductive therapeutic relationship would be characterized by the expert therapist having to administer a treatment to a rather passive client.

Another aspect of this sea voyage anology is seen in the fact that the most important issue is the nature of the voyage itself rather than any specific destination. Personal construct psychotherapy focuses on the *nature* of the problem that the client is trying to deal with in therapy. There is a fascination with the idea of solving the problem or getting more information about the problem so that more adequate strategies can be brought to bear on the problem. There is a task orientation in the therapy that takes the focused attention away from the client as such. Rather than being focused on an introspective search for the 'self' the focus is on the task at hand. There is a high level of interest and involvement in the problem by both the therapist and the client. There is a devotion to the problem by the persons concerned. One might, in this respect, be made mindful of Maslow's (1971) description of the self-actualizing person as one who has temporarily abandoned the self in the pursuit of a problem. The client in personal construct psychotherapy becomes task or problem centered. The problem is understood as the thing to be worked on rather than anything that is wrong with the client. Another image conjured up is the research student and the supervisor who form a research team for the purpose of investigating a problem. The client is the 'research student' who brings in the problem to be examined and investigated. The client is the expert on the content of the problem. The therapist is like the research supervisor who is an expert on the techniques of investigation. The therapist has a command of the investigative tools that are placed at the disposal of the client. The counselor is an expert in aiding the client to design alternative ways for more adequately dealing with the problem. One could even say the client is coming to deal with problems in more realistic ways, except that reality has to be understood as something that the therapist does not want to use in order to limit the client's creative imagination. In this way the problem is not one for solving, as such, but rather one for investigating so that some effective action can be undertaken and some further movement becomes possible as the problem shifts at the touch of the client and counselor.

Playfulness

Closely connected with this task centeredness is a kind of playfulness that is present throughout the whole personal construct psychotherapeutic enterprise. For effective therapy to begin, clients have to be invited not to take life in such a deadly serious manner. In fact a deliberate attempt is made to cast most statements to the client in what Kelly called an *invitational mood* (Kelly, 1964). For effective therapy to take place the clients must, to some extent, come to experiment with their lives, to risk letting go of a present understanding long enough to entertain other possibilities. This experimentation can be greatly facilitated by creating the spirit of *as if* and *let's pretend*. If a client is unwilling to accept this invitation and become playfully experimental, then the possibility of benefit in the therapy is greatly diminished, if not completely eliminated. Such a client would still be understandable within Personal Construct Theory, however, that client would be, for all practical purposes, severely limiting the change that might have been possible. The client must gain some perspective on his or her life and not take things so seriously.

The Psychotherapeutic Process

Perhaps at this point it would be advisable to pay more attention to the actual progression of the therapy, and some of the activities which fill the therapy session. A good place to start is with an examination of the concept of *now* and the place it has in Personal Construct Theory. This might be conveyed in the following hypothetical dialogue between therapist and client. After listening for some time to a client, a therapist might want to convey, in one way or the other, the following message: 'I think I know where you are coming from but *now* let's try to find out where you are you going.' This type of concern with the *now* is in fact central to the way life itself is defined in Personal Construct

Theory. 'Life is a way of using the *present* (the now) to link the future with the past in some original fashion' (Kelly, 1980, p.28). This sentence could just as easily describe the process of psychotherapy, since psychotherapy is seen as an accelerated part of life. In Personal Construct Theory the concept of *now* is best understood as either *what now* or *now what*. There is a quality of always linking things up for the purpose of creating a future for the person or, more accurately stated, helping the person to create a future of individual significance. This is a future created in the present moment which contains that quality which ensures a sense of progression in living. Another way of characterizing this quality is to say 'A person lives his life by reaching out for what comes next and the only channels he has for reaching are the personal constructs he is able to place upon what may actually be happening' (Kelly, 1958, p.228).

The main emphasis is placed on the nature of the personal construct *system*. This is a system laid down through past experiences but whose job it is to anticipate the future. The emphasis is on the totality of the system and the need to understand the system in a holistic fashion. The therapist reaches out for the total structure of the client in an attempt to grasp some part of the wonderment that is called 'the person'. The concern is with the construct system of the client as a guide to meaning and understanding which transcends the concern with just the behavior of the client. It is the personal theme which underlies the behavior that is most important to the therapist. Kelly states that therapy is more concerned with how a person is able to get on with his or her life in general, rather than with providing answers for how that person should behave (Kelly, 1965, p.220). The concern is with the overall philosophy of the person rather than with conditioning specific behaviors.

Psychotherapeutic Projects

There are, of course, quite a variety of things which are covered within a personal construct psychotherapy. It might be helpful to examine the listing which Kelly provides by way of summarizing these activities (Kelly, 1958, p.231).

(1) 'The two of them (client and therapist) can decide that the client should reverse his position with respect to one of the more obvious reference axes.' This type of activity in therapy is seen often as rather superficial change but it has its place within a therapy. For example, the client may decide to begin to see himself or herself as strong rather than weak on the *strong–weak* construct dimension which is presently a part of the construct system. Because clients have usually tried this on their own, this type of change is usually not too difficult to achieve. This change, however, must be carefully examined because of the implication such shifting, often called 'slot change', might have for other aspects of the person's world view. For example, to be strong the person may feel compelled now to be rather cruel to certain other people. This slot change, perhaps easy to accomplish, can often have far reaching and sometimes undesirable implications. One hopes that the therapist might be able to anticipate such complicated implications before the slot change is undertaken.

(2) 'They (the client and therapist) can select another construct from the client's ready repertory and apply it to matters at hand.' Again this ploy is usually of minimum benefit for the client, but then it might be of some benefit. In our example above, the client might begin to see a particular issue in terms of the dimension *adequate* versus *inadequate* rather than the former distinction of *strong–weak*. In this way the issue shifts somewhat but remains the same in many ways. This, however, might be just the right amount of movement the client can stand at the time. Often in psychotherapy much more change is taking place than can be seen on the surface. For the therapist the shift may not appear significant, but within the client's system a much larger change might be indicated.

(3) 'They (the client and the therapist) can make more explicit those preverbal constructs by which all of us order our lives in considerable degree.' This can be very helpful in that some things we feel compelled to do are not well understood by us because they are at a low level of awareness. Assisting the person to become aware of these things can be quite helpful. This aspect of psychotherapy will be described in more detail under the heading 'psychological underground' which follows in the next section.

(4) 'They (the therapist and the client) can elaborate the construct system to test it for internal consistency.' This particular device, used frequently in therapy, is designed to help the client add things up, recognize inconsistencies, and decide what these inconsistencies mean. Although the general aim is help the person reconcile these discrepancies, Personal Construct Theory recognizes that a certain level of inconsistency is necessary and even desirable.

(5) 'They (the client and the therapist) can test constructs for their predictive validity.' This means to see whether the way the person views things can be verified. This involves teaching clients to be observant and to collect data so that evidence for validation or invalidation can be presented for their current beliefs. This is an attempt to enable the client to become reality-oriented. In a successful psychotherapy the client becomes realistic in the sense that client's expectations correspond to the world the client finds.

(6) 'They (the client and therapist) can increase the range of convenience of certain constructs, that is, apply them more generally. They can also decrease the range of convenience and thus reduce a construct to a kind of obsolescence.' There are a number of things that are being attempted here. In the one case the therapist may be aiding the client in extending his or her construct system to cover more events. One such situation would be where the client is facing a new situation in which the existing construct system can be used to interpret the new material. In the other case the therapist may be directing the use of the construct to a very few things. For example with the client using a *strong–weak* dimension, the therapist might invite the person to apply this construct dimension only to the physical realm and not use it in the broader psychological realm.

(7) 'They (the therapist and the client) can alter the meaning of certain constructs; rotate the reference axes.' Here the client and therapist work

together in order to modify the present meaning of an existing construct. With the *strong–weak* example, the client might now come to understand *strong* to mean a kind of 'support for others', rather than having its former alignment with the domination of others. The construct dimension is rotated so that the relationship to other construct dimensions is altered. This is seen as creating a rather profound change within the person's construct system. Some of the techniques, discussed later, will be designed for this purpose.

(8) 'They (the client and therapist) can erect new reference axes.' In personal construct psychotherapy this is seen as the truly creative aspect of psychotherapy. Through this process new meanings are acquired by the person. For example, the person comes to see the *strong–weak* dimension as a distinction which is rather crude and considerably less refined that seeing these same events in terms perhaps of a new *helpful* versus *harmful* dimension. Here it is not so much that *strong–weak* has become modified as much as it has been abandoned and the person comes to the world from an entirely new perspective. This is a perspective that gives the person certain advantages in living that did not exist before.

The Psychological Underground of Personal Construct Therapy

Although much of the therapy is on a verbal level, another aspect of personal construct psychotherapy which characterizes it and makes it appear quite different from other therapies that are classified as cognitive therapies (Mahoney, 1977) is its concern with meaning dimensions that have no clear verbal label with which they can be expressed. In much of the research and clinical work, Personal Construct Psychology has concentrated on the verbally labelled dimensions that are lifted off a paper and pencil assessment technique known as a Role Construct Repertory (Rep.) test or Rep. grid. (The assessment section of the book will contain a more detailed description of this test.) Personal Construct Therapy, however, is heavily invested in those construct dimensions that, for one reason or another, remain outside the verbal realm and reside usually at a low level of awareness. Some other theories like to posit an unconscious realm to deal with this material, but this would not be in keeping with the kind of systems approach that personal construct theory represents. This theory might be thought of as representing a kind of organismic, humanistic, non-mechanistic systems approach to psychotherapy.

These constructs, operating outside the verbal realm, are often new constructs that enter into the client's awareness first as only vague feelings and are very loosely formulated understandings. In actuality, these constructs may be either truly *new* constructs or ones that were laid down before the person was able to use verbal labels; very old constructs that have never been verbally labelled. Only the verbal label is new. These constructs, so described, are often closely associated with another class of constructs that are also not easily expressed in words and these are the so-called body constructs; constructs governing external muscular movements, and internal process such as digestion. All of this refers to the necessary embodiment of all construct dimensions.

Eugene Gendlin's (1977) work on *felt meanings* is seen as very helpful in understanding this aspect of construct systems. Gendlin has worked out a very nice technique called 'focusing' which could be useful in a personal construct therapy. The advantage of appropriating this technique for use in personal construct psychotherapy is the framework that construct theory provides in understanding how a vague feeling, lifted from a body sensation and then translated into verbal expression, can fit into the overall personality structure of the client.

In Personal Construct Psychology all of these constructs are termed *preverbal constructs*. As previously mentioned preverbal constructs are found not only in those areas of construction that are laid down before verbal systems developed but are also involved when people build new constructions into themselves that are destined to become truly a part of them. A new construct can be built by starting at either the verbal or body sensation end. It is important, however, that both ends be taken into consideration.

Also included under the heading of preverbal constructs is the concern that much of therapy is carried out at the non-verbal (body construct) level. Much of what the therapist makes out of the constructions of the client is accomplished by the way in which the client moves; the way the client behaves in relationship to the therapist. This becomes most obvious in the body movements that the client goes through when the client is relating certain information to the therapist. In Personal Construct Therapy it is possible to analyze the therapy purely along non-verbal construct dimensional lines. Comprehensively one can then see the whole therapy taking place on both a verbal and a body level at the same time. In this way it is technically possible to understand how to carry out an entire therapy at the non-verbal level, or at least how to utilize more non-verbal techniques and understand them psychologically. What Personal Construct Psychology offers is a way of analyzing the bodily occurrences in such a way that they can start to take on a truly psychological significance. By using this theory a therapists does not have to rely solely on a traditional type of R–R analysis (Spence, 1956) to make sense out of these non-verbal aspects of therapy.

The Use of Behavior

The view point taken in Personal Construct Psychotherapy is that behavior is to be used for investigative purposes. Through behaving, people find out about themselves. Through behaving in a certain way, something is likely to happen to a person so that information is received and the person is able, only then, to truly understand himself or herself. In a personal construct therapy a client might well be given a behavioral assignment followed by a behavioral assessment of that assignment. This is done not in order to teach the client a specific new behavior but rather to use the behavior as a probe or key to unlock possible new information. Kelly suggests that in treating a snake phobia the problem is to figure out some different relationship the client might have to snakes, and that behaving in a different way toward the snake might go a long way in improving the relationship.

Also related to the personal construct approach to behavior is the fact that the way a person explores and opens up change in the system is through action. It is an investigation, this action. Saying that behavior is an investigation eliminates it from the class of things a person would necessarily want to repeat. A person might not want to repeat an action even if it turned out all right, particularly if the first time through answered the question that was being asked by that behavior. Kelly points out that a person might not want to repeat some of life's grandest moments. These might be true turning point experiences. In Personal Construct Therapy there is a healthy respect for behavior. Behavior is a way of asking a question. A construct is often expressed behaviorally and that means it gains expression through the body. It is a bodily expression. Behaving is then another way of seeing the embodiment of a construct.

Techniques

Before concluding this introduction to psychotherapy, some comments should be made about the nature of the techniques used in this kind of therapy. If one takes techniques to mean the general kinds of strategies and tactics employed by the therapist in order to maximize the conditions for psychotherapeutic benefits for the client, then the personal construct therapist can be described as employing a great variety of these techniques. At times the therapist might be described as very active or perhaps even confrontative with the client, and at other times the same therapist might appear very quiet and non-directive in the approach taken to the client. At times the therapist might move in very close to the client and at other times the same therapist might maintain a kind of distance from the client in order for the client to develop an independence of action and feelings. In total there can be, and perhaps should be, a great variety of techniques selected for use by the therapist. The selection of techniques is guided by a therapeutic plan developed through understanding the nature of the client's construct system and how effective change might take place in that system. The techniques used must be seen as serving the purpose of operationalizing the aims of a personal construct psychotherapy. One might describe the position taken on techniques as a kind of systematic or disciplined eclecticism. This would be contrasted with a kind of random or even wild eclecticism where the therapist just employs some technique at the moment in order to produce a dramatic effect that will 'shake up' the client and keep the therapist and client awake for the next few minutes. Although there are certain techniques which are particularly closely associated with personal construct psychotherapy, most of the techniques used by the personal construct therapist are ones that would be observed in the repertory of a great many other therapists.

In personal construct therapy the main emphasis remains on the rather broad dimensions used for managing the total therapeutic enterprise. These are dimensions designed to deal with the total construct system of the client as that client interacts with the therapist. One of the most important of these dimensions is the *loosening* versus *tightening* dimension. Although much more detail will be presented later, it is necessary to present, here, a brief explanation of this dimension. For many personal construct therapists this dimension of tightening and loosening has become the primary dimension along which psychotherapy is planned. Certainly it is a very important dimension for any therapist in this orientation. The concept of tightening refers to the client's moving in a direction which enables that client to see clear, crisp relationships among the things that make up life. The construct dimensions in the system have clear implication for other dimensions and for the kinds of predictions that can be made. A client who is tightening or has a tight system of constructs is able to be internally consistent and precise in what his or her system of meaning is able to do. In loosening, the client is invited to let go of clearly defined and exactly formulated meanings; the client is encouraged to entertain alternative ways of seeing the surrounding world. The clients who are loosening are in more of a fantasy world and dream-like state where their world has many different meanings which exist almost simultaneously. Bannister explains in some detail the way this *loose–tight* dimension is used to order the different techniques employed in a psychotherapy:

'If we attempt now to tighten the construct *tight–loose* into terms of practices within psychotherapy, we can see that a wide range of techniques is permissible and necessary within the bounds of construct theory psychotherapy. Thus if a client needs to loosen his constructs in order to draw off from his particular involvements in a situation so that he can see it in terms of alternative perspectives, then we may well use loosening techniques. Many of these are traditional in other psychotherapeutic approaches. Free association and dream interpretation in psychoanalysis, fantasy in Gestalt therapy, the non-directive style of Rogerian therapy, are all ways in which clients may be encouraged to loosen their construing . . . . Equally, classic forms of tightening from other forms of psychological therapy are entirely admissible. The procedures of behavior therapy are often excellent strategies for tightening, in that they encourage the client to define vast fears into specific situations and undertakings and to quantify pervasive anxieties into hierarchies' (Bannister, 1975, p.135–136).

Bannister further points out in this section that personal construct theory has its own specific techniques such as maintaining a fixed role, role playing, using a role construct repertory grid, filling out a self characterization and other specific techniques which are designed to enable the person either to tighten or loosen his or her own construct system. These techniques will be discussed in detail in later chapters. In addition, Karst (1980) has provided a very useful examination of the role of specific techniques in personal construct psychotherapy.

Summary

The term psychotherapy is broadly defined in Personal Construct Theory to include different types of professional helping relationships. The approach taken to understanding a person is through the person's meaning dimensions (personal constructs) that the person chooses to employ in order to structure his or her life. The aim of a personal construct psychotherapy is to enable a client to actively elaborate his or her system of personal constructs. The therapist in this orientation is characterized as being creative, courageous, and taking a credulous approach to the client. The client must remain open to the possibility of actively experimenting with life. The therapeutic relationship is characterized as a cooperative investigation of the client's problem. The therapist and client are both experts in their own realms. The therapist possesses the expert knowledge concerning the investigative methods which the client might want to use. The client possesses the expert knowledge concerning the content of the problem. Throughout the relationship a playful atmosphere is promoted in order for the client to be creative.

There are many different projects undertaken during the therapy, which range from enabling the client to better use his or her present system to aiding the client in constructing truly new meaning dimensions. The work in therapy makes use of both verbalizations and behavioral expression which are not easily verbalized. The client's behaviors (overt actions) are emphasized in the therapy. Specific actions are used by the client in order to investigate and inquire into the nature of the life problem. During this therapy the counselor can be observed employing a wide range of techniques emphasizing behavior modification techniques if system tightening is indicated, or creative fantasy techniques if system loosening is desired. The selection of techniques is based on an assessment of the total construct system of the client. The purposes of the techniques is to enable the client to begin movement toward full human development.

CHAPTER 2

A Language for
Personal Construct Systems

In order to understand how a personal construct system works one needs to become familiar with the technical terms of the theory and the underlying philosophical assumptions of the theory. Presented here is a brief overview of the theory in order to acquaint the reader with the language of the theory including both the structural and process conceptualizations of how the person is presented from this point of view. Because of the limited amount of space that will be devoted to these technical aspects of the theory, the reader is encouraged to refer to Kelly's (1955) original two-volume work for more extensive descriptions.

One might think of the material presented here as a brief reference source which can be used from time to time when technical terms appear in subsequent chapters. In fact if the reader wishes to avoid the technical terms, as a point of departure, this chapter can be by-passed and considered in small sections as it may be needed later in the reading. Because of the number of technical terms some may think Personal Construct Theory offers too rich a diet for a single serving and that a piecemeal approach might be advisable. However, for those who are willing, the main course begins here. There are, however, other places where brief summaries of Personal Construct Theory are presented (Landfield, 1978; Bannister and Fransella, 1971; Bannister and Mair, 1968; Kelly, 1966b). The purpose of the summary presented here is to provide an introduction directed specifically to the person interested in the way technical terms in Personal Construct Theory apply to the enterprise of psychotherapy.

Constructive Alternativism: a Philosophical Position

Personal Construct Theory takes the position that it is very important for theories of personality and psychotherapy to explicate the philosophical assumptions made in the building of that theory. By placing these philosophical assumptions 'up front', so to speak: (1) one can more easily assess the connections among different aspects of a theory since the sources of their derivation is clear; (2) one can, with greater ease, assess the relationship of the theory to other bodies of knowledge; and (3) one can more easily and responsibly elaborate the theory during a psychotherapy since a clearer understanding of fundamental principles is more likely to occur.

For Personal Construct Theory this basic philosophical position is known as *constructive alternativism*, which has been succinctly stated by Kelly in the following way:

> 'Like other theories, the psychology of personal constructs is the implementation of a philosophical assumption. In this case the assumption is that whatever nature may be, or howsoever the quest for truth will turn out in the end, the events we face today are subject to as great a variety of constructions as our wits will enable us to contrive. This is not to say that one construction is as good as any other, nor is it to deny that at some infinite point in time human vision will behold reality out to the utmost reaches of existence. But it does remind us that all our present perceptions are open to question and reconsideration, and it does broadly suggest that even the most obvious occurrences of everyday life might appear utterly transformed if we were inventive enough to construe them differently' (Kelly, 1966b, p.1).

Although there is a real world external to our perceptions of it, the way we, as individual persons, come to know that world is by placing our own interpretation upon it. The world does not automatically and directly reveal itself to us. We must strike up a relationship with it. It is only through the relationship we form with the world, that we gain the knowledge that enables us to progress. The responsibility is ours for the type of knowledge we have of the world in which we live. Kelly characterized this aspect of his philosophical foundation as a position of *epistemological responsibility* (Kelly, 1966b). Another reason for adopting this active approach to knowledge is the fact that, for Kelly, the world itself is 'in process'. It is constantly changing so that an adequate understanding of the world requires a continual re-interpretation of it. Knowledge of the world cannot be collected, stored up, and built upon like so many secure building stones. An adequate understanding requires constant change.

In Personal Construct Theory, the additional assumption is made that knowledge of the world is unitary. It is believed that over the 'long haul' we will know what things are really like. At some point in the far distant future it will eventually be clear which conception of the world we should accept; which conception is veridical. At the present time, however, it may be a much better strategy to entertain a number of different interpretations (constructive alternatives) in order to see what advantage each one might be able to demonstrate. In addition it is thought that some advantage is gained by adopting an expanded time frame rather than viewing the person from moment to moment or within the confines of any single situation. This latter concern is well represented by Miller Mair (1976) in his discussion of construct theory and the use in psychology of the metaphor and concept of mystery:

> '. . . . Kelly suggests that if we are to make something more of the mystery of man—or any man—we should not limit ourselves by considering him only within the fleeting moments of a psychological experiment, or in the first five years of life, or even within a ten-year follow-up. Kelly suggests that we may be able to gain a fuller perspective on the possible nature of man if we consider him within the span of his own life and, beyond that, within the sweep of the centuries. At any moment, each man is suspended somewhere between his own birth and his own death, but also between the birth and death of the human race, the birth and death of the world, and more. If we only view him within the very narrow limits of time and place we may dismiss many human struggles as trivial or neurotic which may appear in a different light if we consider a wider context and a longer journey' (p.266).

At attempt will now be made to demonstrate how this philosophical concept of constructive alternativism influences some of the activities in the psychotherapy room. First, constructive alternatives, in respect to the way the client is relating to the world, are conspicuous by their absence. The client is frequently acting in a certain way because she cannot conceive (in other than in the most abstract and intellectual way) of another way it might be possible to act. If, only for a few minutes, the client could start to suspend her judgment of present reality, long enough for new possibilities to become apparent, some progress might begin.

From the position of the 'realistic person' there is a world and it is all too obvious what the world is and how one must act in that world. The present interpretation of the world is seen as if it were chiseled in granite. The client never allows himself or herself a chance to play with any other possibilities. The troubled client's rigid behavior is then too often directed by what he or she takes to be a hard reality. We are suggesting, here, that reality may not be entirely a concrete matter. There might be other reasonable alternatives as to what it all might mean. Perhaps the client can start to realize that there just might be something he or she can do to influence the kind of world in which he or she lives. The question is raised concerning what possibilities there might be, in a situation, other than that which appears on the surface to be so obvious.

For the greater part of our daily lives we are confronted with a world that does not seem reasonable for us to challenge. We find ourselves in a world filled with doorknobs, chairs, table tops, stair steps, or even the walls of a coal mine (in the physical realm), and with perhaps hostile employers, indifferent colleagues, or an unappreciative child (in the interpersonal realm). It is usually all too obvious to us what is before us and what we should do. For example, we walk into a room, find a chair, sit in it, and listen to a lecturer giving an oversimplified explanation of the world political situation. We report for the morning work assignments and find an added task for the next week. Often it does not seem reasonable for us to challenge the meaning of these things which fill our lives. It is not obvious that we have construed anything at all. We have simply seen the situation for what it is worth and done what was called for. Yet from a personal construct theory position, these things are all subject to reconsideration, although, for the most part, it does not seem reasonable for us to challenge them. Either we think that there is no other alternative to the situation possible or that the alternatives are very illogical or implausible.

From the perspective of a personal construct psychotherapy, difficulties arise from the fact that people often over-extend this obvious and solidified world into one that could prove to be somewhat transitory. The client treats a rather abstract realm as if it were absolutely concrete. The idea confronts the client that he or she cannot learn mathematics, or that he or she cannot trust others because 'people are just out to get what they can from you—and its a dog-eat-dog world out there.' In a personal construct approach one is invited to view the world as something that has to be interpreted. In certain circumstances a person might want to change his or her mind about some of the most obvious things in present life situations. It is the aim of personal construct psychotherapy to enable people to 'lift off' fixed ideas at least long enough for some other possibilities to emerge. Kelly (1955) describes the process of embracing and acting upon alternative constructions, however, as having real consequences. Not every alternative construction of events is as good as any other. Some of the constructions are validated while others are not. In fact some alternatives can lead to quite disastrous consequences.

A person casts a prediction about the world at a high level of abstraction and checks out that prediction at a much lower level. We might say that a certain person is obviously quite intelligent. We then listen for the rather clever things that this person will say in specific situations. The construct of intelligence is quite abstract while the evidence is gathered at the more concrete level of specific comments. The confirmation or disconfirmation of our predictions is no simple matter because we also construe the evidence that will serve this purpose. For example, we have all been faced with situations where there had to be overwhelming negative evidence presented to us before our favorable conceptions of some other person could be changed. It has been pointed out correctly, I think, that the main concern we should have is with the internal consistency of a person's system. Does it hold together from top to bottom? (Bannister and Mair, 1968). Over the long haul, however, a system that has simply fabricated the evidence to maintain internal consistency will not endure. The eventual invalidation of the system will be observed. The existentialists have had much to say about the case of the person who builds a life based on lies. In the long run the tissue of lies collapses. Kelly has the idea that the external world has some real impact upon peoples' lives; it changes peoples' lives. People, however, are free to choose the different meanings that this world will have.

Nevertheless it is important to remember that *not* every construction is as good as every other one.

One final practical implication of the principle of constructive alternativism for the psychotherapist and the therapeutic enterprise is the idea that the kinds of lives we all lead are constantly changing. The substance of our lives is never static. There is a constant change in our relationship to others and to our physical environment. The world in which we live is constantly changing, therefore any conception we have of it must continually change. There has to be a plan for change and much of the theory has to do with dealing with just these transitions. What we take ourselves to be, must be constantly in the process of changing. No present solution will last forever. Life keeps changing for all people, young and old.

Personal Construct Systems: Basic Characteristics

Included in this discussion are what Kelly termed the *Fundamental Postulate* plus two of the eleven corollaries that can be seen as derived from this postulate. This material is presented together because it contains the defining attributes of the basic system of constructs and is the bedrock upon which the total theory rests. It is a statement of the *givens* one starts from in order to understand the nature of persons from this point of view. This basic material is stated in the following way:

Fundamental Postulate: *A person's processes are psychologically channelized by the ways in which he anticipates events* (Kelly, 1955, p.46).

Construction Corollary: *A person anticipates events by construing their replications* (Kelly, 1955, p.50).

Dichotomy Corollary: *A person's construction system is composed of a finite member of dichotomous constructs* (Kelly, 1955, p.59).

These statements of the theory give information about what the person is and how we are to approach an understanding of this person. First the person is to be understood as an organized whole. The person, cannot, then be examined in part functions such as memory, cognition, perception, emotion, sensations, learning, etc: nor can the person be seen simply as a part of a social group. Rather the person is recognized in his or her own right as the focus of study; an individual to be understood in his or her own terms. The unit of analysis is the *personal construct* and the person is approached as if he or she were structured psychologically as a system of personal constructs. Using the concept of a personal construct, the clinician approaches the person according to the meaning dimensions that the person imposes upon the world in order to make the world interpretable. For the most part the therapist is concerned with the system of meaning the person uses to understand interpersonal relations; the person's way of viewing his or her relationship to a parent, a spouse, a friend or neighbor, an employer etc. Another way of characterizing this approach is to say that the concern is with the person's world view, particularly in the area of interpersonal relations.

This understanding of the person's world view is seen as applying both to the client and to the professional psychologist. The theory is designed to be a *reflexive* theory. The way the client is explained can be used to explain the therapists as he or she creates this explanation. Any explanation that can be applied to the client must be able to be applied to the person who offers the explanation. This thesis has been discussed at some length by Oliver and Landfield (1962).

These constructs and systems of constructs operate in specifiable ways. The emphasis is placed upon the *process* nature of the psychological life of the person. The person is seen as constantly changing and moving in one direction or another. Furthermore this movement is regulated—it forms a pattern—it is channelized. This process or change operates within a finite realm. The construct system of a given person at a given time is limited by definite parameters. The person is viewed as an imaginative but limited system of constructs, rather than being envisaged as simply trailing off into some infinite, nebulous conglomerate of construct dimension. At any given moment the person is understandable as a system of some more or less definite size. This, however, does not say anything, necessarily, about what the person is capable of becoming in the future. Some people may develop a very extensive and extraordinary personal system.

As a matter of fact construct systems are oriented toward the future. The person is seen as anticipating what is coming next. The person takes what has gone before and uses the present moment to reach out to grasp what is on-rushing at the next moment, day, or year. The person is attempting to capture the familiar in the new events by using the past and, at the same time, adding to them the unique qualities that they deserve. The process involves forecasting events in such a way that some prediction is offered concerning what things are and the form they should take. This process is described as 'construing a replication'. The person listens for the familiar themes to repeat themselves and then uses this to grasp the nature of the world as that person passes into the future.

For example we might consider a particular woman, 'Anne', who is assumed to possess dimensions of meaning (personal constructs) that she used to understand the other people in her life and her relationships to them. One thing she understands (at some level of awareness) is how she relates to and what she things and feels about the men in her life just now. Let us suppose that for the most part she sees them as having very definite opinions concerning just about everything. She finds this both reassuring at times and a bit disquieting or even irritating, at other times. Then she meets this new fellow, 'Anthony'. Anthony, as a man, comes in a rather familiar package—he is then anticipated by her to be a person who is likely to have definite opinions. These personal constructs do more than simply describe, they are predictions about how things are likely to be. In this case, however, Anthony is a man who does not seem to structure his life according to his opinions. It is not exactly that he does not have opinions, but he uses his opinions in a very different way from the other men in her life. This lets her know that a *particular* replication has to be construed. For the present, Anne might just keep him as being a man, but one who somehow does not allow himself to be handled as an exact duplicate of the other men in her life. This is the stuff of which new constructs are made. Perhaps she now realizes that Anthony is a man who values things but does not have to express these values as dogmatic opinions.

Another example which illustrates simply the application of an existing construct dimension is that of 'John' who seems to recognize a theme not noticed before in an older friend. He might say to himself, 'the qualities here put me in mind of the way I felt in the presence of my sister. Yes it is similar to the *compassion* and kind of *affection* I used to receive from her'. There is then a searching (at some level of awareness) for what contrasts with this quality which sets the limits on the total construct dimension and completes its meaning. John might say that this compassionate quality contrasts with the *uncaring* and *neglecting* impression conveyed by his uncle who always just seemed to be interested only in how clever people could be. This contrasting quality of the dimension is used to locate a total set of elements (other people) in the person's life; some located on the *likeness end* and the other on the *contrasts end*. These construct dimensions are not being used to contain the elements, but rather are used to locate them like the points of a compass are used to locate objects in relative terms; only in relation to one another. It is only that the old friend's compassion fixes him in relationship to the sister which in turn contrasts with the uncle. Perhaps under different circumstances, in relationship to some other people, that same uncle might, indeed, become the compassionate person in relation to these other people that the person has recently met. The placement of persons on construct dimensions is like a physical object being located in space. In describing where one lives a person might say 'I live in the *north*', *meaning one's house is in the north part of the town. If this same person were visiting the nation's capital (located north of the home city) then this same person would say, 'Oh, I live down south.' The interesting thing is that the North* versus *South* dimension is quite absolute but the events are realtive to each other as they are located using the dimension. In just this same way the construct dimension is absolute. It is the people who are arranged relative to one another using this dimension. Construct dimensions themselves are absolute but the events that are dealt with are relative to one another. Constructs are reference axes used to locate life events.

These construct dimensions are bipolar (have two poles and are dichotomous); in other words they are not continuous nor unipolar. The relationship between the two poles is that of a *contrast* ; one pole is the opposite of the other. The dichotomous nature of the construct is, however, very difficult to understand. The position is taken that all psychological dimensions which may be experienced as continuous, can be broken down to their ultimate dichotomous form. Nevertheless there has been a great deal of research using construct dimensions in the continuous form (Bannister and Mair, 1968; Epting, 1972; Fransella and Bannister, 1977).

There are a number of ways that dichotomous construct dimensions can be used in a continuous fashion. Kelly outlines six ways in which the bipolar dichotomous construct can be constructed into a scaled continuum. The following is an illustration of one such method labelled *hierarchical scales*.

'Suppose we build a hierarchical scale of *integrity* versus *disintegrity*, *candor* versus *deviousness*, *courage* versus *defeatism* and *objectivity* versus *subjectivity*. Suppose, also, that these constructs are arranged in that hierarchical order. Let the binary digit 1 represent the first of each pair and the binary digit 0 represent the second of each pair. A dishonest, devious, defeatist, subjective person would be represented by the scale value of 0000 and would be at the *disintegral* end of the scale. An honest but devious, defeatist, subjective person would be represented by the number 1000. Because of the high relevance of honesty to integrity, he rates in the upper half of the scale. A person who was dishonest, devious, defeatist, and objective would be represented by the number 0001 and would still be near the bottom of the scale' (Kelly, 1955, p.142–143).

At the heart of the idea of dichotomy, in Personal Construct Theory, is the concept of the 'quality' of things. In Personal Construct Theory the position is taken that there are different qualitative distinctions that can be made. For example for us a certain person is seen as outgoing. In other respects that person is also seen as kind. The complement of these qualities are their contrasts (cruelty and shyness) which serve to complete the meaning of these concepts. In order to know what kindness is, one has to grasp the nature of cruelty. However, for a friend of ours this opposite of kindness may mean neglect. For this friend the construct dimension would then be *kindness* versus *neglect*.

Whatever these two poles are for a given individual, the relationship between the poles is that of contrast. The dividing line between the two poles is termed the 'cleavage line'. In using this construct it is a matter of the person being characterized as either kind or cruel in terms of the psychological essence of things. This dimension refers to a thought and a feeling as well as an action. It is, in a word, a way to characterize the very being of the person at that time. Borrowing a term from social psychology one might describe a construct as a 'hot' cognition (feeling–thought) with a bodily involvement which implies an action component. Let us say a client locates a certain person he or she has met as falling in with other 'kind' people, until a certain amount of evidence is received, and predictions are made that invalidate the hypothesis of kindness. This might cause the client to regard the person then as essentially cruel. Another outcome of invalidation, of course, is that the whole kind–cruel dimension is discarded, but much more will be said about that later. One note of caution here is that the client may *not* be dealing with the other person as a total unit, but instead be dealing with a single aspect of the person. Under our discussion of transference this topic will be covered in greater detail.

Returning to the concept of dichotomy, one of the easiest ways to see its psychological importance is to focus on the action component. As long as the other person is considered to be kind, then the client might be gearing his or her actions and perceptions to treating that person as one who is making supportive remarks. This might continue until some evidence enters the system which shifts the person to the cruel pole. This shift directs the client to begin behaving quite differently toward the person. For the more mature client, the other person is not considered totally kind or cruel, but rather some aspect of the other person, at the moment, is considered to be cruel or kind.

Another way in which the dichotomous nature of a construct is revealed is in situations where clients have to take some kind of action. For example, a client may have to decide whether to go out or to stay home for the evening. There the dichotomy is obvious to us all because the action component is in focus. Either the client is found at home or he or she is seen outside. It is the position, in construct theory, that all dimensions contain this 'either–or' quality in the last analysis. This 'last analysis' is the psychology of action through which the nature of the dichotomy in constructions is best revealed.

Organizational Structure of Construct Systems

Up to this point we have been, for the most part, treating personal constructs as if they were separate units. Included in this section are those corollaries of the fundamental postulate that describe the structure of personal construct *systems* . These are concerned with how personal constructs as single units are related one to the other. These corollaries are as follows:

Organization Corollary: *Each person characteristically evolves, for his convenience in anticipating events, a construction system embracing ordinal relationship between constructs* (Kelly, 1955, p.56).

Fragmentation Corollary: *A person may successively employ a variety of construction subsystems which are inferentially incompatible with each other* (Kelly, 1955, p.83).

Range Corollary: *A construct is convenient for the anticipation of a finite range of events only* (Kelly, 1955, p.68).

Modulation Corollary: *The variation in a person's construction system is limited by the permeability of the constructs within whose ranges of convenience the variants lie* (Kelly, 1955, p.77).

Within this section of corollaries one begins to see the emerging form of the *system* of constructs that is the personality structure of the individual. The first concern is with the fact that a hierarchical arrangement of constructs exists. An ordinal relationship exists among construct dimensions. There are constructs which are *superordinate* to other constructs in the system. These superordinate constructs serve to organize the lower order *subordinate* constructs into recognizable patterns. For example the construct *realistic* versus *unrealistic* is likely to be rather superordinate to many of the person's other concerns about life. Many other subordinate constructs of the person are likely to be subsumed under this overarching concern. The way in which a superordinate construct subsumes its elements (other construct dimensions) can occur in a number of different ways. For one person the construct 'outgoing versus shy' might be arranged so that being outgoing is subsumed under those things which are realistic; whereas being shy is seen as unrealistic. The reverse might be taken to be the case by another person. For yet another the superordinate concern of realistsic matters might include both 'being shy versus outgoing'. Both these ways of being might be seen as realistic ways of dealing with different situations; whereas unrealistic is reserved to handle construct dimensions such as whether others are 'real devils versus real angels'. As reported by Bannister and Mair (1968, p.80) Dennis Hinkle outlines a list of four different ways that two constructs can be related to each other in terms of implicative relationships.

It must be remembered that superordination is only a relative position with regard to those things that are subordinate. If one moves to other places in the system the things that once were considered subordinate are recognized now to be quite superordinate. For example, our former concern with *outgoing* versus *shy* might now be seen as superordinate in relationship to our concern with *talking a great deal* versus *having very little to say*. The important quality to keep in mind here, is that the superordinate constructs influence and even determine the nature of those things that they subsume; whereas the constructs that are in the superordinate position are free to be used in formulating new concepts of what the world is like. One gains personal freedom by being able to find superordinate constructs which will enable one to see particular concerns in life in entirely new ways.

This concern with the relationships among constructs has led some investigators (Bieri *et al.*, 1966; Landfield, 1977; Adams-Webber, 1969) to the study of 'structural' properties of constructs such as the amount of differentiation (how many different constructs does a person use?) and the extent of integration (how much are the different constructs interrelated?). For the therapist this concern can be very important. For example the question is raised of how many distinctions clients are making about their 'bad moods'. Is the client able to distinguish feelings of loneliness from rejection, jealousy, or guilt feelings? How are these feelings integrated with the other thoughts and feelings the person is having at the time? In terms of the total organizational structure, Kelly sums up this condition by stating that the structuring of construct relationships is 'the price men pay to escape inner chaos.'

The term *range of convenience* addresses the question of how many events or what band of events can a construct or construct system deal with effectively. The question is raised in terms of how much of life can the construct order and make some reasonable anticipations about. The *range of convenience* of a construct is limited to those things that the construct dimension can be used to understand. Even more limited is the *focus of convenience* of the construct. Within the construct's total range are those events which the construct dimension can deal with superbly—the focus of the construct. For example one might encounter a client who has an excellent construct system for understanding infants; how to treat an infant, and how to set up relationships with young children; a system that is geared to the fantasy life of the young child. This person, with this focus of convenience in his or her construct system, will be quite capable of handling this type of relationship. Let us say this same construct system is also used by the person to order his or her adult relationships. That is to say adults are within the range of convenience of the system, but the construct system just does not work optimally there. On the positive side of things, the person might be expecting adults to be playful. On the negative side, the person may be expecting some kind of dependency needs to be met by adult friends. This, however just does not happen. With this person perhaps a goal in therapy would be to enable him or her to build some additional constructs through which adult relationships could be more satisfactorily handled. This might be thought of as a kind of fine tuning. It must be remembered that many therapies are just a matter of working with the person so that some construct can be built in order to bring something into focus; to place the matter in the range or focus of convenience of existing constructs.

Next comes the concern with modulation which means that the person is also limited by a construct system which will restrict the entry of events into the realm of meaning. This raises the question of a construct's *permeability*. This quality determines the scope of the construct system. The question is what determines the range of a construct, and the answer is the permeability of the construct. Any construct has to have some permeability, but there must also be some limit. A construct system is always more or less permeable. If a construct is permeable it will allow new information to enter that will enable the construct system to change. In a way, it is the job of the therapist to see that some permeability is made possible in the system; and in other ways to see that excessive permeability is limited. An excessively permeable structure may have its own problems. The person might find himself or herself involved in every piece of new material that comes along. The person sees implications for what he or she should do and be coming from just about everywhere.

It must be remembered that for any change to take place the person has to have a system that is permeable enough for that change to take place within it. The person has to construe his or her own changes. The impermeable system is one that will not allow material in, therefore allowing it to be missed. This matter has implications for the person's dealings with the outside world in that it makes that outside world less understandable. This is because the world will continue to change and affect things that the person will recognize as having changed, but the reason for that change will appear very mysterious.

Within this discussion of structure the concept of *fragmentation* adds the idea that people really don't add up except in the most comprehensive sense of that term. The introduction of the fragmentation corollary means that we are *not* dealing here with a kind of consistency theory. In fact it may be that inconsistencies are being maintained for very good reasons. This is the idea of the fruitful paradox. It is *not* necessary for the therapists to try to rout out all the inconsistencies in the client's life. There might be some long range incompatibilities and contradictions in the person's life that are the key to the person's creative abilities. Over the long haul the person comes up with truly creative solutions to life's problems in the process of reaching some kind of synthesis of apparent contradictions. In total the client's total structure is maintained in a loose over-reaching structure that holds the client together psychologically. But the client does not have to be tightly bound up in the therapy, with the therapist constantly pointing out all the inconsistencies. In this way the therapy is different from a 'rational' therapy. The goal is not the completely self-consistent person.

In summary, why is it important to understand the ordinal relationship between constructs? The heart of the matter is that the property of ordination provides a way for people to avoid chaos in their lives. In this way the property of ordination gives the outlines whereby the person can see more carefully the interconnections and implications that one area of life has for another. It also gives some way of ordering things in life so that the more important things are sorted out from the trivial. Instead of having a clutter of events, there should be a hierarchy within which choices can be made.

Another particular problem that is relevant to this topic is the client who has a particular way of thinking about the superordinate concerns or the broad valued orientations in life, and a very different way of thinking about the concerns that fill the actions of everyday life. It may be that these two things are not very well connected. For this reason the person may be experiencing some kind of 'value vacuum' or 'existential crisis'. The person is not really aware that the way he or she is acting in a particular situation is in any way connected to the things that he or she holds on to most dearly. The therapy might just be a way of helping the person to make connections between the day to day world and the high level values contain in the superordinate realm.

In another client the focus might be on the content of the superordinate constructs. For example a female client might be using a very strict evaluative construct such as 'good versus bad' in order to subsume many of the aspects of her own behavior, as well as significant others. For example, the client might be thinking that 'not showing up for work', is a bad thing, and that 'showing up for work' is a good thing. She then feels badly about missing work because this is not consistent with what she knows to be good. The therapist might find it helpful to initiate the use of a number of different ways to construe the event of missing a day at work. The shift might be, for example, in the direction of viewing the event as either 'useful' or 'not useful' for her goal of gaining independence from her rather unpleasant family situation. In this way the client has a new reason for thinking about her work behavior in other than a moralistic way. This shift might enable this woman to get on with the projects in her life rather than being paralyzed by the evaluative implications of her every activity.

Process and Function of Construct Systems

Although every colorollary has its own motivational components, the two corollaries presented in this section are central to this issue. Even though construct systems have a definite form (structure) they are always in the process of changing. This process is built directly into the construct's structure. It is not a matter of an inert structure being infused with some motivational force or psychic energy from the outside. Kelly was very much opposed to the traditional concept of motivation implying that external forces are either pushing or pulling some static structure.

Instead the person is understood psychologically through his or her own set of personal constructs which are constantly in motion. Both the person and his or her environment are seen as constantly moving and changing. For the person who is seen as constantly 'in process' the problem of psychological importance is to understand the direction in which he or she moves. These 'motivational' corollaries are stated in the following ways.

Choice Corollary: *A person chooses for himself that alternative in a dichotomized construct through which he anticipates the greater possibility for extension and definition of his system* Kelly, 1955, p.64).

Experience Corollary: *A person's construction system varies as he successively construes the replication of events* (Kelly, 1955, p.72).

Because traditionally the Choice Corollary has been considered as the central statement of motivational concerns within personal construct theory, this is where our discussion begins. The Choice Corollary's main focus is on the direction of movement for the person. This is put forth in terms of the choices which experientially exist for the person. In this theory the person, is always seen as having to make choices, but these choices are seen as orderly, understandable, and predictable when the person's own point of view is taken into consideration. The choices that exist for the person are the choices that exist between the poles of the constructs. For example, a relevant dimension in dealing with a certain person might be the meaning dimension of 'sensitive to feelings' which, in bipolar form, might be stated as 'sensitive to the feelings of others' versus 'insensitive'. This dimension is one selected because it has certain advantages in the present situation over — let us say — the dimension 'genius' versus 'ordinary intellect'. Let us suppose further that these two dimensions are being held in place by the superordinate construct of 'concerns of the heart' versus 'intellectual power'.

All the choices that can be made in this sub-system of constructs are structured by the nature of the construct dimensions that the person has available. In addition, the choice that is made in based on the greater possibility for the elaboration of the person's system at the moment. This is to say the choice made is in the direction where the person sees the best opportunity for the most complete understanding of his or her world at the moment. This can be either in the direction of a more comprehensive view (*extension*) of the situation or in the direction of more detailed knowledge of the matter (*definition*). The elaborative choice is made in the direction of the person sees as providing the greater possibility for the total growth and development of his or her construct system. This is the principle that governs the direction of movement in the system, which in turn is structured by the form of the bipolar constructs.

This is a far cry from saying that the choice is directed by the hedonic principle of pleasure versus pain, or even that it is based on validation or invalidation of hypothesis. Personal construct theory, however, does see some distinct adavantages in using the validation versus invalidation concept for other purposes, but we will explain that matter when the *Experience Corollary* is discussed.

Returning now to our example, let us say our client has chosen the 'concerns of the heart' pole of the construct' concerns of the heart' versus 'intellectual power'. In this way the client is indicating that his or her best opportunities can be realized by moving in this direction. The client might be saying that something central to values is to be dealt with rather than the ability to put forth a logical argument. With this decision made, the relevant question concerns the dichotomy of 'sensitive to feelings' versus 'insensitive to feelings'. The client then takes the 'insensitive to feelings' alternative since it implies the greater possibility for understanding the other person at this time. Perhaps the other person has just humiliated someone by turning a clever phrase. This choice offers at the moment the best understanding of the other person.

In this corollary only the choice itself is being addressed. This choice is of course structured by the particular construct dimension the person has available and the final decision point is between the two poles of a particular construct dimension. This does not imply, necessarily, that any of this choosing is accomplished at a very high level of awareness. The choice itself is governed by the elaborative possibilities that the choice holds for the person. Kelly insists that this even holds in the case of the self inflicted death. One particular kind of suicide makes this clear and that is the type illustrated by Socrates (Kelly, 1961). The choice for him was between renouncing all his teaching or drinking the hemlock to end his physical life; that is, the choice was either to end his spiritual life or his physical life. Socrates chose the hemlock in order to provide for the possibility of continuing his real life, his teaching. (This matter will be handled in more clinical detail later in this book.) The choice is taken in the direction of where the person sees his or her greatest possibilities. This points to the essentially psychological nature of this theory. The choice is a personal decision which is the initial step in the person's having some impact in the world. This sentiment is reflected in the following statements: '. . . . man makes decisions which initially affect himself, and which affect other objects only subsequently—and then only if he manages to take some effective action . . . . Men change things by changing themselves first, and they accomplish their objectives, if at all, only by paying the price of altering themselves—as some have found to their sorrow and others to their salvation. The choices that men make are choices of their own acts, and the alternatives are distinguished by their own constructs. The results of the choices, however, may range all the way from nothing to catastrophe, on the one hand, or to consummation, on the other.' (Kelly, 1966b, p.16).

The other main aspect of motivational concerns in Personal Construct Theory is portrayed in the Experience Corollary. The person is described as one who contacts the world in an active way. The emphasis is placed on the person's active interpretation of events rather than on the nature of the events themselves. The events of life, according to Kelly, are necessarily ordered on a time dimension. It is the task of the individual constantly to seek out the repetitive themes in the flow of new events. At first new events are only dimly perceived. There is then a search for some similarity to other known events which can serve to establish a repetitive theme that can, in turn, be contrasted with some other events. Here one has the emergence of a new construct which results in the person's being able to build an enriched system for living. The person is using what he or she has to tentatively explain something new. It is this groping with uncertainty that characterizes Personal Construct Theory. It is a theory of the unknown (Kelly, 1977).

This corollary focuses on the person's being confronted with the validation and invalidation of his or her construct system. This idea is that 'confirmation may lead to reconstruing quite as much as disconfirmation—perhaps even more. A confirmation gives one an anchorage in some areas of his life, leaving him free to set afoot adventuresome explorations nearby, as, for example, in the case of a child whose security at home emboldens him to be the first to explore what lies in the neighbour's yard . . . . A succession of such investments and dislodgments constitutes the human experience.' (Kelly, 1966b, p.18).

The unit of experience is seen as a cycle of five phases: anticipation, investment, encounter, confirmation or disconfirmation, and constructive revision. Much more will be said about this sequence later, for it is used as a model for the presentation of the psychotherapeutic enterprise in the next section of the book. It is sufficient, for the present, simply to point to the fact that the person must first anticipate events and then invest him or herself in a personal way in order for the system to progress. The encountering of events is done with some commitment to the outcome since an investment has taken place. At that point the person is open to validation or invalidation in such a way that constructive revision takes place. To short cut this complete cycle of experience is to prevent the person from benefiting from living a life enriched by true variability in the construct system. Kelly points out such a case of a school official who had had 13 years of experience, but accomplished in such a way that the poor fellow had really only one year of experience repeated 13 times.

Individual Differences and Interpersonal Relations

This portion of the basic theory deals with the nature of the relationships that exist among people. The nature of the social process is to be approached in terms of how one goes about gaining a truly psychological understanding of social relationships. The perspective taken in Personal Construct Theory is to approach social concerns form the person's own unique system of personal constructs. These corollaries are as follows:

Individuality Corollary: *Persons differ from each other in their construction of events* (Kelly, 1955, p.55).

Commonality Corollary: *To the extent that one person employs a construction of experience which is similar to that employed by another, his processes are psychologically similar to those of the other person* (Kelly, 1966b, p20).

Sociality Corollary: *To the extent that one person construes the construction processes of another, he may play a role in a social process involving the other person* (Kelly, 1955, p.95).

Beginning with the individuality corollary, the thesis presented is that each person has aspects of his or her construct system that are not identical with those of any other person. In addition to there being differences among people in the content of their construct dimensions there are differences in the ways these constructs are combined into a system of constructs. This thesis is particularly important for the therapist who must be concerned with individual clients as unique cases. Even though there are similarities between one person and another there are many aspects of each person that must be dealt with as his or her unique content and organization of constructs dictate. This places the demand on therapists to prepare themselves for building new constructs of their own in order to deal with each new client. The therapist should be prepared for that eventuality.

A rough analogy that has been drawn in the literature on uniqueness is to the meteorologist who must understand the general principles of weather systems but who must become particularly concerned with a single hurricane which is named and tracked as an individual system. This same concern is reflected in Gordon Allport's work with the morphogenic analysis of particular individuals (Allport, 1962). The individuality corollary is a declaration that part of this theory is concerned with how a particular person goes about structuring his or her life.

In contrast with this individuality corollary is the commonality corollary, which emphasizes the psychological similarity which occurs among different people. As might be expected, the similarity of concern pertains to the construct system rather than to the similarity of the events with which a person has had to deal in his or her life. This corollary implies that the life circumstances of two people may be quite similar, but if their interpretations of these circumstances are quite different then one will find two quite psychologically dissimilar people. On the other hand two people may encounter quite different external events in life, but may interpret them in the same way, and in that way produce this psychological similarity.

How this statement of commonality goes beyond even construct similarity must, however, be explained. For two people to be considered psychologically similar they must not only be able to predict the same things on the basis of similar construct dimensions, but they must also be similar in the ways in which the predictions were produced. Kelly states that 'We are interested, not only in the similarities in what people predict, but also in the similarities in their manner of arriving at their predictions' (Kelly, 1955, p.94). Since the corollary is stated in terms of similarity of construction of experience rather than similarity of events, for Kelly another way of stating the principle of psychological similarity is as follows: 'I wanted it to be clear that the construction would have to cover the experience itself, as well as the external events with which experience was ostensibly concerned. At the end of an experiential cycle one not only has a revised construction of the events he originally sought to anticipate, but he has also a construction of the process by which he reached his new conclusions about them. In launching his next venture, whatever its concern might be, he will have reason to take account of the effectiveness of the experiential procedures he employed in his last.' (Kelly, 1966b, p.21).

What has to be similar is the final conclusion people draw concerning what has happened to them, what that means to their life, and what questions it leads them to ask next. The psychological similarity is the similarity in the things that it leads people to pursue from this present moment in life onwards. The nature of this similarity is very important to recognize because it may lead to conclusions different from those of an analysis based only on past exposures to situations. This is perhaps best illustrated by the psychological similarity of two persons despite the contrasting cultural backgrounds. People from Bali, Chad, Russia, and the U.S.A. may all be quite similar if they have structured their different experiences in the same or similar ways. The emphasis is on the *way* the person has structured his or her experiences. As expressed by Kelly ". . . . the psychological similarity between the processes of two persons depends upon the similarity of their constructions of their personal experiences, as well as upon the similarity in their conclusions about external events" (Kelly, 1966b, p.21). It does not matter that persons might have used different pathways in their construct system in order to arrive at a prediction. What does matter, however, is that they make the same thing out of the *way* these conclusions were reached, as well as reaching the same conclusion, as such.

Concluding our discussion of the basic theory is an examination of the Sociality Corollary. This corollary reaches beyond the question of commonality to the issue of interpersonal relations; how people relate to one another. In Personal Construct Theory there are two orientations which stand in contrast to each other. On the one hand, we have the kinds of relationships with others which are based on the ability of one person to be able to predict and perhaps control the relationship with the other. The intention here is to be able to accurately predict the behavior pattern which will be emitted by the other. This kind of orientation is seen as a very limiting human condition. It is important when the other does not matter as a 'person' but only as a behavior emitting machine. In certain situations, such as in a large shopping center, this might even be appropriate. On entering a department store one simply wants to be able to have an accurate understanding of the traffic flow so that one is not crushed by the opposing line of shoppers. The point is that at some times people might best be regarded as behavior machines so that prediction and control are appropriate for understanding the situation. On the other hand there are qualities of interpersonal relationships which transcend the purely behavioristic orientation and the *other* is regarded as a 'person' in his or her own right. This is described as establishing a *role relationship* with the other person and requires that the one person not only construes the behavior of the other but attempts to construe the way the other person is experiencing his or her own world. The sociality corollary focuses on the process whereby one person attempts to construe the construction process of another person. The person attempts to subsume the construction processes of the other. Within this orientation to interpersonal relationships, what we do in relation to others is based on our understanding of what the other person is like 'as a person'. This does not mean that by understanding the other we would automatically agree with the other. We might even decide to oppose what we see in the other, but this opposition is based on what is called a role relationship with the other. We are not opposing a behavior emitting robot, but another person who in some respect is credited with having a personhood similar to our own in some ways, but quite different, perhaps, in most other ways. It is posited that such a role relationship creates a more compassionate relationship with others, even with others whom we oppose. This is offering a purely psychological definition of the term *role*. A role depends on *one* person's psychological activity, the activity of undertaking an understanding of the other's outlook.

This corollary is very important for the psychotherapist because it is the role relationship that forms the cornerstone for building the psychotherapeutic relationship. In order that the therapist should be effective, he or she must be able to establish a role relationship with the client. That is to say the counselor must base his or her understanding of the client on the understanding gained through attempting to subsume the construction processes of the client. It must be added that the client might return the compliment and construe the constructions of the therapist at the same time. The one does not preclude the other.

It must be added that there does not necessarily have to be an unusually high degree of accuracy of the other's construction processes; at least in the beginning stages of a relationship. Kelly states it in the following way, ". . . my construct of your construction processes need not be accurate in order for me to play a role in a social process that involves you. I have seen a person play a role, and do it most effectively—even in a manner quite acceptable to his colleagues—when he grossly misperceived their outlooks, and they knew it. But because he did what he did on the basis, of what he thought they understood, not merely on the basis of their overt acts, he was able to play a collaborative role in a social process whose experiential cycle led them all somewhere." (Kelly, 1966b, p.24).

**Characteristics of Single Construct
Dimensions and Systems of Constructs**

The following section provides an additional lists of terms for a psychology of personal constructs by presenting the formal characteristics of personal constructs. First brief definitions are offered for those terms that have been covered up to now in our discussion of the basic theory.

Elements: *The things or events which are abstracted by a person's use of a construct are called elements. In some systems these are called objects.* (Kelly, 1955, p.562).

Pole: *Each construct discriminates between the poles, one at each end of its dichotomy. The elements abstracted are like each other at each pole with respect to the construct and are unlike the elements at the other pole.* (Kelly, 1955, p.563).

Contrast: *The relationship between the two poles of a construct is one of contrast.* (Kelly, 1955 p.563).

Likeness End: *When referring specifically to elements at one pole of a construct, one may use the term 'likeness end' to designate that pole.* (Kelly, 1955, p.563).

Contrast End: *When referring specifically to elements at one pole of a construct one may use the term 'contrast end' to designate the opposite pole.* (Kelly, 1955, p.563).

Permeability: *A construct is permeable if it admits newly perceived elements to its context. It is impermeable if it rejects elements on the basis of their newness.* (Kelly, 1955, p.563).

Range of Convenience: *A construct's range of convenience comprises all those things to which the user would find its application useful.* (Kelly, 1955, p.562).

Focus of Convenience: *A construct's focus of convenience comprises those particular things to which the user would find its application maximally useful. These are the elements upon which the construct is likely to have been formed originally.* (Kelly, 1955, p.562).

Closely connected with the above list, of previously introduced characteristics, is the term *context* of a construct. It is defined in the following way.

'The context of a construct comprises those elements among which the user ordinarily discriminates by means of the construct. It is somewhat more restricted than the range of convenience, since it refers to the circumstances in which the construct emerges for practical use, and not necessarily to all the circumstances in which a person might eventually use the construct. It is somewhat more extensive than the focus of convenience, since the construct may often appear in circumstances where its application is not optimal.' (Kelly, 1955, pp.562–563).

The psychotherapist needs to understand the context in order that a construct evolved in one context may be used in another context. The client may benefit from being able to transfer his or her discriminations in one context to another. The client may learn to apply a construct more widely and find it to his or her advantages. At the same time, it is important, in other situations, to enable the client to discriminate in the use of different contexts. The meaning of a construct may be badly distorted as the context is changed.

One of the most important contexts to take into account, in order to understand a construct, is the context of family members. Understanding what a particular construct means in that context helps both the client and therapist come to terms with the use of a particular construct. For example a client may be using the construct 'fearful versus assured' as a way of sorting out the power struggles in the family. The client's way of being self-confident, for the most part, is to assume the opposite end of 'being fearful' which means putting the other family members in their place so to speak. The use of this construct in other contexts might not be to the client's advantage; for example among his or her associates at work. Assurance always has power-struggle implications because of the original context. Placed in other contexts the client may learn to modify the meaning of this dimension. The client may learn to be self-confident without being vindictive.

A slightly different concern is reflected in the concept of the *symbol* of a construct defined, in the following way.

> 'An element in the context of a construct which represents not only itself but also the construct by which it is abstracted by the user is called the construct's symbol.' (Kelly, 1955, p.563).

The symbol then is only one element which is serving as an example of what the construct is designed to handle. The symbol is important because it is often the only way the construct is verbalized. For example a female client might have 'my Father' as the symbol of a construct dimension that might be described as 'influencing others' versus, not 'not knowing how to manage things'. Let's say the father is a symbol (one element), under the pole 'influencing others'. The opposite pole may not have any consistent symbol, so that the whole construct dimension is represented by the essence of what the client takes her father to be like. When the client is trying to talk about being influential and effective, instead of dealing directly with the content she keeps talking about how her father does things and what he is like. It is not the client's father, as a person, who is being discussed but rather how he serves as a symbol for 'being influential' and effective in life as against messing things up and not knowing how to manage things. Being able to understand such a symbol might be very important in the counseling relationship with this client.

The symbol of a construct is often contained in what is known as the *emergent* pole of a construct, defined as follows:

> 'The emergent pole of a construct is that one which embraces most of the immediately perceived context.' (Kelly, 1955, p.563).

In psychotherapy it is common for the client to have available to himself or herself only one of the poles of a construct. The meaning, however, of the construct dimension may not be at all clear from a consideration of the emergent pole alone. The opposite end of such a pole is termed the *implicit* pole.

'The implicit pole of a construct is that one which embraces contrasting context. It contrasts with the emergent pole. Frequently the person has no available symbol or name for it; it is symbolized only implicitly by the emergent term.' (Kelly, 1955, p.563).

Such a pole of a construct dimension may hold many of the implications that use of this construct dimension carries with it. For a particular client, it may be puzzling, for both the client and the therapist, just why it is necessary for the client to be so forceful with people upon initial acquantance. It may be that the *implicit* pole of this construct carries with it the idea of being a 'nobody' in the presence of others. With this alternative one can better understand why the client 'comes on so strong' with others.

The next three characteristics of construct dimensions pertain to the nature of the control that a construct exerts over its elements.

Preemptive construct: *A construct which pre-empts its elements for membership in its own realm exclusively is called a pre-emptive construct. This is the 'nothing but' type of construction — 'If this is a ball it is nothing but a ball.'* (Kelly, 1955, p.563).

Constellatory construct: *A construct which fixes the other realm membership of its elements is called a constellatory construct. This is stereotyped or typological thinking.* (Kelly, 1955, p.563).

Propositional construct: *A construct which carries no implications regarding the other realm memberships of its elements is a propositional construct. This is uncontaminated construction.* (Kelly, 1955, p.564).

For the psychotherapist these characteristics are very important because they further determine the kinds of alternatives available to the person for living his or her life in any given situation. Each of these particular characteristics has some advantages and some disadvantages. Starting with the pre-emptive attribute, the control exerted is to foreclose on one alternative, at least for the moment, and consider that one dimension as the only relevant matter. For example, in considering all the possible ways one may think about one's fellow workers (conscientious versus uncaring, attractive versus ugly, etc.) it may be very important just now to consider the single dimension of whether they are friendly towards you versus being rather unfriendly. On the one hand, this pre-emption on a single construct dimension places the person in a position from which effective action may be taken. By doing this the person is predisposed either to reciprocate that friendship or to face the situation of not being in a friendly environment. On the other hand, a premature pre-emption might mean that other, more relevant, dimensions have been ignored. In the previous example, the work situation may not be one where personal concerns are relevant, and there may be more advantages found in concentrating on the dimension of whether the fellow workers are 'effective versus ineffective' in their work.

The constellatory nature of a construct dimension can be thought of as a slightly expanded pre-emptive quality. There is not just one dimension that is being considered (in terms of control exerted over elements), but there are definite limits set on how many other construct dimensions will be taken into consideration at a given time. Contained in this category is not only stereotyped thinking, but also simply set patterns of thinking about oneself and other people.

If a constellatory construction is being dealt with, there are automatically a number of other dimensions that are brought to bear. For example, in using the dimension 'friendly' versus 'unfriendly', the dimensions of kindness and extraversion are perhaps being simultaneously taken into consideration. On the one hand these constellatory constructs can be seen as stereotypes, in that once you know that a person is, for example, a banker, you know that he or she is likely to be mindful of details and to prefer conservative values. On the other hand the constellation has some advantages because there are tightly related dimensions of meanings which serve to organize the person's thinking. It is often the case, however, that the concern of the therapist, for a client, is with how the *set* or *fixed* meaning structures are distortions of the present reality.

The propositionality of a construct, in contrast to the other two characteristics, indicates very little if any control over the elements being embraced by the construct. It in no way fixes or controls the meaning of the elements. A given event or set of events may be interpreted in any number of different ways. A propositional construct in no way fixes the realm membership of its elements. To say that a given event is one thing in no way excludes it from being a number of other things as well. For example when propositionally considering one's mother, she is considered not only as a provider of goods and services, but also as a person who needs things, a person who needs love herself, a person who may be more or less open to new ideas, etc., all at the same time. This one element (mother) is then opened up to multiple interpretations rather than being thought of pre-emptively as nothing but a provider for others.

For the most part it is the aim of the therapy to enable the client to move in the direction of increased propositionality. Particularly early in the therapy, the counselor also should be propositional in his or her construction of the client. The advantage inherent in this approach is the increased knowledge one gains by considering alternative possibilities for the client. The disadvantage of this approach is that the whole time could be spent in considering different possibilities without reaching any effective conclusion. Propositionality, under some conditions, may place both the client and the therapist at some disadvantage.

Professional Constructs

This last set of terms in the language of personal constructs consists of those designed for use by the counselor in order to understand the construct system of the client. Even further these are terms which enable the therapist to formulate some strategy or plan of action for the therapy. In fact Kelly designated these as the 'diagnostic' constructs. These terms refer to characteristics of constructs and construct systems which enable the professional worker to formulate plans for effective psychotherapy.

Two of these professional terms have already been introduced in the Ordination Corollary. Since no concise description was presented at that point, the following definitions are offered.

Superordinate construct: *A superordinate construct is one which includes another as one of the elements in its context.* (Kelly, 1955, p.532).

Subordinate construct: *A subordinate construct is one which is included as an element in the context of another.* (Kelly, 1955, p.532).

Added to this list, for diagnostic purposes, is a third characteristic which is described as a special kind or superordinate construct. It is defined as follows:

Regnant construct: *A regnant construct is a kind of superordinate construct which assigns each of its elements to a category on an all-or-none basis, as in classical logic. It tends to be non-abstractive.* (Kelly, 1955, p.564–565).

The regnant construct might be thought of as an express train that runs directly from the superordinate (value like constructs) down to the constructs that are concerned with everyday activities. Thus, the person who has 'friendship' in a regnant relationship to 'sharing food and shelter' never hesitates to take in a neighbor whose house has just been destroyed. The operation of these constructs keeps life from being a confusing set of choice points which could paralyze a smooth and effective life flow. These are the kinds of constructs that might be utilized in order to aid the person in what others have called *values clarification* (Simon *et al.*, 1978). Following this flow of constructs reveals how one's values influence one's behavior. Considering a more serious problem, these constructs might be utilized in aiding people caught in existential dilemmas where life's meaning seems to be seeping out of their personal systems.

Another type of superordinate construct specifies the nature of a construct's range. It is described as follows:

Comprehensive construct: *Comprehensive constructs are those which subsume a relatively wide variety of events.* (Kelly, 1955, p.477).

This characteristic of a construct or a construct system contrasts with the following characteristic:

Incidental construct: *Incidental constructs subsume a small variety of events.* (Kelly, 1955, p.478).

Diagnostically this problem concerns how wide or narrow the influence of the particular superordinate construct under consideration is. If the psychotherapist begins to talk with the client about a concern that is in a comprehensive position, then the therapists might expect there to be ramifications throughout the personal system. For example: on the one hand a person might have the dimension *honest* versus *dishonest* located in a comprehensive position in that person's construct system, which means it affects almost every kind of interpersonal relationship the person has. On the other hand, this same person may have a concern with fashionable clothing which applies to a narrow set of his or her peers. Of course this is only one person's system, for another the honesty dimension might be incidental whereas the issue of fashion could be quite comprehensive.

In therapy it is very helpful to know how extensive the implications of a particular issue are. It is possible for the discussion of certain issues to reverberate throughout the system.

From a discussion of comprehensive constructs, we turn now to a concern with the access a person has to the world in which she lives. This is a concern with how the person receives her world. This is described as follows:

> Dilation: *Dilation occurs when a person broadens his perceptual field in order to reorganize it on a more comprehensive level. It does not, in itself, include the comprehensive reconstruction of these elements.* (Kelly, 1955, p.532).

The contrast to this process is defined as follows:

> Constriction: *Constriction occurs when a person narrows his perceptual field in order to minimize apparent incompatibilities.* (Kelly, 1955, p.532).

This is a problem-solving tactic which is concerned with how much of the world is to be processed at any one time. The process of dilation points the client in the direction of attempting to handle more different kinds of information from many different sources. In order to handle better some life problems the person backs off from the immediate problem in order to broaden his or her perspective on how a particular matter fits in with other life events. In other situations the client might use the strategy of avoiding the confusion that too much information can bring by attending to only a few incidents during the day and letting the rest of the world take care of itself for the time being.

Before leaving the concern with the broad topic of superordination there is the further concern of personal identity and integrity, defined in the following manner:

> Core construct: *Core constructs are those which govern a person's maintenance processes — that is, those by which he maintains his identity and existence.* (Kelly, 1955, p.482).

> Peripheral construct: *Peripheral constructs are those which can be altered without serious modification of core structure.* (Kelly, 1955, p.482–483).

The core constructs are those which are serving to stabilize the person's own sense of himself or herself as a person. These refer to the ultimate central concerns for every person; those concerns on which life depends. The therapist is well advised to be aware of which constructs may be connected to core structures.

On the one hand core constructs are characterized as being relatively comprehensive since the person needs to have central organizing principles that relate to a wide variety of life events. On the other hand core constructs should not be too permeable since it would not be a good idea for every new event to be seen as directly related to one's most central concerns. The core is resistant to change and usually changes only gradually over a period of time. When the therapist deals with the content of the core constructs, clients are likely to experience it as emotionally moving—an experience touching upon their deepest passions.

For the most part, the material dealt with in psychotherapy will center around what is termed the *role governing core*. These are the sub-set of core constructs which deal with the way we relate to others through establishing role relationships with them. Much of the material here, however, may *not* be well verbalized owing to the early age at which it was established. Particular interest will be centered on dependency themes. More will be explained about this in subsequent chapters.

There are some areas of content that, in all likelihood, will appear in core structure, such as a person's sexual identity and any other values and beliefs that serve to define the person's very being. These are things such that, if they were changed, the person would be fundamentally altered and would not longer be the person he or she now is. Another example of this material might be the person's cultural or sub-cultural identity, such as being Armenian, Jewish, or Lithuanian. This would be laid down early in life and serve as an assumptive base on which the rest of life is built.

The peripheral constructs might also be comprehensive constructs but they would relate to matters that are not central to one's identity. The material here might involve personal material in which the person is not primarily invested, for example whether one is very practical or impractical. Of course one would have to know the person's system in order to designate any content material as residing in either core or peripheral structure.

Yet another set of construct characteristics concerns how available, to the person, is the material that must be worked with in the therapy. Our first concern here is with *cognitive awareness*.

> Level of Cognitive Awareness: *The level of cognitive awareness ranges from high to low. A high-level construct is one which is readily expressed in socially effective symbols; whose alternatives are both readily accessible; which falls well within the range of convenience of the client's major constructions; and which is not suspended by its superordinating constructs.* (Kelly, 1955, p.532).

The concept of *level* is very important in personal consstruct psychotherapy because it replaces a concern with conscious versus unconscious material found in other theories. The concept of conscious versus unconscious often indicates that separate mechanisms operate in the two realms; whereas level of awareness indicates that the same principles govern the whole system and the primary problem is the placement of these principles on any number of different levels. The concern with a threshold of awareness is minimized.

Closely related to level of awareness is the concept of suspension.

> Suspension: *A suspended element is one which is omitted from the context of a construct as the result of revision of the person's construct system.* (Kelly, 1955, p.532).

This characteristic is related in some respects to the fragmentation corollary, since one way for incompatible material to be handled is for it to become suspended from the total system. It is, nevertheless, still available to the person in some respects. Material held in suspension is seen as having implications for the system as a whole even though it resides at a low level of awareness. The suspended construct dimension might be allowed to reappear if a new superordinate construct comes into use which could tolerate the presence of this information. This suspended material may be either negative or positive as far as the person is concerned. In this way it is very different from the concept of repression as used in other theories.

Another concern that was encountered earlier under the topic of 'emergent' pole versus 'implicit' pole of a construct is the concept of submergence.

> Submergence: *The submerged pole of a construct is the one which is less available for application to events.* (Kelly, 1955, p.532).

With submergence one is dealing with more than just an implicit understanding of the missing pole of a construct dimension. The submerged pole of a construct is at a low level of awareness because of the kind of implications involved in the total construction. Perhaps the emergent pole of a construct involves the client's depressed outlook, but opposite to this is the submerged end of this construction which involves the client's anger, even rage, at his or her life situation. The anger is submerged as a pole of this dimension because it implies for the client a type of unacceptable behavior, such as totally obliterating the surrounding environment.

Within this discussion of 'unconscious' or nonconscious material the final term introduced is *preverbal constructs*. Since this topic was covered in some detail in the first chapter only the formal definition is presented here.

> Preverbal Constructs: *A preverbal construct is one which continues to be used, even though it has no consistent word symbols. It may or may not have been devised before the person had command of speech.* (Kelly, 1955, p.532).

The last of the professional terms dealing with the general nature of constructs is the dimension of 'tightening versus loosening'.

> Tight Constructs: *A tight construct is one which leads to unvarying predictions.* (Kelly, 1955, p.565).

> Loose Constructs: *A loose construct is one leading to varying predictions, but which retains its identity.* (Kelly, 1955, p.565).

This dimension is, perhaps, the single most important concern in conceptualizing the total enterprise of psychotherapy. For this reason only a very brief description will be offered at this point since it will be discussed in greater detail later. When a construct is being tightened the exact meaning of the content of the construct is specified. In tightening, the client is asked to speak slowly and in complete sentences so that it becomes clear just what is being said and what implications follow from what is being described. In loosening, the client is asked to relax and report on fantasies and dreams about the material. The client is encouraged not to try to make 'good sense' but to let things flow and follow the thought as it develops. This dimension is used to refer to specific individual constructs and to the general system of constructs. Bannister and his colleague (Bannister, 1960; Bannister and Fransella, 1965; Bannister *et al.*, 1971) have made extensive use of this construct in their work with schizophrenic clients.

Traditional Constructions

This group of professional constructs deals with those issues which are particularly designed to handle change in personal construct systems. It deals with the person as he or she changes. These issues are concerned with some of the things people feel intensely. It is as if the person has strong feelings when he or she is most alive and is undergoing some particular transition in life. The human emotions are seen as particular kinds of transitions in the personal construct system. Again only a brief sketch of these issues will be presented since the topic of personality change will be dealt with more extensively in subsequent chapters.

The first of these concerns is with *anxiety*, one of the most frequently addressed topics in any psychological investigation of the human condition. Anxiety is approached as a transition term. It is a term that refers to the person undergoing a significant modification—a personal change. It is defined as follows:

Anxiety: *Anxiety is the recognition that the events with which one is confronted lie outside the range of convenience of one's construct system.* (Kelly, 1955, p.495).

The most obvious quality of anxiety is, of course, the strong feeling component of pain, confusion, bewilderment, and sometimes panic. This feeling state is seen as the reaction one has when one's construct system sketches in only enough of the outline of the problem so that one can perceive that one's available set of constructs is inadequate to handle the situation. There must be some recognition of the problem, otherwise the person would simply not perceive the situation and therefore be unaffected by it.

Anything that reduces the range of convenience of the construct system would effect anxiety by increasing the probability that any given event would then be inadequately handled. One would further expect that a less elaborate system, having fewer constructs, would increase the likelihood of producing anxiety. A person can be made anxious by present issues with which that person has little familiarity. For example, having to answer questions about mathematics would make the person unschooled in such matters extremely anxious.

While anxiety is painful, it can also have its beneficial components. The anxiety one feels is often part of the creative quest for new information. By placing oneself on the road to discovery one is likely often to be in the situation of confronting problems which lie mostly outside one's present construct system. '. . . anxiety, *per se*, is not to be classified as either good or bad. It represents the awareness that one's construction system does not apply to the events at hands. It is, therefore, a precondition for making revisions.' (Kelly, 1955, p.498).

A human condition that is sometimes confused with anxiety is that of *threat* which is defined as follows.

Threat: *Threat is the awareness of an imminent comprehensive change in one's core structures.* (Kelly, 1955, p.489).

In threat, unlike anxiety, the life events that are being dealt with are recognized all too clearly. As the material is recognized, the implications for profoundly changing the person become obvious. People feel threatened in situations that promise to change them in such a way that they are to become something quite different from what they are now. Kelly comments that one's impending death is likely to be such an event. It is perceived as unavoidable and has the power of radically altering what the person now takes himself or herself to be.

Other aspects of threat are revealed in Landfield's exemplification and expectancy hypotheses, defined as follows:

'His (Landfield's) *exemplification hypothesis* was that a person would be perceived as threatening if he appeared to exemplify what the perceiver himself once was but no longer is . . . . Landfield's second threat hypothesis was the *expectancy hypothesis*. A person is seen as threatening if he appears to expect the perceiver to behave in the old ways.' (Kelly, 1955, p.490–491).

Here the emphasis is on persons who are threatening to the client. They are threatening because they are inviting the client to move in a direction that could comprehensively change the core structure. In this way the therapist can often be a threatening figure, as it becomes obvious that comprehensive changes are necessary for the line of therapy undertaken. It is important to keep in mind that threat is involved in self change, whether that change is in a desired or undesired direction. The threat involved in sudden success that promises fundamentally to alter core structure serves as an example of desirable change that is nevertheless threatening. If the success has no implications for change then no threat will be experienced. Threat is usually more obvious to us when a failure experience implies a fundamental change.

Closely related to threat is the concept of fear, which is defined as follows:

Fear: *Fear is the awareness of an imminent incidental change in one's core structures.* (Kelly, 1955, p.533).

Fear is different from threat in that the implied change is incidental rather than comprehensive; not as much of the core structure is to be involved. We are made fearful by what we know less about because it is not likely to be obvious to us how profoundly it can change us. If we know little about radiation poisoning it will frighten us. As we gain more knowledge about this matter and how it can affect our present life and the lives of future generations it is more likely to threaten us. If the change is only to affect a small area of our lives it is frightening.

Another component of this transitional emotional experience in people's lives is described in the personal construct definition of guilt.

Guilt: *Perception of one's apparent dislodgment from his core role structure constitutes the experience of guilt.* (Kelly, 1955, p.502).

With this concept, which is so often approached from an external-social perspective, it is important to note in construct theory that guilt is dealt with as an emotional condition defined solely from the point of view of the person— from the inside out. Guilt occurs when people find that the things they are doing are discrepant from what they take themselves to be. The core role structure involves those constructs the person uses to interact with others. These constructs also serve to maintain that person's sense of integrity and identity. Defined in this way, the person feels guilty when he or she slips out of this role or is in some way confronted by the fact that a dislodgement from this structure has taken place. A person feels guilt when he or she steals only if being a thief is discrepant from what the person takes the self to be. If stealing is not discrepant from the core role structure then no guilt will occur. If the person has not formed a clear role relationship with others then little guilt can be felt.

Defined in this way guilt has little to do with violation of social norms as seen from an external perspective. The concern instead is with the way the person has structured core role relationships. The handling of guilt does not point solely to an external manifestation of expiational rituals. Instead, the therapist concentrates on the nature of a self-structure which can begin to understand the nature of the dislodgment and which might guide the person in this transitional experience. With guilt, as with the other issues in this section, some personal change is being indicated.

Yet another concern, in this area of transition, is with the forward movement of the person. This concern is reflected in the definition of aggressiveness.

Aggressiveness: *Aggressiveness is the active elaboration of one's perceptual field.* (Kelly, 1955, p.508).

The type of transition indicated here is seen by the person who is actively pursuing the choice points that his or her own personal construct system offers. There is a kind of spontaneous quality to aggression which enables the person to investigate more fully what implications his or her system has for what can be done. The people around such a person might feel threatened because the person might be involving them in a rapid-fire line of action that would alter them in some profound way. Aggression is likely to occur in areas of anxiety where the person is attempting to build a structure to handle events that are presently outside his or her realm of understanding. For the most part, aggression is treated as a constructive enterprise that might well be identified with a person's assertive qualities. The aggressive qualities are, in fact, the assertive building of the construct system. Some of the more negative qualities that are commonly identified with aggression are handled with the next concept—the feeling of hostility—defined as follows:

> Hostility: *Hostility is the continued effort to extort validational evidence in favor of a type of social prediction which has already proved itself a failure.* (Kelly, 1955, p.510).

The power that one finds in hostility as a result of the extortion effort might be confused with aggression which is simply the active (spontaneous) elaboration of the system. In hostility the person may be passionately angry or methodically cool, calm and collected. Anger or the lack of it is not the most important dimension to take into consideration. What is important is the fact that part of the person's world is beginning to crumble (become invalidated) and the person believes it necessary to insist that supporting evidence be produced. The husband is being hostile when he insists that his wife overtly express her love when, in fact, the two no longer have a loving relationship. The core of the hostile persons is involved in this enterprise. In this way one may see the hostile person fighting for his or her life. Perhaps this is a compassionate picture of the hostile person; something that is missed in many other of our understandings of hostility. At any rate the job of the therapist often focuses around the question of what is being invalidated, and what makes this invalidation impossible for the person to bear just now.

Recently the topic of the emotions has been addressed both by Bannister (1977) and McCoy (1977). McCoy in fact has attempted to add to this transitional conception of emotional experiences by offering definitions of bewilderment, doubt, love, happiness, satisfaction, complacency, sadness, self-confidence, shame, contempt or disgust, contentment, startle or surprise, and anger. The reader is urged to consult her work for a discussion of these additional terms. One of these additional terms is presented there as follows:

> 'Love: *Awareness of validation of one's core structure* . . . . In short, in love one sees oneself completed by the loved person and core structures are validated.' (McCoy, 1977, p.109).

This is a kind of total affirmation of oneself as a total being. There is a kind of completion of the person implied in this definition. Epting (1977) offered a slightly different definition which is as follows:

> 'Love: *Love is a process of validation and invalidation which leads to the best elaboration of ourselves as complete persons.*'

This definition covers not only the love found in confirmation and support as in a validation but also covers the love that serves to invalidate those things about us that is not worthy of us. The loving act is not always supportive, but it always is in a direction that is intended to complete us as a person. This love also places us on the edge of our construct systems. It enables us to become truly experimental with our lives.

Cycles of experience. This last section of transitional constructions pertains to the cycles of experience involving *action* and *creativity*. Presented first is the cycle pertaining to the ability of the person to take some effective action in life— defined as follows:

> The C-P-C Cycle: *The C-P-C Cycle is a sequence of construction involving, in succession, circumspection, preemption, and control, and leading to a choice precipitating the person into a particular situation.* (Kelly, 1955, p.515).

In any therapy an understanding of human action must be undertaken, otherwise the person is left at best with only a better understanding of life without any way of putting that understanding into practice. This sequence begins with circumspection, which is the matter of employing constructs in a propositional way. The matter at hand is construed in many different ways at once—various interpretations of the life situation are offered. Then comes the pre-emption, when one of these alternative dimensions of meaning is selected for special consideration. Without selecting one dimension, at least momentarily, no action is possible since the person would be constantly considering alternatives. Life at that point presents itself as a choice between the poles of a single dimension. In this way the person is exercising the personal control in his or her system by making the choice and taking some action. The person involves himself or herself in a personal way in the affairs of life. This choice is made of course in the direction of elaborating the total system. This cycle offers an understanding of human action by attending to the weights placed on different parts of the cycle. On the one hand you have the contemplative client who is unable to accomplish many things because the alternatives are all separately so appealing that no one choice is made. One the other hand one finds the client who might be described as a 'man of action' who perhaps precipitates himself all too quickly into making a decision that leads to some specific act. In fact impulsivity is defined in the following way:

> Impulsivity: *The characteristic feature of impulsivity is that the period of circumspection which normally precedes decision is unduly shortened.* (Kelly, 1955, p.526).

This means then in some circumstances the person attempts to find a sudden solution to a problem. This might be expected to occur when the person is made anxious or guilty or threatened. An understanding of this cycle perhaps gives some way of defining the problem of impulsivity and offers some productive solutions.

The second major cycle is that of creativity, defined as follows:

> Creativity: *The creativity cycle is one which starts with loosened construction and terminates with tightened and validated construction.* (Kelly, 1955, p.565).

The creativity process is then a matter of loosening and tightening. As mentioned earlier, the planning of psychotherapy is largely centered around this tightening and loosening dimension. This is to say that the process of psychotherapy is seen mainly as a creative enterprise where the therapist is attempting to aid the client in becoming more inventive with his or her life. The creativity cycle addresses the question of how one creates new meaning dimensions so that the system can be elaborated to cover truly new material. This is using the term creativity to cover those processes that are used to account for something fresh and new being introduced into the system; something that did not exist before.

The answer to that problem lies in the direction of allowing the client to loosen the present meaning system so that new material has a chance to be recognized in some hazy form. In this loosened phase the person is usually reluctant to verbalize what is taking place. These approximations to new conceptualizations are then progressively brought into a tightened structure—a structure which will allow testable formulations to be made so that some validation is possible. Creativity then involves both loosening and tightening. In order that new meaning may emerge, the counselor must be able to aid the client to undertake both and to see both as valuable aspects of his or her personality.

Summary

This chapter has presented the main terms in the language of a personal construct psychotherapy. The initial concern was with constructive alternativism—the basic philosophical position of the theory. The fundamental postulate and each of the eleven corollaries were presented in order to explain the theory's structure, dynamics, and principles of interpersonal relations. Also presented were the formal characteristics of construct systems, followed by what were termed charcteristics of professional constructs. These are basically diagnostic terms that deal with both formal characteristics as well as the transitional themes that enable the therapist to understand personal changes in the client.

PART II

The Psychotherapeutic Venture as a Total Experience

One way to organize the enterprise of psychotherapy is to view it as a total or complete experience for both the counselor and the client. In Personal Construct Theory the total unit of experience is envisaged as a five phase cycle embracing the separate processes of anticipation, investment, encounter, confirmation or disconfirmation, and constructive revision (Kelly, 1966b).

For psychotherapy the *anticipation* phase (covered in chapter 3) is approached as the hypothesis formation stage or planning stage of the therapy. In the anticipation phase the therapist begins to formulate a tentative picture of the client as a total person and of the client's presenting problem. As the therapy progresses, this initial picture is constantly being revised. In this phase the counselor might employ a formal assessment procedure, the role construct repertory (Rep) test, in order to gain a more precise view of the client's personal and interpersonal experiences. The Rep test gives the counselor a sample of the construct dimensions which the client is currently employing. In addition, some therapists ask clients to produce a short written sketch of themselves in order to aid in this assessment enterprise. The formal assessment of the person is followed by the appraisal of the client's various activities, which often includes an assessment of the total social context of the client's life. The conclusion of the anticipation phase involves the *'diagnosis'* of the client along personal construct lines. Diagnosis is a more or less complete description of a person's construct system using both the formal terms of the theory and what Kelly called 'transitional' terms, which describe the person's psychological processes. Woven into this description are implications for personal change. Diagnosis does not involve the use of traditional psychopathological terms which serve only to pigeonhole the client for the purpose of some administrative action by a 'mental health' official.

The second phase of the experience cycle, that of psychological *investment* (covered in chapter 4), brings the client and therapist fully into the enterprise of psychotherapy itself. The general approach taken to the client is presented, with attention focused initially on the client's complaints in life. By complaints we mean the problems in living which need to be dealt with in the therapy.

Investment is the involvement of both the client and the therapist in the therapy. In this way what happens in psychotherapy matters, in an important way, to those engaged in the process. Investment is a courageous act for both client and therapist. In the investment phase there is a real involvement of the two people in the process of therapy.

The third phase of the cycle of experience, *encounter* (covered in chapter 5), brings the client and the therapist to the point where some effective action can be taken. There must be a *commitment* made which totally immerses the persons in the psychotherapeutic enterprise. It is an aggressive (assertive) response in that an active elaboration of the construct system is undertaken; with this, of course, comes some risk. This is to say, effective therapy involves some risk for the client and for the therapist. The therapist, however, does everything possible to minimize excessive risk. It is during this third phase that the client faces significant aspects of his or her life and the implied life changes which have only been alluded to in previous phases. A dialogue is set up in this phase between the client and the therapist which allows the person to explore life outside the narrower confines of the initial complaint. Particular attention is paid, at this time, to the relationship between fantasy and behavior.

The fourth phase of the cycle, *confirmation* and *disconfirmation* (covered in chapter 6) goes beyond the commitment necessary for the encounter phase. At this point the person comes to terms with just what has happened as a consequence of the commitment made earlier. During this phase in psychotherapy the dimensions of tightening and loosening are focused upon. Major emphasis is placed on seeing psychotherapy as a creative enterprise. In order for new constructs to be introduced into the system there must be a recognition of just how the present constructions have, in fact, turned out. One of the major questions raised here, concerns how the client's concepts have stood up to the test of disconfirming as well as confirming information.

The final phase is that of *constructive revision* (covered in chapter 7). After the confirmation or disconfirmation has taken place, the client is faced with a total appraisal of his or her undertakings. Some account is taken of the total construct system revision which has taken place. If the therapy has been effective it has enabled the person to gain new 'vantage points' for taking stock of what life is like. The main focus in this section is on productive movement and change in therapy and in active exploration of the results of the therapeutic enterprise up to this point.

CHAPTER 3

Anticipations

Every major term in Personal Construct Theory contains, either explicitly or implicitly, the quality of anticipation. It is an orientation to the future which directs the person to reach out for what is coming next. In the construct theory view, the person literally lives by and through anticipation. It has been pointed out, however, that this anticipation is not a future orientation that robs the present life of the person (Landfield, 1977). The person does not live 'in the future' but rather uses the future to enrich the present moment. This anticipation need not be an active, vigilant type of process but rather can be very passive and filled with contemplation, as in the expression 'I wonder what will happen next.' It may be more accurate to say that 'anticipation' can be seen as global and unfocused at some times and at other times precisely focused on anticipating the occurrence of specific events.

Aside from this general understanding of anticipation, the way this term is used in this chapter includes those things which are propaedeutic to an actual therapy, or rather to the actual moment-to-moment therapeutic enterprise. In the approach taken to psychotherapy by construct theory, it is very important for there to be time explicitly put aside in order to anticipate the nature of the therapy which is about to take place. This anticipatory phase is a way of preparing the therapist for the therapy in such a way that it maximizes the chances for a successful therapy.

Although anticipation (as a phase in therapy) is mentioned first, it does not mean that anticipation is only done at the beginning of therapy and then forgotten about for the remainder of the time. Nor does it mean that everything that one undertakes as a therapist must be anticipated before any action is taken. Kelly (1955, p.1190) warns against making the 'historical fallacy' whereby one never undertakes anything unless one has first anticipated all the consequences. For the most part it is thought that a much better way of going about things is to keep this anticipation constantly in process throughout the therapy. In fact, it may be that the best 'diagnosis' is only possible after one is well under way in the therapy. The anticipation phase is simply a way of beginning the activity that is called psychotherapy. Covered under this term anticipation are those general ways of collecting the elements of a therapy in such a way that something productive has a possibility of taking place.

In this chapter will be found some tentative classifications for dealing with the client and the therapy. Kelly (1955, p.1004–1005) called these *structurations*. These are simply a set of convenient pigeonholes which the therapist can use to keep things sorted out. As the therapy progresses, the structurations are refined and modified to become the actual *construction* of the therapy. These more precise *constructions* are centered around those matters that the client will be elaborating in more detail during the actual therapy. These early 'structurations' make it possible for the therapist to prepare himself or herself for the therapy.

Client's Expectations

One of the first types of anticipations for the counselor to be concerned with is how the client perceives the counseling situation. Just what is the client expecting from the therapy and from the therapist? In his 1955 psychotherapy volume Kelly listed some twelve alternative perceptions the client may have of the therapy and some twelve different conceptions the client may have of the therapist. For example the therapy may be a setting in which the client is planning to carry out rather drastic changes which have already begun to take place. The therapy may be seen as a safe haven for such change. This situation is a frequent occurrence in marital therapy, where the purpose of the counseling is to help the person come to terms with an inevitable divorce. On the other hand, the therapy may be seen as a situation in which the client has decided to take a rather passive stand toward things. In still other situations the therapist may be seen as a stooge or foil, or possibly as an authority figure. Kelly thought that it was an advantage for the therapist to be seen as a representative of reality. This would then set the stage for the experimental work that should take place in the therapy. The reader is urged to consult Kelly's book for a more detailed discussion of these different expectations. (Kelly, 1955, p.566–581).

These expectations are mentioned here not so much to present the content of these different concepts, but rather to point out the importance, in personal construct psychotherapy, for the therapist to be concerned with just what the client's expectations are of the therapy and of the therapist. These expectations can be very important in determining how the therapy will begin. The anticipations of the client will shape the nature of the personal concerns that the client will be presenting for initial consideration in the therapy.

Assessment Procedure

The role of anticipation in Personal Construct Psychotherapy is further seen in the appraisal of the construct system of the client. Described here are a set of tools the therapist has available for gaining an appreciation of just who the client is psychologically. The client is approached as a unique person with hopes, desires, stresses, pains, and joys. Just what is the nature of this person whom we take, just now, to be our client? What are the best ways (major constructs) which can be used to adequately describe this client in order that new pathways can be opened up for greater freedom of movement? The primary purpose of the assessment is to provide *useful* information for the client and therapist. The purpose of the assessment is the same as the purpose of the therapy. For Kelly (1955, p.204), 'Therapy is concerned with setting up regnant personal constructs to give new freedom and new control to the client who has been caught in the vice-like grip of obsolescent constructs.' It is hoped that the picture of the client that emerges though the assessment will be that of a complete and real person. The question raised is: 'How is the therapist to know the client in order to best offer some help to that client?'

Although the concern in this section is with *specific* techniques which have been developed for formal assessment, it must be remembered that no formal procedures *have* to be used in personal construct psychotherapy. After all it is a basic understanding of the client that is sought, and many counselors find that they prefer not to rely heavily on any formal procedure other than the clinical interview. In fact all of the assessment procedures discussed in this chapter might be best thought of as simply structured interviews of various types. The different procedures described in this chapter are presented only for the convenience of the therapist interested in this theory and should not be interpreted as an absolutely necessary part of the personal construct theory approach.

It must be pointed out, however, that some psychotherapists have become very concerned about the assessment procedure and actually structure the entire therapy around it. For these therapists the assessment procedure is used as a probe and offers structure for the interview. The general consensus is that the structured assessment interview is particularly helpful with the less verbal client. The assessment devices help the client grasp concrete issues and help in giving form to the thoughts the client wishes to express. It is a safe guess that less than one-third of all construct therapists make extensive use of formal assessment procedures.

Due to the fact, however, that assessment tools are specific, concrete and manipulatable, there has been an extensive amount of work in this area. In fact at the present time, it is the most widely publicized and published aspect of personal construct psychotherapy. The work in this field has centered around what Kelly termed The Role Construct Repertory Test or Grid. Unlike many other authors of theories of psychotherapy who ignore measurement techniques, Kelly developed a specific assessment procedure which is integrally related to the theory. The actual procedures used are designed to assess the construct characteristics presented in chapter 2.

There have been several books published which concern themselves mainly with this instrumentation. One of the most recent is the Fransella and Bannister (1977) *'Manual for Repertory Grid Technique'*. This book provides a detailed account of the clinical and research use of this instrument. In addition Patrick Slater (1976; 1977) has edited a two-volume work *'The Measurement of Intrapersonal Space by Grid Technique'* which provides examples of work done with this instrument as well as a detailed description of a principal component procedure for analyzing the protocols. The Rep Grid procedure has also been given extensive attention by Landfield (1971) in his book describing the structural and contentual dimensions of a group of clients undergoing psychotherapy. Further accounts can be found in Bannister and Fransella's (1971) general overview of personal construct psychology, in Bannister and Mair's (1968) earlier book on the quantitative aspects of this orientation, and in a recent account by Neimeyer and Neimeyer (1981).

Role Construct Repertory (Rep) Technique

As noted above, a way both to anticipate what is to take place in the therapy and to gain a psychological understanding of the client is to invite the client to produce a sample of her or his construct system in bipolar form. This technique is commonly referred to as the Rep test (Kelly, 1955). It is not, however, a test in the usual sense of that word since the content and form of the instrument should be modified to fit the needs of the counselor and the client. This instrument might best be thought of as a structured interview technique whereby the counselor can gain a quick overview of some, at least, of the client's major construct dimensions.

In one of the most frequently used forms of the Rep. test, the *Grid* form (Kelly, 1955, p.272) the client is asked to nominate 22 people who fit the designated role descriptions listed in Figure 1 under the heading 'conceptual grid overlay sheet — figure list'. As indicated in Figure 1, the client is then asked to attend to these 22 figures three at a time by noticing the placement of the three circles in successive rows of the 'Conceptual Grid'. Each of the 22 rows contains a 'sort' of three figures which are designated for clinical purposes described in further detail in Figure 2.

The client begins by considering sort no. 1, the 'value sort'. The client is asked to place an 'x' mark in the circle of the two figures who are similar in some important way and to leave the third circle blank. In the example of the completed grid in Figure 3, the client has indicated that his nominated 'successful' and 'happy' person are similar when compared with his 'ethical' person. The client is then asked to name the characteristic which makes the two figures similar and different from the third, and then to give what he considers to be the opposite of this named characteristic. These characteristics are placed, respectively, under the heading 'construct' and 'contrast'. In the example, the client reports that the 'successful' and 'happy' person are similar in that they 'Don't believe in God', while the opposite of this is being 'very religious'. This construct dimension is considered to be more than just words or a complete thought. It is seen as a meaning dimension which is an expression of a way of being involving a feeling and implying some specific actions. Considering this first construct dimension the client is then asked to put a checkmark (✓) under the names of all figures who also manifest the construct pole 'Don't believe in God'. The client, in the example, nominates the ex-flame, the rejecting person, and the threatening person for this distinction. Each of the remaining 21 *Sorts* are completed in the same manner. In Figure 3 a blank is interpreted as the application of the contrast pole.

Analysis of the Rep grid is accomplished in two main ways. First the *content* of each of the constructs is examined for the types of constructs and the level of abstraction of the constructs. This is a study of the *qualities* of experience covered by the constructs in the grid. In the example used here only a few of the constructs are abstract and deal with the personal qualities of the figures. Many of the constructs are characteristics dealing with physical or surface qualities of the figures (e.g. have brown eyes, from the south), special role characteristics (e.g. lawyers, teachers, etc.), or refer back to the client (e.g. understand me better, don't understand at all). Often an examination is made of the varieties of constructs used, whether there are repeated themes in the list, and whether some constructs are noticeable by their absence. The content of the constructs can also be examined in the way they are used to thread certain figures together around various themes and in this way serve to link the constructs together.

In a recent case I had the opportunity to supervise, Rigdon (Rigdon and Epting, 1983) using the Rep grid to initiate an investigation of the major construct dimension of a client regarded as extremely 'obsessive' by a clinical staff assessment. Starting with the Rep grid administration and extending over six sessions with the client, the client gradually clarified for himself and the therapist the following main dimension: 'unattached diplomatic, separates personal feelings from what is going on' as the preferred or positive pole *versus* 'thin-skinned, lost in the conversation without knowing where they are', as the non-preferred or negative pole. During the administration of the grid, Rigdon asked the client to indicate which pole of each construct he most preferred, liked, or found attractive as a personal characteristic. With this knowledge of the client's construct system, it was much easier for the therapist to understand why the client was resisting so strongly any attempts to get him to move close to his feeling about things. For the client moving in the direction of feelings implied becoming lost and losing his bearing in the situation. Subsequently the therapist began to concentrate on the lack of commitment the client was willing to make to life projects. The client then spontaneously generated 'venturesome' as a feasible alternative to this 'non-committal' stance. This new dimension of 'venturesome' versus 'non-committal' then became a new way to construe the world which cut across and served to free the client from his former concern with emotions and whether to express them or not. It is a good bet that further work with the client would center around ways to integrate these two dimensions. It is hoped that this case example will serve to demonstrate that constructs are not single words but a felt meaning dimension, and that content of these construct dimensions can help both the client and the therapist to a better understanding of the broad outlines of a productive therapy.

For the most part, the content analysis of construct systems has remained informal amd 'clinical' in nature. Landfield (1971), however, has provided

FIG. NO.

	FIG. NO.		
	1		Se
	2		Mo
	3		Fa
	4		Br
	5		Si
	6		Sp
	7		XF
	8		Pa
	9		XP
	10	MF	Mi
	11	MF	MD
	12	MF	No
	13	MF	RP
	14	MF	PP
	15	MF	UP
	16	MF	AP
	17	MF	AT
	18	MF	RT
	19	MF	Bo
	20	MF	SP
	21	MF	HP
	22	MF	EP

SORT NO.: 22 21 20 19 18 17 16 15 14 13 12 11 10 9 8 7 6 5 4 3 2 1

Construct Contrast

Name

Number Date

CONCEPTUAL GRID

12-14-53

CONCEPTUAL GRID OVERLAY SHEET — FIGURE LIST

1. Write your own name in the first blank here.
2. Write your mother's first name here. If you grew up with a stepmother, write her name instead.
3. Write your father's first name here. If you grew up with a stepfather, write his name instead.
4. Write the name of your brother who is nearest your own age. If you had no brother, write the name of a boy near your own age who was most like a brother to you during your early teens.
5. Write the name of your sister who is nearest your own age. If you had no sister, write the name of a girl near your own age who was most like a sister to you during your early teens.

*FROM THIS POINT ON DO NOT REPEAT ANY NAMES. IF A PERSON HAS ALREADY BEEN LISTED, SIMPLY MAKE A SECOND CHOICE.

6. Your wife (or husband) or, if you are not married, your closest present girl (boy) friend.
7. Your closest girl (boy) friend immediately preceding the person mentioned above.
8. Your closest present friend of the same sex as yourself.
9. A person of the same sex as yourself whom you once thought was a close friend but in whom you were badly disappointed later.
10. The minister, priest, or rabbi with whom you would be most willing to talk over your personal feelings about religion.
11. Your physician.
12. The present neighbor whom you know best.
13. A person with whom you have been associated who, for some unexplained reason, appeared to dislike you.
14. A person whom you would most like to help or for whom you feel sorry.
15. A person with whom you usually feel most uncomfortable.
16. A person whom you have recently met whom you would like to know better.
17. The teacher who influenced you most when you were in your teens.
18. The teacher whose point of view you have found most objectionable.
19. An employer, supervisor, or officer under whom you served during a period of great stress.
20. The most successful person whom you know personally.
21. The happiest person whom you know personally.
22. The person known to you personally who appears to meet the highest ethical standards.

Figure 1. The grid form of the Role Construct Repertory (Rep) test (from Kelly, 1955; reproduced by permisison of W. W. Norton & Co., Inc.)

64

SELF	SITUATIONALS	VALUES
1. Self	10. Minister	20. Successful Person
	11. Physician	21. Happy Person
FAMILY	12. Neighbour	22. Ethical Person
2. Mother		
3. Father	VALENCIES	
4. Brother	13. Rejecting Person	
5. Sister	14. Pitied Person	
	15. Threatening Person	
INTIMATES	16. Attractive Person	
6. Spouse		
7. Ex-flame	AUTHORITIES	
8. Pal	17. Accepted Teacher	
9. Ex-pal	18. Rejected Teacher	
	19. Boss	

The rationale for each of the triads is given as follows:

1. *Value Sort.* The client is asked to compare and contrast representatives of success, happiness, and ethics.

2. *Authority Sort.* The client is asked to compare and contrast a person whose ideas he accepted, a person whose ideas he rejected, even though he was expected to accept them, and a person whose support was badly needed at some period in his life.

3. *Valency Sort.* The client is asked to compare and contrast a person whose rejection of him he cannot quite understand, a person whom he thinks needs him, and a person whom he does not really know well but whom he thinks he would like to know better. All three of these are somewhat phantom figures and one may expect that in interpreting them the client relies heavily upon projected attitudes.

4. *Intimacy Sort.* This is a more difficult sort involving the Spouse, the Ex-flame, and the Pal. It tends to bring out features of personal conflict, both between the client's attitude toward two intimate figures of the opposite sex and also between an intimate figure of the opposite sex and an intimate figure of the same sex.

5. *Family Sort.* This sort involves the Father, Mother, and Brother figures. It is an invitation to form a construct which governs the client's relationship within his family.

6. *Sister Sort.* This is an invitation to construe a Sister figure. It provides an opportunity to see the Sister as like the Accepted Teacher and in contrast to the Happy Person, like the Happy Person and in contrast to the Accepted Teacher or in contrast to both of them.

7. *Mother Sort.* Here the comparison figures are the person in whom the client was once disillusioned and the person whose teaching was highly acceptable.

8. *Father Sort.* Here the comparison figures are the Boss and the Successful Person.

9. *Brother Sort.* The comparison figure are the person who appeared to reject the client and the teacher whom the client himself rejected.

10. *Sister Sort.* The comparison figures are the same as for the Brother sort.

11. *Kindliness Sort.* The Sister, Pitied Person, and Ethical Person are thrown into context.

12. *Threat Sort.* The client has an opportunity to construe threat in the context of the Brother, Ex-pal, and Threatening Person.

13. *Spouse Sort.* The Spouse figure is compared and contrasted with the Threatening Person and the Happy Person.

14. *Mating Sort I.* The Mother is placed in context with the Spouse and the Ex-flame.

15. *Mating Sort II.* The Father is placed in a similar context.

16. *Companionship Sort.* The Pal, Ex-pal, and Attractive Person are placed in context.

17. *Sibling Sort.* The Self, Brother, and Sister are compared and contrasted.

18. *Achievement Sort.* The Boss, Successful Person, and Ethical Person are placed in context.

19. *Parental Preference Sort.* The Mother and Father are placed in context with the Threatening Person.

20. *Need Sort.* The Self is compared and contrasted with the Pitied Person and the Attractive Person. This gives the clinician an opportunity to study the relatively subjective and objective reference which the client gives to his personal needs.

21. *Compensatory Sort.* By placing the Ex-flame, the Rejecting Person, and the Pitied Person in the same context the clinician can sometimes get some understanding of how the client reacts to the loss of relationship.

22. *Identification Sort.* This is a crucial sort. It involves the Self, the Spouse, and the Pal. From it one sometimes gains an understanding of the client's domestic difficulties.

Figure 2. Explanations of the 'sorts' extracted from the completed grid of figure 1 (from Kelly, 1955; reproduced by permission of W. W. Norton & Co., Inc.)

CONSTRUCTS

SORT NO.	Construct pole	Contrast pole
1	Don't believe in God	Very religious
2	Same sort of education	Completely different education
3	Not athletic	Athletic
4	Both girls	A boy
5	Parents	Ideas different
6	Understand me better	Don't understand at all
7	Teach the right thing	Teach the wrong thing
8	Achieved a lot	Hasn't achieved a lot
9	Higher education	No education
10	Don't like other people	Like other people
11	More religious	Not religious
12	Believe in higher education	Not believing in too much education
13	More sociable	Not sociable
14	Both girls	Not girls
15	Both girls	Not girls
16	Both have high morals	Low morals
17	Think alike	Think differently
18	Same age	Different ages
19	Believe the same about me	Believe differently about me
20	Both friends	Not friends
21	More understanding	Less understanding
22	Both appropriate music	Don't understand music

Elements (by sort no.):

FAMILY
1. Self
2. Mother
3. Father
4. Brother
5. Sister

INTIMATES
6. Spouse
7. Ex-flame
8. Pal
9. Ex-pal

VALENCES
10. Rejecting person
11. Pitied person
12. Threatening person
13. Attractive person

AUTHORITIES
14. Accepted teacher
15. Rejected teacher
16. Boss

VALUES
17. Successful person
18. Happy person
19. Ethical person

Figure 3. An example of a completed grid in the Rep test (from Kelly, 1955; reproduced by permission of W. W. Norton & Co., Inc.)

a system for classifying personal construct dimensions into 20 major categories which can be used for comparing content of construct systems coming from either the client or from the therapist when the therapist is also asked to fill out a Rep Grid. The other major content classification systems have been restricted to experimental work in social (Duck, 1973) and developmental areas (Livesley and Bromley, 1973).

The second main way of analyzing the grid is to examine the *structural* relationships which exist among the construct dimensions. For the most part, this *structure* is operationalized in terms of the amount of overlap or similarity which exists among the construct dimensions in the way these dimensions are used in the Rep grid to sort the role figures. A number of different quantitative methods have been used to assess the overlap and resulting structural groupings of the construct dimensions. Non-parametric factor analysis, multi-dimensional scaling, cluster analysis, principal components analysis, and simple counting procedures are the most frequently used methods. The best single source for a description of these procedures can be found in Fransella and Bannister's book (1977).

In examining the structure of a construct system, therapists have often been interested in the amount of differentiation that exists among the constructs. The interest here is in finding out which constructs are grouped together and how much overlap exists in the total system. This is an investigation of the total number of different constructs which are available to the client and is often referred to as the amount of *cognitive complexity* found in the client's system.

Recently, however, there has been growing recognition that *complexity* in terms of differentiation is an inadequate conceptualization of the issue and that an investigator also needs to be attending to the amount of *integration* that exists in the system. Integration refers to the extent to which the separate constructs in the client's system are tied together by superordinate or hierarchically arranged linkages. A construct system can be thought of as manifesting either high or low differentiation combined with either a small or a large amount of integration. Empirical work has recently begun to investigate the psychological characteristics of four groupings: (1) low differentiated and low integrated clients; (2) low differentiated but highly integrated clients; (3) highly differentiated but low integrated clients; and finally (4) both highly differentiated and highly integrated clients (Landfield, 1977). It has been generally found that the third group (high differentiation–low integration clients) seem to have the most trouble in handling life experiences. This group is able to see a great many possibilities but has no effective way of handling this multi-dimensionality.

Case Example. Landfield (1971) presents a very good example of the use of the Rep grid in evaluating a therapy case. The client's (Joe's) Rep grid appears in Figure 4. In Landfield's modification of the Rep grid the client is asked to place a '1' in the row under the figure name to which the construct pole applies, while a '2' is inserted if the contrast pole applies. An 'N' is placed in the grid if neither the construct nor the contrast really fits the role figure. This procedure

#	Construct pole 1	1	2	3	4	5	6	7	8	9	10	11	12	13	14	15	Contrast pole 2
1	KIND	(1)	1	2	N	N	N	(2)	N	N	N	2	2	N	1	N	STUPID
2	DEPENDABLE	1	(1)	1	1	2	N	N	1	N	N	2	2	(1)	1	N	IGNORANT
3	PERSONALITY	1	N	(1)	1	N	N	N	N	N	N	(2)	N	N	1	N	BUM
4	UNAWARE	2	2	2	2	2	2	(1)	N	N	2	(1)	2	2	2	2	FRIENDLY
5	PERFECTIONIST	N	1	1	N	2	2	2	(1)	1	1	2	(2)	1	N	N	IRRESPONSIBLE
6	WILD	N	N	2	(1)	N	(1)	1	N	N	N	N	2	N	2	1	FUNNY
7	ASTUTE	N	2	N	N	1	2	N	N	(1)	N	N	2	2	2	(1)	SPORTSMAN
8	AFRAID	(1)	2	N	1	(1)	(1)	N	N	N	N	N	1	2	2	N	CONFIDENT
9	DON'T CARE	N	2	N	N	(1)	N	2	N	N	N	1	1	2	N	(1)	AWARE
10	ATTITUDE	N	(1)	2	N	2	2	N	2	2	(2)	N	2	N	2	N	CAREFREE
11	GET ALONG	N	2	1	1	1	1	N	1	N	N	N	1	1	(1)	2	ABILITY
12	ATHLETIC	N	N	2	N	2	1	N	N	2	N	N	N	(2)	N	2	SELFISH
13	MIXED UP	2	N	1	1	(1)	1	1	1	(1)	1	N	1	N	N	1	CHUBBY
14	TAKE CHARGE	2	2	2	2	2	1	N	N	N	(1)	N	(2)	N	N	N	FOLLOWER
15	MATH	N	1	N	N	2	1	N	N	N	(1)	N	2	1	(1)	N	TRAMP

NAMES OF ACQUAINTANCES

has an advantage over Kelly's original procedure in that one knows precisely whether or not each pole fits the figure it is placed under.

It will be seen that only two circles appear in each row. This is because Landfield is not using the original triad procedure but rather asks the client to consider how two people are either alike or different. If the two people are found to be similar, a contrasting description is then gained by instructing the client to search the role figure list for someone who contrasts with the two similar figures. If the two figures are seen as different, the description of the one person becomes the construct pole and the description of the other person becomes the contrast pole.

Joe

The client whose grid appears in Figure 4 terminated therapy soon after it began. In examining the *content* of the constructs Landfield notes that there are a large number of construct dimensions which are difficult to understand, e.g. the construct dimension no. 10, *attitude* versus *carefree*, and the dimension no. 15, *math* versus *tramp*. There is some reason to believe that these may *not* be a contrasting relationships at all or they might be descriptive poles cast at very different levels of abstraction so that the outside observer is given no clue as to the meaning of the dimension.

In trying to use these construct dimensions to understand Joe, Landfield speculates as follows:

'When Joe is *not perfect* (Construct 5) does he feel irresponsible? Does he behave more effectively (Construct 8) when he is *not afraid*? Is he trying to close out the frustrating outer world (Construct 9) when he does *not care*? When Joe is *not trying hard on the athletic field* (Construct 12), does he feel *selfish*?' (Landfield, 1971, p.104).

Perhaps more revealing of the unusual nature of Joe's system is the structural analysis of his grid. Using a measure of construct dimension overlap, Landfield reports that 'no relationships whatsoever appear among either his fifteen descriptive constructs (row patterns) or his fifteen people constructs (column patterns). This total lack of grid organization is a rare occurrence and suggests conceptual confusion.' His frequent use of the nonapplication rating N suggests a definite type of constriction in the use of his personal constructs' (Landfield, 1971, p.104).

From his total analysis (structural and content) Landfield hypothesizes that 'Joe is confused, narrowly fixed in his approach to life, and may have difficulties in communicating with other people.' Landfield provides the following excerpts from the intake and termination research interviews as support for the hypothesis of 'confusion, constriction and difficulties in communication' (Landfield, 1971, p.104).

Joe's Intake Interview

Interviewer: Tell me very briefly what it is that brought you here to make an appointment.

J o e : I don't know. It seems like *I'm* pressure, built up over a period of time. It's come to a point, you know, points where . . . I don't think this was the most serious time.

I. Um hum. I see. What, what is the, the experience you have when you refer to pressure?

J. (Pause) Uh . . . . s it's not tangible; it's just a. Something's push-pushing me. E-mea . . . it's not, eh, it's not an outward forced like any, you know, like any particular person, but it's just a, something, you know, keeps on shoving ya. An it just turns into mistakes.

I. How do you experience this push though? In other words, what does it feel like?

J. (Pause) Like you're just, uh . . . (now slurring) in a, you know, in a, in a depression period, you know what I mean like everything, nothin' seems to set like you want it to be. It jus goes . . . uh, I don't know how to explain it. It just goes against . . . what you think it should be.

I. Does it frighten you some when it comes back?

J. Not so much frightened as aggravated.

I. Aggravated. I see.

J. Mostly with myself, not with others, not with anybody else.

I. Why do you feel that? Why does it aggravate you?

J. Yes, sir.

I. Um hum.

J. I only know, know exactly why but . . . I guess it's just a feeling of dissatisfaction . . . with yourself I mean, if you're it's just that I so, I might not react fast enough in a game or somethin' 'n' that just does somethin' to me and I can't forget it. I mean I, like I played most sports and then every (words are choppy) time you know, I'll stop just to daydream and just, I just think of the things, that, I didn't react the right way to. And everything. I mean I can't bring up any, anything that was good. It's just that the bad points keep on playing over and over in my mind.

. . . .

J. I have, I have, I, it's not that I can't do anythi— It's just that I have . . . no confidence in myself for things that I do. I mean I have, I have, nn, it's just a lack of trust in myself.

. . . .

J. Well, I mean, uh, people, people couldn't see what I did, you know, what I mean, it sorta, it wasn't as, uh, public as if you'd play sports or something. You know, um, I couldn't, it was more personal that it was public. (Landfield, 1971, pp.104–106).

Joe's Terminal Interview

I.   You were beginning to say about . . .

J.   Um, it just don't matter to me. I mean, so what if I don't—But, uh, I don't think it'll affect me one w—. I don't know if it will or won't. I guess I just don't care.

. . . .

I.   (Pause) How did it come about, that you shifted your feeling of one of rather intense concern, like you say the feeling that you were going batty, to one now of not caring?

J.   Uh, there's no particular point where it just went like that, uh, I just don't know how to explain it, uh . . . I guess I just thought I . . . something was wrong and it wasn't . . . something like that, because it doesn't seem to bother me.

I.   What about your experience here at the clinic? Mmm, how did you feel about it?

J.   Rather hard to adjust.

. . . .

I.   You mean you just feel like he somehow didn't particularly care about you? Or did this feeling start before you started seeing him?

J.   Well, uh, not that so much that, uh, I just couldn't talk to him; uh, I never could talk to anybody in my life, but a, I just couldn't say what I wanted to say. Somehow I just, I couldn't get myself in the mood to put across what I was thinking.

. . . .

J.   Uh, well, this might spec—this is one reason I came, but I, I got a little dog a home. I can sit there an I can talk ta the thing, and I think the thing is hearing me. I mean, it's just . . . she understands a lot better, and she just can't talk back. That's the reason it's easy . . . but, uh . . . I feel a lot more . . . I feel a lot more at home with my dog, than I would with a human being.

I.   Do you think that if you would have started with another therapist, that you might have been able to establish this feeling?

J.   Can't say. I mean, uhn, I have no idea. I don't think nobody could say that. No one could even come close ta thinking what would happen . . . It didn't, 'n I guess you just can't idealize life . . . .

. . . .

I.   Is there anything else you think, Joe, about this whole business that might be, uh, might be significant?

J.   It's kind of general . . . uh . . .

I.   Um hum.

J.   (Pause) I can't put my finger on anything in particular, specific . . . .

(Landfield, 1971, pp.107–108).

Client involvement in analysis

Before going into some of the other specific techniques which the therapist needs to take into consideration, it is important to note that many therapists report significant benefit from simply having the client go through the procedure. The grid provides the client an opportunity to view his or her own construct system in an explicit and organized way that is usually not available in the context of the therapeutic interview. Clients often report being surprised by what the grid enabled them to say and understand about themselves and their life. It is as if the client was dimly aware of how certain figures were construed, but seeing things explicitly laid out in the grid makes a lot of things sensible that had been quite puzzling. Clients are made aware, by this procedure, of many things they did not know that they knew. It has long been recognized that we know more than we can tell. One can then see the Rep grid as a procedure which enables us to tell ourselves a little more of what we know.

In using the grid in therapy, it is common for the therapist to actively involve the client in analyzing the results, including helping the therapist to identify (name) the cluster patterns. A clinical judgment must be made about the extent of involvement of the client. In some cases a literal interpretation of the grid structure may not be advisable. The construct theory of therapy, however, leans in the direction of sharing the analysis procedure with the client; excluding the client *only* when it would be clearly indicated as harmful.

Other Techniques

There are à number of other techniques that are employed in order to aid the therapist in anticipating the nature of the client and the issues which might arise in the therapy. Perhaps one of the most frequently used is the *self-characterization*. In this procedure the client is invited to write a brief description of herself or himself following these instructions:

> 'I want you to write a character sketch of Harry Brown (client's name) just as if he were the principal character in a play. Write it as it might be written by a friend who knew him very *intimately* and very *sympathetically*, perhaps better than anyone ever really could know him. Be sure to write it in the third person. For example, start out by saying, "Harry Brown is . . . ." ' (Kelly, 1955, p.323).

This technique is designed to obtain a sample of the client's constructs organized in script form. The analysis of the self-characterization, in fact, takes place on many different levels including an examination of the topical areas the client produces, the general themes and cause-and-effect relationships mentioned, as well as the meaning dimensions portrayed as bipolar constructs (implicitly or explicitly stated). In addition each sentence and term is examined in the light of the total organization of the sketch. In conducting this analysis the therapist is urged to think about what this sketch reveals about the total organization of the client's construct system in terms of the professional constructs mentioned in the second chapter. For example, what does a sketch reveal about how the client is handling anxiety, hostility, fear, or guilt?

In some cases the *self-characterization* is used to write an *enactment sketch* for the person. This is a role playing technique used in Fixed Role Therapy which will be described in more detail in Chapter 8. Briefly stated, the self-characterization is used to locate the growing edge of the client's construct system. These are the places the therapist identifies as 'good bets' for facilitating spontaneous elaboration of the client's construct system.

Another technique employed in therapy is the use of the *Situational Resources Repertory Test*. This device helps the counselor assess the extent to which clients are spreading their dependencies over a variety of people in life versus concentrating them on relatively few people. As will be discussed in later chapters the theme of dependency is central to a personal construct psychotherapy. Briefly stated, Kelly hypothesized that there are a number of advantages, in terms of effective living, for the client to move from a narrow range of dependencies to a relatively wide range (Kelly, 1962).

In this procedure the client is asked to think of specifically of a time in life when he or she was in need of help from others. Kelly (1955, p.314) provided 22 such situations, five of which are listed below:

(1) Think of the time in your life when you were most perplexed about what kind of job or vocation you might go into.
(2) Next think of the time in your life when you had the greatest difficulty understanding how to get along with people of the opposite sex.
(3) The time when things seemed to be going against you— when your luck was particularly bad.
(4) The time when you were most hard up financially.
(5) The time when you were in poorest health or had a long period of sickness.

After specifying a time and place when each of these situations occurred, the client is asked to consider the 22 figures used in the Rep Test (mother , father, best friend, etc.) and to indicate which ones of these, if any, the client feels could be turned to for help. The ability of this figure to help is indicated by having the client place an 'X' in a space next to that figure's name. An example of a completed Situations Test is provided in Figure 5.

Using the information from this procedure the counselor can being to see how the client is structuring personal relationships in the area of dependency. This procedure can also provide the client directly with needed information. This information is particularly important when working with depressed clients. Because there will be a number of 'other techniques' introduced later, in chapter 9, we shall limit our presentation now to these two examples.

Trouble with	1 Mate	2 Father	3 Mother	4 Sister	5 Brother	6 Boss	7 Noncomm. Officer	8 Comm. Officer	9 Minister	10 Relative	11 Neighbour	12 Buddy	13 Confidant	14 Physician	15 Advisor	16 Self
A. Finances		×	×							×			×		×	
B. Mate		×	×	×									×		×	
C. Police		OMITTED	OMITTED													
D. Neighbour		OMITTED	OMITTED													
E. Jealousy		OMITTED	OMITTED													
F. Parents	×			×		×							×		×	
G. Sibling		OMITTED	OMITTED													
H. Loneliness	×	×	×	×		×							×		×	
I. Anger	×	OMITTED		×						×			×		×	
J. Fear of death		×	×			×							×		×	
K. Shame		×	×			×							×		×	
L. Persecution	×	×	×			×							×		×	
M. Discouragement		OMITTED	OMITTED													
N. Sickness		OMITTED	OMITTED													
O. Suicidal thoughts																
P. Misunderstood		OMITTED	OMITTED			×							×		×	
Q. Effeminacy	×					×							×		×	
R. Cowardliness			OMITTED			×							×		×	
S. Stupidity		×	×	×		×							×		×	
T. Hurting someone	×	×		×		×							×		×	
U. Gullibility						×							×		×	
V. Confusion	×			×		×							×		×	
W. Failure		OMITTED	OMITTED	×		×							×		×	
X. Women																
Y. Passivity		OMITTED	OMITTED													
Z. Needed help		OMITTED				×							×		×	

Date, place

Appraisal

This third main aspect of anticipation deals with the task of collecting information about the client so that the counselor can handle, in an optimal manner, the kinds of issues which will occur in the course of the therapy. Appraisal refers to the examination of both the client's external environment and the client's interpretation of that environment. What has the client had to anticipate in order to make sense out of life? Expanding upon this question it becomes, 'what has served in the past to offer validation and invalidation for the client's construct system?' What has served to support the client's ideas, dreams, hopes and aspirations? What has the client had to consider when she or he is trying to build a sensible life? In this aspect of personal construct psychotherapy the therapist is reminded that any assessment of the client has to be placed within the context of the client's life situation, sub-culture, and culture. The client's total surroundings must be considered; no accurate assessment can be made of the client taken in isolation from the environment. This aspect of the therapy is clearly illustrated by Ivey (1980) in a recent examination of the counselor and psychotherapist from the viewpoint of the person–environment fit hypothesis. The therapist's concerns turn from a primary focus on the content and structure of the construct dimensions to an examination of the validation of the client's system. What has the client had to look to in order to find some kind of support for life? What have been those things which have been taken as having special meaning in the life of the client? In fact, the very construct dimensions obtained in the Rep test are given their best interpretation when seen in the context of the client's environment. In this respect one might consider this a contextualist position in psychology (Mancuso, 1976). One might think of this section as a personal construct approach to case history material which covers the overlap between social work and individual–clinical psychotherapy.

Personal Construct Psychotherapy requires an ecological approach to the person. We must, in planning a therapy, grasp both the nature of the person's construct system and the nature of the world which that person must use in order for that system to receive some type of validation. The investigation of validation takes on the form of a *structuralization* or working hypothesis. This is a starting point for the counselor which precedes the more precise *construction* of the total system and environmental context. For personal construct psychotherapy there is always an assessment of the construct system of the person, and an assessment of the world (situation) in which that construct system must operate. One could say that it is not really possible to understand a person's construct system without placing it in a specific time and place. We ask ourselves, 'how will this particular person's (our client's) construct system operate in this particular situation?' What would this person be like in this particular situation? For example, a special question might be, 'what are the person's family's beliefs about the way to go about making decisions?' Another questions might be, 'how do people in his community go about dealing with minority groups?' This gives a way of assessing the social and political implications for the counselor in terms of how the system of validation operates for the client.

One of the important areas to be covered is the client's view of his or her culture. It is very important to know how the client describes the social world. It is important to understand how the client describes strangers and deviant people—particularly 'bad people', personal prowess, frustration and anger reactions, how quarrels are mended, how mating behavior occurs and the nature of family folklore (Kelly, 1955, p.699). Also included in this assessment would be a description of the client's community background, community economics, religious organizations, schools, community interpersonal relations, educational experience, domestic relationships, and family history.

All of this material is seen as the ' "validating evidence" against which the client has had the opportunity to test out his or her personal constructions.' The interest here is *not* in these events as moulders of the person's system but as the basis of what this person has taken to be reality. This is what the person's system has had to keep in order. This is the evidence against which the client has had to test new constructions. One must not be too bound by any given lists of things that must be taken into consideration, but rather note that it is important, very important, to take the situation into account in order to understand the construct system. A construct system cannot be considered separately from the situation.

Spontaneous activity

One of the main aims, in this aspect of the therapy, is to get the problem stated in a way that reflects the client's problem in a 'fluid rather than in a static condition' (Kelly, 1955, p.724). The counselor is seeking the most permeable set of constructions for viewing the problem; a way of stating the problem in a way that it can be solved. The emphasis is on 'avenues of movement which the person can open up for himself.'

This points to free movement of the system termed *spontaneous activity*. The counselor wants to examine the client's world in such a way that particularly close attention is paid to areas where the client simply takes off into a line of interest and movement. Attention is paid here to the directions of the client's activities rather than the amount of pressure behind the person's interests as is formulated in 'psychodynamic' orientations.

The concern with spontaneous activity refers to that area where the person is truly moving freely. This is in fact the area of the system where the constructs are most permeable. These permeable constructs are those along which growth and elaboration of the system can occur. These are areas where the client is concerned with 'creative' thinking, the client's fantasies, the client's dreams, the client's fanciful perceptions. It is here that 'emotional' insights can take place. In fact Kelly states that 'It is possible to approach personal constructs through the analysis of spontaneous activities without depending upon the person's verbal explanations' (Kelly, 1955, p.739).

Vocational choice

In Personal Construct Psychotherapy, special interest is taken in the client's vocational choice because this is often an area where spontaneous construction has taken place or an area in which spontaneous activity is presently taking place. For Kelly a vocation is looked upon as if it were a 'system of ready-made constructs and a system of validators', which are surprisingly clear (Kelly, 1955, p.747). This makes it then a place where productive work can take place relatively rapidly. This is based on the assertion that 'A person's vocation is an area in which he ordinarily has many constructs which are permeable enough to permit a considerable amount of successive evolving to take place' (Kelly, 1955, p.748). The vocational area then is a good bet for enabling a client to experience some positive gains in therapy. It is a place where the person has made a happy compromise between what is challenging and what is safe so that it does not overstress the system. This is an area where changes can be undertaken and consequences of these changes can be quickly and efficiently evaluated. The importance of the vocational area is further anchored by Kelly in asserting that 'A vocation is one of the principal means by which one's life role is given clarity and meaning. Hence it serves as a stabilizing support against chaos and confusion' (Kelly, 1955, p.751).

Diagnosis

This fourth and final aspect of *anticipation* deals with the process of diagnosis undertaken by the personal construct psychotherapist. In many important ways this final aspect of anticipation points the way to the actual process of psychotherapy, which will be discussed in the next section of this book. In Personal Construct Theory, diagnosis *is* the planning stage for the total management and framework for the therapy. The therapist's task in diagnosis is to provide a helpful conceptualization of the client; a conceptualization that will facilitate the client's being able to undertake constructive revision of various types. Most emphatically diagnosis, in construct terms, does not involve placing the client in the common nosological categories or pigeon-holes such as schizophrenic, manic, depressive, etc. These terms play no formal part in the diagnostic procedure. Instead, diagnosis is couched in terms of the dimensional properties of the construct system which was described in chapter 2. The purpose of the diagnosis is to provide a way to aid the client in moving from his or her present position in life to a future which has greater practical potentialities for personal growth. The aim of the diagnosis is to provide a transition.

It is important to recognize that diagnostic construction which are employed in this therapy can be used without any necessary consideration of disturbance or illness of the client. These dimensions are ways of describing the client's system so that further possibilities and optimal functioning can be promoted. It must be recognized, however, that much of the time of a professional therapist is taken up with personal difficulties. In construct theory these personal difficulties are termed *disorders* which can be defined as 'any personal construction which is used repeatedly in spite of consistent invalidation' (Kelly, 1955, p.831). For a number of reasons which can be specified, the client is unwilling and/or unable to change the system even though it obviously is no longer working in the way it was designed to work. For one thing a client might be very reluctant to abandon a present construction before she has really any viable alternative available. By not changing, the client is, at least, avoiding immediate anxiety as we have defined that term in chapter 2. In dealing with disorders it is the job of the counselor to help the client deal with invalidations in more effective ways.

In fact, Kelly (1955, p.831) states that 'the goal of psychotherapy is to alleviate complaints—complaints of a person about himself and others and complaints of others about him.' It is important, however, not to misinterpret that statement to mean that psychotherapy is simply a matter of adjusting the person to environment. It is recognized that, in many cases, what needs to be worked on is not the person who is doing the complaining but rather the others, or the environment in which the person is living. Nevertheless, the personal complaint of the client is taken as the initial focus of the therapy. One starts with the way the client sees things. Much more will be said about the nature of the complaint in the following section of this book. For the present it might be best to summarize the construct approach to diagnosis with the following statement,

> 'Perhaps the proper question is not *what* is a disorder but *where*, and the therapist's question is not *who* needs treatment but *what* needs treatment' (Kelly, 1955, p.835).

Steps in the Diagnosis

In order to organize the total amount of information needed for meaningful diagnosis of a client experiencing a disorder, the following 'steps' in the diagnostic procedure are offered. These are offered as important areas of concern rather than any necessarily ordered developmental sequence.

Step 1 is a normative formulation of the client's problems and is stated in terms of 'exactly what is peculiar about this client, when does he show it, and where does it get him?'

Step 2 involves a psychological description of the client's personal constructs. The question is 'what does the client think about all this and what does he think he is trying to do?'

Step 3 is the psychological evaluation of the client's construct system with the question being 'what is the psychological view of the client's personal constructs?' For example the therapist would want to locate the client's areas of anxiety, aggressiveness or spontaneous elaboration, and constriction.

Step 4 is an analysis of the milieu in which the adjustment is to be sought, with the question being 'In addition to the client himself, what is there to work with in this case?'

Step 5 is a determination of the immediate procedural steps in the therapy. 'Where does the client go next?'

Step 6 is the actual planning of the management of the client and the treatment of the case, with the question raised, 'How is the client going to get well?' (Kelly, 1955, p.777–779).

Types of Disorders

The disorders which the construct counselor deals with can be divided into either a primary concern with *structural* properties of the construct system or as primary concern with the *content* of the constructs themselves. The concern with structural properties covers both the use of the *general diagnostic constructs* covering conceptual organization, and the *transitional* constructions which are concerned with the feelings and emotional states of clients. It must be remembered, however, that both the general diagnostic constructs and the transitions constructs are concerned with systematic qualities—how the construct system operates as a system.

Disorders in the structure. The structural disorders which have received the most extensive elaboration in construct theory are listed as follows: disorders involving dilation or trying to take in too many things at one time; construct systems that are either excessively tight or excessively loose; disorders involving the core constructions or central identity issues; disorders involving aggression and aggression linked with guilt; disorders involving excessive hostility; disorders involving anxiety, excessive constriction and guilt; disorders involving undispersed dependency; disorders involving psychosomatic and 'organic' problems; and disorders involving control and impulsivity. It must be remembered that the diagnostic terms mentioned above are simply used in describing disorders and do not imply that these terms (e.g., anxiety, guilt, hostility, loosening and tightening, etc.) are disorders themselves. It means that these terms are used to aid in understanding a system that has begun to malfunction in the sense that constructive revision is not taking place in the light of repeated invalidation from the internal and external environment.

Since this book is not centrally concerned with diagnostics but with the process of psychotherapy, only an illustration of the use of a diagnostic dimension with a disorder will be presented. (For the reader who desires further information, Kelly (1955) provides two chapters of descriptive material). In using a diagnostic term the press is always in the direction of finding an effective treatment plan. the following example deals with disorders involving dilation and illustrates it through the discussion of a particular case.

'Consider a person who once, perhaps as a child or adolescent, leaned heavily upon a belief that God could be inveigled into complying with all his requests. Suppose he had developed a dilated field with respect to this construction. God would take care of *all* his requests. Suppose the construction, as well as being one imposed upon a dilated field, is also a *tight* one—for example, God's compliance is perceived both literally and specifically. Now suppose that, through testing and invalidating evidence and perhaps through other developments as well, this religious structure is abandoned. The person is left with a considerably dilated field.

Let us suppose that the formidable task of reconstructing the person's dilated field is postponed or, perhaps, is undertaken on too small a scale. As the person confronts a succession of major issues in his life, he finds himself without the capacity to construe them satisfactorily. He attempts to make great generalizations with little ideas.

But what other remaining bases does such a person have for construing adult issues? Obviously he must use certain preverbal dependency constructs, since these are the only ones with sufficient range of convenience. There is nothing else to use and here he is with a dilated field on his hands. He attempts to work out his problems in terms of constructs which are of even longer standing than the ones he has abandoned: preverbal constructs which once governed his infantile relations with his parents. He still wheedles to satisfy his day-to-day wants; except that now he wheedles his associates instead of God or his parents.

Such a person avoids testing his solutions to current adult issues in terms of impersonal facts. He looks only for the 'don't you love me?' facts. Actually he is not prepared to face any clear-cut invalidating evidence, for that would call for revision of a large portion of his construction system. He is not ready for such revision, for, in terms of our Modulation Corollary, the impending variation in his construction system, being necessarily subordinate to something more permeable, cannot be worked out.

Those permeable aspects of his system which might once have given him overall stability have been abandoned. Perhaps they were so tightly drawn that they would not have worked anyway. He is not in a position where he can afford to stake his adult thinking on the outcome of a practical experiment. Instead, he snuggles up to people, whimpers, panders to their whims, indulges his own, and generally postpones his psychological maturation.

Such a person is not necessarily immobilized by his lack of a suitable working superordinate system. He may do a lot of thrashing about. But his experiments are not designed to give definitive results. The only thing that he is testing is his preverbal construct that some people are indulgent and others are not. He may now express it by saying that some people are 'accepting' and others are 'rejecting'. It means the same thing. He looks for the 'accepting' people.

Actually, as far as adult issues are concerned, the person can be seen to be procrastinating a good deal of the time. He is not in a position to experiment because he is not in a position to make revisions that the results of the experimentation would call for. He cannot take such revisions in his stride because he has abandoned— and has not replaced—the superordinate structure with which his dilated field was once held together. His world would really collapse in a heap of anxiety if he had suddenly to abandon either the little structures which he has recently erected or the one remaining superordinate structure of parent-like indulgence.

Such a person as we have described does not wholly avoid anxiety. As he looks at his dilated field, he gets anxious because he has no structure to force it all into an orderly array. Every time he skims too close to invalidating evidence bearing upon his construct of 'indulgence–rejection' he gets anxious, because it threatens to make him abandon another major line of defense. In therapy he may be anxious as he lays some of his other preverbal constructs on the line for testing. Moreover, if he sees the therapist as likely to reinstate some of the abandoned religious structure he may be threatened, in the sense in which we have defined *threat*.' (Kelly, 1955, pp.837–839)

A feasible way of organizing the treatment of this type of disorder might be proposed as follows:

'There are several ways in which a psychotherapeutic program can be designed for a person of the type we have described. The design will, of course, need to take into account a good many more factors than we have listed, but we shall not bother to mention all of them here.

One way to deal with such a case is to start by accepting whatever omnipotency transferences the client is inclined to use for construing the therapist. At the same time the therapist may control the threat by making it clear that he will not use his supposed omnipotencies for making the client over into something he does not want to be. This step has some hazards, for it puts the relationship on a cafeteria basis—the client will get nothing that he does not ask for. Soon the client starts bringing detailed shopping lists to the interviews: "I lack this," "Help me get that," "Give me a whole basket full of those," "I must know how to do this—and not later than Tuesday!"

a. *Indiscriminate "insights".* Each new construction that is developed in the interview room is likely to be applied to a dilated field. "That makes *so much* sense," the client will say, "My Great Aunt Penelope was that way. Mother certainly was. Oh, I see, it is like making deductions on your income tax. And wouldn't you say that kind of thinking has influenced the recent strike in the steel mills? Oh, and I can think of so many times I have made that mistake. Perhaps this is real important—one time when . . .' and so on. This is the I-see-it-all-now type of reconstruction that can be expected in an overdilated field. Each interview is likely to produce a whole set of "fascinatingly new insights" which are smeared on the cilent's life picture with sweeping strokes and gaudy colors. Yet all of this kaleidoscopic shifting appears to be pretty much confined to the interview room and is actually subordinate to the stabilizing preverbal dependency construction with which the client views the therapy relationship. Knowing no other way to deal with the necessity for the change, the client is essentially making incantations to Psychology.

The psychologist will have to wade through all this "insight" and help the client establish little islands of intact and workable structure. Thus the remaining seas of confusion or anxiety are broken up into something of more manageable size. The client can be made aware of his dilation and his propensity for "world-shaking insights". At this stage of therapy it will probably do more harm than good to confront him with his magical thinking and the possibility that his whole preverbal dependency system ought to be abandoned. Such a turn of affairs might very well precipitate a psychosis. He needs the preverbal system, inappropriate as it is, as a permeable, comprehensive, superordinate structure beneath whose stabilizing sway new reconstruction on more limited scales can be experimentally tried out.

b. *Attacking manageable areas.* When the psychotherapist has broken up the oceanic expanses of potential anxiety into areas of reasonable size, he may start taking more aggressive steps to get the client out onto dry land. There are two interrelated phases that must be articulated during this stage of treatment. The one has to do with the devleopment of a new comprehensive superordinate construction system or 'system of values'. The other has to do with the verbalization, testing, and eventual occlusion or abandonment of the preverbal structure upon which the client's prior readjustments had been hinging. If the latter phase is pursued to the exclusion of the former, the therapist will have a confused and anxious client on his hands, one who may be too anxious to make any further experimental investments. If the former phase is pursued to the exclusion of the latter, the therapist will find himself involved in an endless series of erudite intellectual discussions with a client who still wheedles when he gets anxious and wants something desperately.

This is the stage of treatment which taxes the psychotherapist's skill and perspicacity. It may also be the stage of treatment where he finds that he must settle for something less than optimal results. The new superordinate system should be verbalized so that it can be readily subjected to occasional test and periodic revision throughout the client's life. It has to be worked out experimentally during the period of therapy. The client should actually do things which are reflected by the proposed new system of values. He should give the system a good trying out.

c. *Use of anxiety*. Along with the experimental development of a new superordinate system the therapist will have to take steps to help the client test his old system. If he fails to do this, he may find that the client does not have enough anxiety in the interview room to cause him to look for any alternative solutions to his problems. In order to get results the therapist must keep in mind the principle that the anxiety in the interviewing room must often exceed the anxiety outside the interviewing room. Otherwise the interview room becomes a haven and nothing more.

An attempt should be made to make the old system verbal. This attempt may not always work. But if the client can verbalize his dependencies upon his parents and his transferred dependencies upon the therapies, he can more readily start testing them. Are these dependencies the ways to get things done, to anticipate life's sequence of events? (Kelly, 1955, pp.842–844)

Disorders in content. It is very important to remember that not all disorders involve structure. It is quite common to find that the client's troubles involve the actual *content* or meaning contained in the construct dimension. Approached in this way an entire therapeutic program could be planned which centers primarily around the content of the constructs and does not involve extensive use of structural qualities. An excellent example of a construct therapy which focuses primarily on the content of the constructs is found in Dorothy Rowe's (1978) work with depressed clients. She uses various techniques including the *Rep grid* in order to elicit the *content* dimensions that forms a client's outlook on life (the construct system). Her particular concern is with the nature of the propositions (construct dimensions) which the clients use to enclose themselves and cut themselves off from others.

The general classes of propositions which she finds her clients using are illustrated in the following list:

> *not trusting* others
> *envying* others

wanting revenge on others
rejecting others
feeling unloved, unloving, unforgiving, unforgiven
feeling ignored by others, disparaged by others, unable to communicate with others, not understood by others
feeling confused, in conflict, incompetent, different from others
feeling that other people are dangerous, that one is disliked, that one cannot be loved for oneself alone but only for what one does, that one's burdens are greater than anyone else's
feeling that one is bad, abnormal, mad, ugly, that one cannot change
feeling disappointed with one's past life, that nothing good can be expected in the future, that the world is uninteresting, that it is dangerous
fearing other people's anger, the power of others, rejection by others, loss of individuality
fearing that one will go out of control, go mad
fearing to become attached to others, to be seen to be happy, to do anything less than perfectly, to make a decision, to excel, to be an individual, to be self-assertive, to reveal oneself to others, to change
feeling guilty because one is disliked, gets angry, makes others angry, distresses others, has not met one's responsibilities to others, has not lived up to one's own expectations
fearing isolation, chaos, annihilation, death.
(Rowe, 1978, pp.235–236)

Rowe works with the actual statements that come from the client or can be closely inferred from the client's statements. An example of a list of propositions comes from one of her clients, 'Joan' and is presented as follows:

I don't trust other people.
If someone dislikes me it must be my fault.
If someone gets angry with me I don't want to have anything more to do with that person.
If I discuss my angry feelings I shall become angrier.
If I show my anger I may go out of control.
A good person never gets angry.
I am different from everyone else.
There is something wrong with me.
I have never been normal.
If I did not get depressed something worse would happen to me.
People take no notice of me.
I don't want people to notice me because I am so big and ugly.
My husband does not love me the way I want him to love me.
My mother does not love me.
My dream of becoming part of a large, loving family will never come true.
I must never get attached to anybody.

If I loved someone I should be hurt when I lost that person.
If I loved someone that person would have power over me.
If I depend on anyone else that person will reject me.
I prefer to be depressed than to form close relationships.
In a close relationship the other person would expect me to give up being myself.
In a close relationship one person always tries to destroy the other.
By being a martyr I can avoid being destroyed by guilt.
No matter what my husband does I feel hard done by.
When I am depressed my husband is nicer to me.
My relatives do not allow me to be myself.
My husband does not like to see the children or me enjoying ourselves.
I have no choice; my burdens are thrust upon me.
When life gets too complicated I can escape by becoming depressed.
I cannot change myself.
Some great, beautiful thing is missing from my life.
I cannot find an ideal mother.
I must revenge myself on my mother and my husband.
(Rowe, 1978, p.237)

The goal of the therapy Rowe undertakes with this client is to help her move in the direction of reconstructing her life in such a way that she is able to embrace content constructions which will open her up to other people and provide her with a fresh and spontaneous approach to life.

Of course it is not possible, with all clients, to move in this direction. The goal then becomes to help the client live in a less destructive way with his or her 'enclosed system'. The major portion of Rowe's book is given over to a detailed description of how this work proceeds with nine of her clients. The cases are described in terms of how the *content* of the constructs is worked with in order to make reconstruction possible. This approach is a far cry from simply giving the clients new things to say to themselves as would be the case in a 'rational' therapy. Instead, the very existential grounding of the client is examined in order that new constructions can be chosen by the client.

Summary

Throughout this chapter the main focus has been on how the therapist can best *anticipate* what is to take place in the therapy. First the client's expectations concerning the therapist and the therapy were discussed. The second main section focused on the *Rep grid* as a way the counselor has avaliable to anticipate the nature of both the *content* and the *structure* of the clients' construct system. The *self-characterization* and the *situational resources test* are additional techniques which have proven useful for this purpose. The third main setion concerned and the *appraisal* of the client's environment. The interest here is on obtaining a picture of those events which have served, in the past, as either validators or invalidators of the client's system. The construct system of the client must always be interpreted in the context of that client's life events. Special attention was drawn to the client's spontaneous activitiy and vocational choice. The final theme in this anticipation phase of the therapy dealt with the dciagnostic process or the planning of the therapy itself. In personal construct therapy, diagnosis is accomplished through examining both the formal construct dimension characteristics and the content of the constructs. The purpose of the diagnosis is to plan a therapy which will enable the client to reconstrue life so that fresh life plans can be enacted. A disorder, in construct terms, is the repeated use of a construction even though that construction has been consistently invalidated.

CHAPTER 4

Investment

This second aspect of the cycle of experience, as it applies to psychotherapy, describes the kind of relationship that develops between the client and the counselor. It is a description of the initial involvement of the two in the process of psychotherapy. With the first, (anticipatory) phase of the therapy completed, the therapist and client now become immersed in the process of the therapy itself. It is at this point in the total cycle that the actual process of psychotherapy begins to engage the therapist's conscious concern, it is during this investment phase that the whole affair becomes truly personal and the actual personal qualities of the client and therapist get involved in the enterprise.

The first main topic of concern is the client–therapist relationship. This is an examination of the therapist's involvement with the client and the client's involvement with the therapist. The second main concern is with the entry point for the therapy. This is the work that surrounds the client's *complaint*—the problem that is presented in order to initiate the counseling contact.

Both of these main topics are undertaken in this investment phase in a special kind of mood which Kelly describes as the *invitational mood*. This self-investment and self-involvement in the therapy is undertaken not in a deadly serious mood but rather in a mood of possibility, in a mood of inviting the client to consider things differently. The idea is that room must always be made for alternatives to be entertained. These alternatives are approached as if they mattered in a productive way rather than being construed in a particularly demanding manner. The client and therapist are invested personally in the therapeutic enterprise for what possiblities it might hold.

The Client–Counselor Relationship

As the client and therapist begin to become acquainted with each other the first issue we will discuss concerns how much information the therapist should share with the client about personal issues. How self-disclosing should the therapist be in the sessions, concerning personal wishes, opinions, evaluations, values, personal involvement with others, etc? On the one hand we have the model of the psychotherapist as guru, where the therapist serves as an exemplar in living so that the more completely known the therapist becomes, the better for the therapy. On the other hand, we have the model of the orthodox psychoanalytical therapist who remains virtually unknown as a person to the client. Clearly the personal construct psychotherapist stands between these two extreme positions.

Just how much disclosing or sharing can be accommodated has been debated by personal construct therapists. Certainly no hard and fast rule should be put forth. It is generally felt, however, that there is an advantage for the therapist not to overdo this disclosure in the first part of the therapy. It is thought that not knowing too much about the therapist enables the therapist to remain more flexible in assuming different roles with the client. The nature of the therapist must not become too fixed in the client's eyes early in the therapy. If the therapist does become just one specific kind of person, then the therapist will not be able to play as many different roles in the therapy with the client as the therapist might ordinarily want to undertake. There is at this point an involvement with the client but at the same time, some distance is maintained. In Personal Construct Therapy there is a task centeredness to the therapy whereby the client feels the engagement of the counselor with the tasks in the therapy. The nature of the counselor's personal material is not put in the forefront for fear of clouding the issue. Another important point is that the counseling hour is for the client. The therapist has other places to work on his or her own personal involvements and concerns rather than continually sharing this material with the client.

The therapist is a real person with the client, but early in the therapy the exact nature of who the therapist is, is not completely spelled out for the client. This allows the client to perceive the therapist in a number of different ways. The therapist is not supposed to overwhelm the client with his own presence and to serve as an exemplar or guide. The counselor is rather to employ such a palliative techniques as *support* and *reassurance* which are based on an acceptance of the client and a warm regard for the client. After all the *credulous approach* is the bedrock of the therapeutic relationship, with the counselor's receiving what the client says as veridical and worthy of respect. It is the flexibility of the counselor that is of prime significance in this beginning phase.

Consistent with this principle in personal construct therapy is Bugental's statement that the therapist might well *not* answer all questions about himself that the client requests. This is particularly true when the client is trying to shift the emphasis in the therapy away from himself or herself to a focus on the therapist. The following is given as an example:

CL-1: I had the feeling just then that I was irritating you by my question.
TH-1: Yes, I guess that's right. I know I felt kind of edgy when you kept on pressing me.
CL-2: Why was that?
TH-2: It has to do with something in your manner which suggests you find a delight in pursuing me, and it comes also from some things in my own history which makes me more than usually sensitive about being teased.
CL-3: What happened to you to make you sensitive that way?

TH-3: I really don't think it would be useful to your therapy for me to go into those experiences now. Another time, we might talk about them. For now, I think it would be most helpful for you to see what your feelings may be about me and about our exchange right now. (Bugental, 1978, p.68).

Differential prediction

In further describing the client–counselor realtionship it is important to remember, in Personal Construct Psychotherapy, that the counselor has the obligation to be able to formulate the nature of the particular therapeutic relationship in hand. The counselor must employ a set of professional constructions or understandings which encompass the nature of what is going on in the client–counselor relationship. This takes the form of the counselor having to spend time setting forth some plans for the interview — plans which have some structure but which can be changed when the *client* wishes to change direction. These plans are structured around the guide posts of what the counselor 'thinks might be a good thing to have happen' and 'what he will definitely try to avoid' (Kelly, 1955, p.632). As the therapy develops and more information is gained, guide posts are refined to include a 'painstaking plot of danger areas' and the counselor's 'ability to predict what his client will say' (Kelly, 1955, p.632). This prediction takes the form, however, of a *differential* prediction. This is to say the prediction would not be a general expectation that some of the same concerns will be brought up that have been brought up before, or that something new will occur. The nature of differential prediction involves the therapist in being willing to predict, for example, that the client will start to talk about his relationship with his brother again rather than continue to examine the nature of his vocational choice. This is to say, predictions are to be made that clearly *differentiate* the choices the client is making in developing the therapeutic interview material. This is a long range goal in the therapy and not a specific requirement which must be met at each interview. The counselor strives to reach a place in his understanding where differential prediction is possible. This says a lot about the nature of the relationship between client and therapist and serves as a test of the counselor's ability to understand the nature of the relationship. This planning also involves attention to the tempo, spacing, and length of the interview.

Teaching the client how to be a client

As another aspect of the client–therapist relationship, this section will deal with how the therapist strives to prepare the client to benefit maximally from therapy. Within construct psychotherapy there is a genuine appreciation of the fact that many clients do not know how to be clients. This is to say that counseling can be enhanced if the client is prepared to respond in a way which allows something therapeutic to happen. This can be done explicitly by the therapist's specific instructions to the client, or it can be implied or invited by the way the counselor responds to the client. One must be careful in this matter. This teaching or instruction, however, cannot be done with overly *simple* instructions to the client without destroying some of the main features of the counseling relationship. After all it is not the purpose of therapy for the client simply to follow the instructions of the therapist.

In teaching the client how to be a client it is important to remember that a great deal of material is conveyed in the form of constructs whose meanings are not really verbal in the usual sense. Clients sometimes have a way of talking intellectually about matters yet missing the real meaning of the very words they use.

Kelly uses as an illustration of this the case of a well-educated professional woman who could verbalize the concept of 'having respect for others' but only later in the therapy realized what this meant experientially. She stated 'I'm beginning to see that people just are what they are. They can't help it. They must be what they must be. I never knew what you meant by 'respect' before. I talked as if I knew what it meant but all the time to 'respect' someone was a little like being afraid of them' (Kelly, 1955, p.645).

Even though verbal instruction is often not enough, it is sometimes helpful for a client to obtain from the therapist some general ground rules for what counseling is all about. This is particularly important for clients who find counseling a truly new and strange experience. One way to provide some structure is the following message from the counselor.

> 'Probably as we talk about these problems it will gradually become clear to both of us that they are related to some things that have been bothering you for a long time. For that reason it is a little difficult to tell just how long this series of conferences will have to last before you discover just how to deal with your troubles. Let me tell you about what to expect.
>
> In the first place I think you will find that these conferences are quite different from anything you have had experience with before. Sometimes you will be telling me very frankly about how you feel about yourself or about other people. Sometimes it will be hard to find the words for what you are thinking. Lots of times you will say things here that you would not think of saying on the outside. Don't be upset by any of this. Treat this room as a kind of special place. What you say here will not be held against you. We are here to help you, not to criticize you' (Kelly, 1955, pp.645–646).

At another time it may be necessary to indicate to the client how the initiative in therapy is to be structured. The counselor might say:

> 'You realize, of course, that all of your life you are going to be facing new experiences. That is what makes life interesting. Nobody can

ever tell you in advance just what these experiences are going to be and exactly what to do when you meet them face to face. In the final analysis only you can make your decisions. The same is true as regards the problems you are going to deal with here. I am not here to solve them for you. Even if I could solve them for you it would not be good for you to let me. Only you can find the right answers; and, once you have found them, only you can put them into practice. I shall help you all I can, but you will have to take the matter of your own recovery in hand' (Kelly, 1955, pp.646–647).

Yet another aspect of instructing the client on being a client involves enabling the client to get at the material that needs to be brought to bear on a problem. This often involves some kind of loosening of the client's system. The client is invited to relax physically and mentally so that fresh material can come forth and a calmer, freer atmosphere can be produced. This purpose can be accomplished in a number of ways, some of which are illustrated below in specific statements to clients. For example, the client might be told, 'Let us see where your thoughts lead you when you just let them go.' . . . . 'Don't try to make sense, just let your mind wander.' (Kelly, 1955, p.647).

During a long, tightly organized story, during which the client is telling about his life, the therapist might interrupt to say, 'But what does all this mean to you? How does it make you feel? What other experiences does it vaguely seem to resemble?' Or the therapist may say 'Suppose the incident you are describing had never happened. How would your life be different?' (Kelly, 1955, p.647).

In order to obtain fresh, less intellectualized and tightly organized material the counselor might say 'Since our last conference you may have thought about some of the things that might have come up in the last conference or which might come up in this conference. Perhaps you thought of some things which you were glad did not come up or which you hoped you would not have to talk about . . . Let's talk about them.' (Kelly, 1955, p.648)

In general this kind of instruction is designed to enable the client to develop a kind of freedom and flexibility in his or her thinking, one that might produce a kind of 'mobility of mind'. This kind of approach will enable the client to be able to anticipate the nature of new life events and help put the client in a position to manage more creatively his or her future life.

Palliative Techniques

A further element in the client–counselor relationship is the use of palliative techniques, techniques that are used by the counselor in order to provide a secure footing for the more adventurous enterprise of constructive revision and change. One might say that these techniques are the backdrop against which constructive revision and change can be most clearly viewed. The two palliative techniques of *reassurance* and *support* are manifestations, in action, of the therapist's basic *acceptance* of the client. These techniques are not in themselves sufficient for a full therapy. However, it is very necessary to use them from time to time in order to help clients to solidify gains and provide for themselves a launching pad for new adventures in self revision and growth.

> *Reassurance* is 'a simplified subordinate construction placed upon the client's situation. It is communicated to the client so that his behavior and ideas will temporarily appear to him to be consistent, acceptable, and organized' (Kelly, 1955, p.649).

This is a way of stabilizing the client and providing a structure for life events to become understandable for the client. This is particularly important when the client is experiencing heightened levels of anxiety or other forms of discomfort. In the following example Kelly demonstrates the use of this technique with a client.

> *K:* We'll give you the ball today, so start with . . . .
> *C:* I have noticed developing . . . a nervous tenseness throughout my upper legs, upper arms and chest and abdomen.
> *K:* Yeah . . . . Now let me suggest something at this point because, while I don't know everything that may be involved in this—it may be due to studies or lack of studies; it may be due to things happening on the outside; it may be due to things that neither of us is quite ready to appraise—but let me throw this into the picture as a matter of a wee bit of reassurance. Sometimes in therapy as we begin to reopen closet doors that have been shut, even though we haven't opened anything with very creaky hinges (client laughs), as we do this there sometimes are impulses that slip through. One finds himself acting impulsively where once he may have had some control. For if we are to go through this house and take a look at all the closets and all the plumbing, it may be that some articles will fall down (Neimeyer, 1980, p.82).

Reassurance can often be accomplished by helping the client predict events that are coming up. This gives the client more assurance of his or her ability to understand such things. For example the counselor might say:

> 'You have been on the verge of dealing with some rather fundamental problems. You may find your moods fluctuating somewhat more than usual between now and next session. While you may be uncomfortable at times, I don't believe it will be more than you can handle' (Kelly, 1955, p.651–652).

Reassurances can also be accomplished by offering a postdiction of material that has already happened. This might be illustrated by the statement:

'I would guess that the last few days have been a little rougher than usual for you. Am I right?' (Kelly, 1955, p.652).

On the one hand, this technique has to be used sparingly because it can cause the client to arrest all change attempts and become very dependent on the counselor. On the other hand, reassurance is, at times, an absolute necessity for successful therapy.

Support is the other palliative technique that can be used in order to monitor the stability and immediate wellbeing of the client. With support it is not so much that the therapist is providing a fixed construction of life events (as in reassurance) but rather it enables the client 'to experiment widely and *successfully*' (Kelly, 1955, p.657). This is done in order to keep the risk factor down in the client's experimental enterprises. It imposes a kind of order and maximizes the chances for a successful outcome for the client.

Support can be shown by the therapist's being willing to be on time for his appointment with the client. More importantly, support is revealed by having the counselor be present with the client in such a way that precise material is remembered and brought to bear on the client's problem in exactly the way the client would have done it. The counselor demonstrates the ability to construe the world using the client's own construct system. The therapist is also mindful of immediate changes the client has made and helps the client recognize these orderly changes. For example, the therapist might say 'I think I am beginning to understand what you mean. Let me see if I can put it into my own words without losing the meaning' (Kelly, 1955, p.657).

Like reassurance, support must not be over-used because of the additive dependency it can promote. It should be limited 'to cases or to phases of treatment in which the client cannot otherwise handle all modes of reality or, more specifically, cannot take unexpected events in his stride' (Kelly, 1955, p.662).

Transference

Although the term transference is used in psychoanalytical theory, it has a different meaning as a term in Personal Construct Psychotherapy. It does, however, focus on the nature of the relationship between client and therapist and how this relationship can be used in order to be beneficial for the client. Transference is the term used to describe the process whereby the client uses constructs worked out to handle another person and then transfers these constructions unchanged to the therapist. The client lifts a construct from some other place and then readjusts the construct to fit the new situation. In the case of transference, clients, in fact, see the therapist through the constructs they formed elsewhere.

The use made of transference in therapy is summarized by Kelly in the following way:

'To summarize . . . we may say that the therapist is always looking for transferences, trying to get them formulated as testable hypotheses, designing experiments, and confronting the client with negative as well as positive results, upon the basis of which the transferences may be abandoned and replaced. Transferences, and the constructs which they employ, are then both means and obstacles in the therapeutic process' (Kelly, 1955, p.665).

There may be instances when the client cannot make material available to work on in any way other than to transfer it directly into the therapy. The difficulty arises from the fact that the transferred material comes in constellations that badly distort the nature of the present situation.

It is important to note here that transference is a necessary vehicle for the client to use in order to understand any new person, in this case the therapist. It is best for the client not to use *whole figure* or *primary* transference whereby the therapist is seen, for example, as exactly like the father in most important respects. It is wiser for the client to make use of a *propositional* or *secondary* transference where only selected qualities are transferred and then used as tentative constructions. For example, the client might say the therapist is 'caring' like the client's father but in other respects quite different from him. In this way the client is able to use the transference process in a productive manner.

One of the most important specific content areas of transference concerns the transferring of dependency constructs. These are constructs that are preverbal and used to define the conditions of the client's basic survival as a person. On the one hand we have to be concerned with the nature of the dependency that the client is forming with the therapist — and on the other hand the nature of the dependency constructs that the therapist may be using in his or her own view of the client. Close attention has to be paid to the spread of these dependencies. Care must be taken to keep the therapist from becoming the supplier of all the client's needs. The idea is to get the client to depend on a number of others, and to get these others, in turn, to depend on the client for certain things. Often, however, the client perceives the therapist preemptively, impermeably. The client responds to the therapist as if his or her life depended upon it.

The therapist is wise to develop a set of professional constructs which are used with the client in order to keep some perspective. The client and therapist should not become 'precious' people to each other, with their lives becoming intertwined in a primary kind of way. The client and therapists develop, instead, a co-worker relationship. The client should be instructed in how to move out into the world outside the therapy room. The use of role enactment and homework assignments in therapy is a useful technique here. For example, the client and therapist might role-play a social conversation at a party and then assign the client the task of implementing some of this material at a real social event.

The transference process is envisaged as a cycle where the person is at first very dependent in the initial stages of exploring a problem in therapy, then goes to a point of complete independence from the therapist. Therapy should be terminated at only the highest point of independence in this cycle and steps are taken *not* to start on a new topic unless the therapist is willing to see the client through another full cycle.

The Complaint

The second major concern in the investment phase of psychotherapy is concern wtih the client's *complaint*—the concern or problem that the client brings to the therapy. The complaint represents the initial investment which the counselor has in the actual process of the therapy. The complaint receives special attention because, as mentioned earlier, the alleviation of complaints is *the* goal of personal construct psychotherapy. This casts the goal of psychotherapy at a 'phenomenological level' (Kelly, 1955, p.832). This implies that the counselor must start therapy with the problem or complaint that the client brings to the therapy in the client's own terms, at the client's own level of understanding.

The complaint can pertain to either the client's direct experience of trouble and discomfort in life or it may pertain to what others find objectionable or problematic about the client, as the client sees it. The work of the counselor is *not* simply to get the client to stop complaining, but rather to enable the client to reconstrue or rethink his position. This can either involve the client's directing his efforts toward changing himself or directing his efforts toward changing his life situation or relevant social conditions. Stating that the goal of psychotherapy is the alleviation of complaints does not imply simply adjusting the client to life conditions. An equal amount of energy might be directed toward strengthening the client and helping him to solidify his position so that he can bear the work of changing social conditions. The psychotherapists must always consider the need for social change as seriously as he considers the need for personal change. The complaint, however, is where the therapist must start no matter which direction the therapy goes.

Another important characteristic of the complaint is that it can be either very focused and specific or very unfocused and global. On the one hand the complaint may be focused on a particular problem—for example 'I can't seem to pass my mathematics courses', 'My wife thinks I should be able to make friends more easily.' On the other hand the complaint can be vague, global and unfocused—for example, 'Things are not going well', 'Just everything is going wrong', 'I just feel uneasy most of the time.'

Whether the complaint is focused or vague, the immediate work in the therapy is to enable the client to elaborate the complaint. It is important to understand what we mean by saying 'elaborate the complaint'. In terms of the kind of psychotherapeutic change mentioned earlier: (1) enabling the client to shift her present constructs to the opposite ends of existing poles; (2) helping the client to organize her present system more precisely; (3) helping the client to replace some of the present constructs with new ones; the main work of elaboration involves this second kind of change. Elaboration is the work of helping the client to explore more completely just what the complaint means in her present system. Following along the constructs of the client's present system, it is a way of helping the client to deal with the issues in a more organized, consistent, and orderly manner. If elaboration is successfully accomplished as an end point in therapy, the client might well come to new constructions of events, but these new constructs are more likely to be direct extensions of the present system or result from the use of a different set of already existing constructs.

Controlled and uncontrolled elaboration

From the view point of Personal Construct Psychotherapy it is always important for the client to take and keep the initiative for things that happen in the counseling. The counselor never wants to get into the position where she is directing the therapy and where the client is reduced to asking 'What next? Where do you think we should go from here? After all you *are* the doctor and I have come for *your* treatment.' Without taking this very important initiative away from the client, the therapist has the responsibility to question whether or not an uncontrolled elaboration of the complaint is a good idea. Generally the client is initially allowed to explore the nature of the complaint in a more or less uncontrolled way. One of the first major issues, however, is how much control should be maintained over this elaboration.

There are some indicators that can be used to detect when it may *not* be a good idea just to let the client go on with his story. First, it is not a good idea for uncontrolled elaboration to continue if by telling his story the client begins loosening up to such an extent that he or the counselor cannot pull things together for any positive therapeutic effect. Second, in uncontrolled elaboration of the complaint the client may be precipitating a highly guilt-producing situation. The more the client says, the further he is alienating himself from his central identity as a person. Finally there may be excessive repetition in the story, indicating that the client is getting stuck in his present construct grooves, so to speak. Further uncontrolled elaboration may then yield very little (Kelly, 1955, p.961). On the one hand the counselor wants enough material out, so that the problem is understood. On the other hand the counselor does not want just an outpouring of material which will serve to defeat the purpose of positive therapeutic gain for the client. Even with a client who is reluctant to talk, the counselor must question whether or not encouraging the client to follow a path of uncontrolled elaboration would be the wisest course of action.

Basic to this whole procedure of elaboration is the following assertion: 'Since he (man) is basically a creature of curiosity, he tends to pursue the implications of his ideas' (Kelly, 1955, p.944). This means that there is something preventing the person from being spontaneously aggressive in developing his understanding of the world and his projects in the world. In Personal Construct Therapy it is generally believed that a controlled elaboration of the complaint will more often yield long range gains in getting the person to contact his zest for living and spontaneity in order to build an interesting and worthwhile life.

Case Illustration

Kelly presents an interesting illustration of controlled elaboration with a *hostile* client whose complaint is that he has never received a 'sense of security' in his home. The overall plan of the therapy is laid out as follows:

> The presence of hostility is established when the therapist determines that the client is unable to accept the natural outcomes of his own experimentation and that he has turned to extortion as a way of confirming his constructs. The therapist seeks to have the client elaborate on what he expected his parents to do in order to give him the 'sense of security'. The elaboration is pursued down to a very concrete level. As each hypothetical illustration is developed, the client is given an opportunity to view it in the light of the rest of his system to see whether such behavior on the part of his parents is what he really wished had happened (Kelly, 1955, p.946).

After listening to a more or less uncontrolled elaboration of a story in which the client reports that the mother did not support the client when the client was falsely accused of a wrong-doing, the controlled elaboration process is initiated in the following manner by

> asking such a question as, 'What did you want your mother to say?' He (the therapist) follows this up sooner or later with such a question as, 'As you look back on the incident *now*, what do you wish your mother had said?' Thus, the therapist is always careful to interweave the elements of the past with the constructs of the present. These questions may be sufficient to start the client on spontaneous elaboration of the implications of his wish. 'What would have happened *if* Mother had only done it differently? How would the ensuing days have been different? How would my life have been different?' (Kelly, 1955, p.947).

After grappling with this elaboration in order to determine the nature of some of the client's major constructs e.g., *those who handicap you forever by rejecting you* versus *those who assist you by believing in you*. Kelly attempts to bring all this up to the present point in the life of the client.

> Sooner or later, then, the therapist, or the client himself, should be asking such questions as, 'Exactly how would you be doing things differently today, if all these things that you complain about had, instead, been the way you wanted them to be? Let's work it through in detail. Take incidents that happened this morning. How would you have handled it *if* . . . . ?' In controlled elaboration the client is given every opportunity to pursue the implications of his own

construction all the way down to the minute details of his daily
behavior. (Kelly, 1955, p.947–948).

Kelly is very interested in having the client explore both ends of his
construction and in this way find for himself what his alternatives are within
his present system. In doing this Kelly notes some difficulties that the therapist
may encounter but can overcome.

The more he elaborates how he would behave different *if* all this
had not happened to him, the clearer the alternative pattern becomes.
Suppose he (the client) says, 'If I had been given more security as
a child I would have had more self-confidence and I would have
advanced in my job instead of being fired. Now look at me. I cannot
hold a job. I cannot . . . . I cannot . . . .' and so on, and so on
— and the client is back on the other side of his construction. The
therapist may persist: 'It is not clear to me what it is that you cannot
do. Can you give me some illustrations? . . . . Now I am still not
clear — just what would you have done in that situation *if* you had
had the kind of self-confidence that you failed to acquire? . . . .
Now is that the way you would like to act?' (Kelly, 1955, p.949).

The next step for the client is to try out some of these alternatives in some
more or less safe ways. It is hoped that the client can start spontaneously to
experiment with ways to change his life. Kelly notes that these first steps in
experimentation are necessarily crude, not a final solution, and may yet need
a great deal of work.

He (the client) may swagger down the street in the manner he thinks
he would have if his childhood had been different. He may indulge
in boasting before his friends. The therapist must be alert to the new
trends and help the client pursue the implications of his alternative
behavior as realistically as possible. (Kelly, 1955, p.950).

Kelly summarizes this illustration with a statement of his aspirations for the
therapy and his realistic anticipation of how difficult this may turn out to be.

What the therapist hopes is that the client will unleash his aggression
in the direction of exploration. He hopes that the client, with
alternative models of behavior clarified and clearly within reach, will
give them a trial. Thus he may be enabled to pick up from the point
where he hypothetically would have been if his mother had not
disappointed him. The therapist hopes that gradually the client will
abandon his investment in the idea that he was saddled with
insecurity. This is a big order, for it is likely that there is much
structure that rests on that particular idea. The therapist cannot

expect that the transition can be made quickly, with unstudied finesse, or without anxiety. (Kelly, 1955, p.950).

Other Suggestions for Elaboration

Controlled elaboration is designed to help the client in avoiding either getting lost in detail or grinding to a verbal halt in conveying the nature of the complaint to the therapist. It is a way of enabling the client to reach for some major themes in his or her complaint and to follow these along some rather specific lines. It is an active investigation of some specific issues that may help the client to get on with living.

In this regard Kelly suggests a number of questions which it may be helpful to pursue with the client when he or she first conveys the complaint. They are as follows:

a. Upon what problems do you wish to help?
b. When were these problems first noticed?
c. Under what conditions did these problems first appear?
d. What corrective measures have been attempted?
e. What changes have come with treatment or the passage of time?
f. Under what conditions are the problems most noticeable?
g. Under what conditions are the problems least noticeable?

The formulation of these questions is designed to get the client:
  (1) to place the problems, if possible, on a time line;
  (2) to see them as fluid and transient, and then to interpret them as responsive to (a) treatment, (b) the passage of time, and (c) varying conditions (Kelly, 1955, p.962–963).

The complaint should be elaborated in such a way that some answers to important questions can be gained and in such a way that even more interesting questions can be generated, which will keep the person searching for a better understanding of the nature of life. The questions are posed in such a manner that some real data can be used, and then some revision of the system can occur, so leading to further understanding. It is *very* important that this aspect of the therapy should *not* be understood in purely rational and logical terms. This therapy is based upon an experiential encounter with life and not on a logical recognition of facts. The purpose of this technique of controlled elaboration of complaints is to give the client a new experience of being with the problem which he or she initially brought to the therapy.

Confrontation

Another issue for the counselor to be aware of in dealing with the complaint is the extent to which one should confront the client with material the client has *not* mentioned. On the one hand, the counselor should be aware of the possible benefits that may accrue by simply mentioning an obviously omitted topic or issue which the client wants to deal with, but can only deal with if the counselor introduces it. On the other hand the counselor has to be aware of the danger of getting the client in too deep and having the client become desperate because there is not yet enough structure built in to handle the matter. Personal Construct Psychotherapy takes the position that the therapist has responsibility both for confronting and for not overwhelming the client. The general rule, however, is that confrontation is undertaken only when the counselor knows very well where he or she is going with the client. The counselor does not just toss out new material just to see if the client will react strongly. Kelly provides a much fuller discussion of confrontation than can be developed here (Kelly, 1955, p.966–975). In similar fashion the reader can find further work on the general issue of the complaint in articles by both Landfield (1975) and Wright (1970).

Summary

The investment phase of therapy is where the client and therapist first start to engage themselves personally in the actual process of the enterprise. The task for the counselor is to work for the establishment of a productive relationship between the client and the counselor. This involves: (1) determining the amount of personal material to be disclosed to the client; (2) building skills to make differential predictions of the client's movements in therapy; (3) teaching the client how to be a client; (4) employing palliative techniques that will strengthen the client–counselor relationship; and (5) understanding the nature of the transference which is inevitably a part of this relationship. The task for the client is to be able, with the therapist's help, to convey the nature of the complaint which brought him into the therapy. Generally a more productive time is spent in this phase of the therapy if the elaboration of the complaint is carried out in a controlled manner which enables the client to understand more fully just what the nature of his difficulty is as he is explaining it. The counselor should be able to take an active role in helping the client to structure this initial task of conveying the nature of the complaint.

CHAPTER 5

Encounter

The next phase of the cycle of experience is based upon a combination of *affirmative anticipation* and *self-involvement*, resulting in a special type of commitment which we call the *encounter*. In the context of psychotherapy and counseling, this commitment comes as the client brings more of her total self into the ongoing counseling process and no longer confines her attention to the limits of the initial complaint or problem.

For the client this is a commitment to the counseling and a commitment to truly being present in the therapy hour with the counselor. At the same time there is a commitment from the counselor to being more totally present and available to the client. The counselor is attempting to establish a true role relationship with the client by attempting to understand the client from the client's own point of view. The counselor is attempting to construe the construction processes of the client. In this way the client and the counselor are set for an encounter with each other and with the different life tasks and problems which the client has brought to be dealt with in the therapy.

Throughout Kelly's comments about encounter, emphasis is placed upon the fact that it is much more than a simple collision with events. Events here refer to other significant people and/or life problems of the client. Instead of a collision there is a receptiveness to these events. There is a knowledge received from these events and this knowledge makes a significant difference in the client's life. There is an openness or receptiveness to the other people encountered and to the life problems in such a way that more than just the realistic facts become known. The client begins to contact some of the possibilities for seeing how these people and life problems may be changed, or how his relationship to these events may be changed. Events are seen not only for what they are, but also for what they may become.

In the encounter the client is supported in such a way that he does not have to employ self-distancing manoeuvres such as a retreat into a cold intellectual–cognitive mode. Instead, the client is encouraged to remain fully human and in contact with all aspects of the situation. In short there is a true dialogue set up between the client and counselor as persons, a dialogue concerning the life problems of the client. There is an open exchange and interaction between the client and the therapist. In creating this dialogue there is neither an attempt to impose preconceived meanings on events nor permission given to outside events to impose their meanings on the client. Instead there is a true interaction between the two so that new meanings can emerge as new constructions.

In the encounter there is an aggressive (assertive) stance taken in terms of enabling the client to elaborate her own personal construct system. The particular problem which the client is having is, in fact, anchored within the more extensive personal meaning system of that client. The basic task, in the encounter, is to enable the client to elaborate the personal construct system which goes beyond the emphasis, described in the previous chapter on Investment, on elaborating the complaint. In Kelly's (1955) terms

> The therapist needs to know what kinds of *problem* the client is facing, to be sure. But he also needs to know what kind of *person* the client is. This means elaboration of the construct system as a whole, not just those unfortunate constructions which are applied to the problem areas (Kelly, 1955, p.985).

There are several specific advantages seen in taking this additional step of elaborating the personal construct system. *First* there is a clearer picture obtained of where, in the person life, the particular problem resides and how it is being maintained. *Second* elaborating the personal system provides the client and therapist with more alternatives. With the total personality system brought into play there is a rich array of ways in which the client might envisage alternative solutions to her present problems. *Third* it provides more materials for the client and the therapist to work with in order to create new constructs (a new meaning) for handling further problems. *Fourth* it provides a broader base for the development of the therapeutic relationship, and provides a way for a true role relationship to be established between client and therapist. It provides a way for the client to form more productive relationships with others and for the therapists to provide the help he knows how to provide in the therapy hour (Kelly, 1955, p.976–977).

With this additional task, of course, come some risks. The client is now facing important aspects of life as they relate to initial complaints. This means that the client begins to see the implied life changes which must be undertaken. The client is likely to feel threatened by these implied changes. Encounter is then the place in the therapy where the movement or action is begun. These initial steps, however, are usually taken within the relatively safe limits of enactment or role playing in the therapy room. This can be seen as an exploration of the relationship between the person's fantasies and his behavior.

Useful Encounter Techniques

The term technique is used here in the best sense of that word; that of organized procedures which can help the client to benefit maximally from counseling. In construct theory these encounter techniques are ones which therapists can employ to aid the client in elaborating the client's own personal construct system rather than being used only further to elaborate the nature of the complaint. Through the use of these techniques the client is aided in bringing more of himself or herself to the counseling. All of the techniques presented in this section can be used as an addition to the ongoing, session-by-session, process of therapy. In this way one may think of the techniques listed here as *special techniques* which can be employed in addition to interview techniques as such. The interview techniques will be covered in the second half of this chapter.

Rep Technique

One of the obvious ways is, of course, to employ the role construct repertory technique (Rep test). Since this procedure was covered in some detail in chapter 3, we will only mention it briefly here by simply stating that eliciting the constructs from the client, using the Rep test, can serve to elaborate the personal system. By listing her constructs, the client often starts to think of her problems in the larger context of her life. The exact directions for accomplishing this are set out in chapter 3. In this chapter our main concern is with other techniques which have their own particular advantages in aiding this elaboration.

Self-description

Although self-description was briefly covered in chapter 3 in the section on self-characterization, more attention needs to be focused on this technique here since it is a very valuable tool in the encounter. The various forms of self-description help the client to bring more of herself or himself into the counseling with a focus on broader life content.

Kelly (1955) provides the following statement which may be used by a therapist when it is appropriate to promote more of an encounter in the counseling.

> 'You have been telling me about the troubles you have. I intend to do all I can to help you. But if I am to help you I need to know more about *you*. I need to understand you as a person as well as understand the troubles you have. So let's lay aside your problems for a little while so that you can tell me much more about what kind of person you are. What kind of person are you really?' (Kelly, 1955, p.985).

This technique is used without 'leading' the client or asking probing questions. It is necessary for the counselor to let the content of the client's life come forward. The therapist is trying to create a situation in which the therapist's own values are not directly imposed upon the client. Rather the client's own values and view are being sought and brought to bear on the counseling.

Any number of procedures can be used to facilitate self-description. Kelly (1955, p.986) suggests the use of Bugental and Zelen's (1950) 'Who are you' (WAY) technique where the person is asked to give a number of responses to this friendly probe. In addition the client can be invited to relate to the thearpist what kind of child he was or what kind of person he expects to become. The client may also be invited to fill out some type of structured autobiography. One example of this technique, suggested by Emily Stogdill[1] in her work with college students, is to have clients devote a half page to each year of their life beginning with the year of their birth. The client is asked to put down just any important event that they can recapture for each year. The purpose of these techniques is to help the client, by the use of a structured procedure, to bring more of their personhood into the counseling. Many clients find self-description very difficult and need some suggestions such as those listed above. Of course there are other clients who respond freely when asked about personal matters and so need no extensive structure.

In Personal Construct Psychotherapy perhaps the most commonly used procedure is the self-characterization, for which Kelly (1955), suggested the specific instructions that we presented in chapter 3. Fay Fransella (1981) has recently provided a good illustration of the use of this technique in therapy with a client, 'Ronald', aged 31, who was having trouble vocationally and had maintained since adolescence the symptom of vomiting when he was under stress.

The client begins by reading his self-characterization to Fransella:

> 'Roland often says he would like to be a Victorian Curate. I think he means by this he would like a leisured life, with time for reflection, with opportunities to follow his own interests. A life with few demands apart from the demands he makes of himself.'

He (Ronald) comments on this:

> 'That, I think, is coming out very strongly on the grid (Rep test). I think I felt there was something very idealized about a certain kind of reaction to other people, productive, relaxed, a whole string of things, a whole cluster. And the notion — a sort of *relaxed productivity*.'

In the second paragraph of the self-characterization he makes it clear that the image he has chosen is important — just in case I (Fransella) should think it a flight of fancy:

> 'There is something slightly old-fashioned about him (the choice of a Victorian Curate may be significant) which is quite hard to identify. It is something to do with his manner, his values and his attitude towards work. He sees the need to earn a living as an imposition and an intolerable burden.'

He then reads out the third paragraph:

> 'People who know him well seem to think that he is able and respect his intelligence and opinions. This surprises him for although he has a very good opinion of himself and expects others to take what he says seriously, he also regards himself as worthless.'

He comments on how confusing it was to be surprised that people

take him seriously 'because I *expect* them to take me seriously'.
F. (Fransella). Is that true?
R. (Ronald). yes.
F. I'm not sure how you explain the contradiction.
R. I suppose the simple answer is that I can't. Those sorts of contradictions are very much a characteristic of me.
F. Of course, it is possible to be worthless in some respects—
R. No. It's actually—I think part of it is—the psychiatrist I saw talked of me being perfectionist, that sort of thing. I think some of the contradictions are connected with some feeling that I ought to be able to do perfect things.
F. —be successful?
R. Yes. It's necessary to be *impossibly* perfect.

Here the problem of getting down to *do* something is highlighted. If one has to be perfect—impossibly perfect—it is obviously not possible to do anything at all. There was not time to discuss more the writing during that session, but I was, of course, aware of what it contained. For instance, he pointed out that it was in his inner world of loose construing that he felt at home rather than in the realistic world of jobs and interpersonal relationships. He says:

'Perhaps some of what seems "old fashioned" about him is not really old-fashioned at all but is more that he doesn't feel at home in the world. He feels at home in his thoughts, his reactions to people and situations, and in his streams. Indeed, this aspect of the world fascinates and delights him.'

As he wrote this his way through this world of confusions, puzzlements and contradictions, he seemed to move towards his own identification of the problem.

'Had I been asked not long ago to say what most characterised Roland I would have said his unresolved contradictions, his confidence in himself and his wish to be inconspicuous, his burning ambition and his unwillingness to do anything about it (the list could go on), or I could have said his puzzlement about the world, or even, if I knew him very well, his fear of the world. Even when I began to try and describe him I concentrated on his alienation from the world including himself. My first attempts began "Ronald is someone who, when writing his name, sees a stranger . . ." and "Ronald is a private person much preoccupied with his own thoughts and reactions", "There is a photograph of Ronald as a little boy taken at his birthday party. The other children look as if they are enjoying themselves. He looks puzzled." '

All these descriptions and what would lead on from them tell us something about Ronald and if they went on to talk about his vomiting, his shyness, his fear of doing things in situations he does not understand, his compulsive smoking, his inability to use his abilities except in a very restricted way, they might provide some explanation of why he wants to change. But in one sense they do not tell us very much about who he feels he is and what he wants to be. (He would find it very difficult to express who he feels he is and what he wants to be, but he feels who he is and what he wants to be.) What they do tell us is something about the barriers in his life and some of the things he must learn to accept and overcome.

'Now I would say that what most characterises him is the phrase "a grown up child" . . . In recent years he has grown up and grown more childlike (when he was a child he felt very, very old). He is still growing in both directions, but he is 31 . . . time's winged chariot is hurrying near, and he hasn't got it right yet. He has to begin to make his world and he doesn't quite know how. So now I would describe him as 'a *grown-up child* who doesn't know how to go on.''

My (Fransella's) task was to help him discover who he 'really' is as well as just who he 'feels' he is; to help him tighten his construing (so that he can better understand and so predict himself and others) and yet retain the ability to fantasise and dream and be creative; to help him get into action and so test out his true worth. (Fransella, 1981, pp.221–222).

Fransella goes on with this case using self-description as a major technique in the therapy, which lasted for 35 meetings extending over a 20-month period of time. Over this period Ronald wrote on: *Me ten years from now*; *What does being successful mean to Ronald*; *Vomiting*; *Ronald as a man of action*; *The meaning of being sick*; and other relevant and related topics. Fransella reported definite progress for the client, who moved away from his troublesome vomiting pattern and away from a major construct dimension of 'not yet successful' versus 'being a success'. Through his writing and working with Fransella he began to see himself as *ordinary* in some ways, which was a step leading him to a new life still filled with problems aplenty but ones which he could cope with more effectively. The reader is urged to read the full description of this most interesting case by Fransella illustrating the technique of self-description.

In yet another way of using self-description, Miller Mair (1977) describes a technique employing a 'community of selves'. In this technique the client is invited to enter into a kind of metaphorical conception of the self as not just one thing but instead as constituting a community of selves. The clients are asked to think about their problems and themselves as if a number of different selves had come to speak about the issues. The following short case description is offered from a client who had agreed to attempt this kind of conversation:

. . . David talked as if he were composed of a number of political factions. Initially he outlined the group. The 'Hard Liners' were aggressive, right-wing, impatient, bigoted, unforgiving, and cynical. The 'Soft Liners' were concerned in all circumstances and on all occasions with finding and taking the easy way out, with appeasement, maintaining the status quo, and with letting sleeping dogs lie. Between these was the 'Middle Group' who were less clear cut but were more or less reasonable, without very definite opinions, liable to be swayed in one direction or another and fairly down to earth. (Mair, 1977, pp.132–133)

Through encouraging clients to proceed in this way to describe themselves and their problems, Mair observed that the clients could come to terms with issues in most productive ways. This technique gave the clients a tool for bringing more of their total selves to bear on the issues they were trying to deal with.

Life-Role

While the self-description and autobiographical procedure previously mentioned can aid greatly in self-exploration as such, special emphasis needs to be placed on this same procedure as an aid in helping the client elaborate life-role structure. It is very important for the client and therapist to grasp the, 'development of the client's personality over the changing years, his construction of himself in terms of his life cycle instead of his daily cycles, and his view of himself as a gradually aging person' (Kelly, 1955, p.990). This was anticipated somewhat in the above example by Fransella when she asked her client to contemplate 'Me ten years from now'.

This technique is particularly important to use with clients who are having difficulty in finding a purpose or aim to their life and are complaining about finding their lives meaningless. Seeing life along its time line provides an opportunity for the client to find those themes which serve to bind his or her life together. This process is often aided by having the client recall some earlier attempt to capture these themes. The following specific questions are offered: 'What were some of your plans for the future when you were a child?', 'What did you want to be when you grew up?', 'What did you think it would be like to be a _____?', 'What led you to change your mind?', 'What do you think about it now?', 'How do you think it has worked out?', 'If you had it to do over again what would you do?', 'Why?', 'How would things be different now if you had followed this other course?', 'What would people think of you?' (Kelly, 1955, p.991).

The use of this technique is particularly important for clients who are anticipating major life changes. Women who are coming to redefine themselves by entering a profession in mid-life after their child-bearing years, and both men and women who feel that some change is called for in their initial career choice, are examples of clients who might find this type of inquiry particularly helpful. In general the time line is a very important part of Personal Construct Psychotherapy. One of the goals of therapy is to help the client see life as a developmental process; a process that the client can understand rather than just being caught up in the confusion often produced by major transitions.

108

Confrontation with alternatives

With this technique we are attempting to move the client into action by employing the C-P-C cycle. You will recall from chapter 2 that this involves starting with *circumspection*, or the consideration of different alternatives, moving then to a *preemption*, which means choosing one of these alternatives, and finally arriving at *control*, which is the precipitation of the person into a particular situation. By this process the person moves into action.

This is a type of encounter where the person at least contemplates what it would mean to pursue a particular line of action in dealing with his or her problems. The client is invited to encounter the world of action, which means choosing among alternative lines of action and then contemplating what it would mean to involve himself in a total way, with this particular line of action. The following questions are posed as possible ways to facilitate this type of encounter: 'What does one *do* about such things?', 'What could you have done?', 'What else could you have done?', 'What kind of action does that call for?', 'What do other people do when they are faced with that kind of problem . . .,' 'Having done that, what comes next?', '*Now* what kind of decision would you have to make?', 'And suppose you did that—what next?' (Kelly, 1955, pp.993–994).

This type of encounter has to be done without the client feeling as if the therapist were pushing the client into action or advocating a particular action. This technique is designed to acquaint the client with action possibilities which means that many other possibilities should probably be considered before any final decision is made. The job of psychotherapy is to help the client entertain and explore conceptually many different alternatives in action before actually making a choice for one particular line of action. The encounter phase, however, would be incomplete without some attempt to come to terms with making a choice and moving into action.

Play and Prescribed Activities

This last set of techniques is not restricted to verbalization in the therapy room, as was the case with the technique just described (confronting alternatives), but instead is aimed at actual encounters in the outside world which may not be highly verbalizable. These techniques involve creative activities and ventures into the environment. It concentrates on the use of actions rather than words. It is cautioned, however, that such activities should not be done as a substitute for verbalization which would serve to decrease the client's level of awareness. Rather it is seen as a need in addition to the verbalization work commonly done in the therapy office.

In this technique the client is encouraged to take up some occupational, recreational, or social activities which will give the client an opportunity to see himself in a new light and reveal new possibilities (alternatives) that may not otherwise be available. For example, the client might be invited to involve herself in a jogging and exercise program which may give her the opportunity to relate to others in a new way and relate to her physical body with heightened awareness. Generally such activities are designed to bring more of this material into realm of verbalized constructs and aid in producing, in the client, a heightened awareness of life. A project of this kind is not indicated when the therapist cannot 'be with the client' in the sense of keeping up with her as she struggles to make new sense out of her world as she goes through the activities. (Kelly, 1955, pp.994–998).

The use of play and creative production can be used in this same way. The counselor can choose a particular kind of material for the client to work with, as in clay modelling, or, if the equipment is available, to let the client select from among several different kinds of materials, e.g., finger paints, drawing, dramatic enactment, poetry writing, etc. This provides means for the client to encounter his or her world in a way that is not focused on immediate self report and introspection; instead it involves the person in a series of actions perhaps not unlike other types of action which can be taken in order for the person to reach a more satisfying way of living. In fact some of these activities actually might be serving as a rehearsal phase of a new life activity. The client might later choose to use one of these activities as a way to continue to explore life.

Another specific advantage of the use of these 'activities' is summarized by Kelly as follows: 'The function of this approach to the elaboration of the construct system is primarily to activate and modulate the C-P-C Cycle for certain *preverbal* features of the client's construction system' (Kelly, 1955, p.1002). These activities may help the client *see* at a higher level of awareness just what he or she is up to in life and how he or she might better move either toward or away from these things. The reader is encouraged to consult the more extensive writings of Kelly on this point (Kelly, 1955, pp.998–1004). In general the direction of these activities is to make more of the total system (new and old) verbalizable, realizing that not everything in therapy is meant to be verbalizable in order to be made meaningful for the client.

Encounter in the Process of Psychotherapy

In this second main section of this chapter, concern will be focused on how personal material, for the encounter, is elaborated as the therapy develops from session to session. (These are techniques and procedures to be used inside the therapy hour as a part of what may be called *interview techniques*). Emphasis is on how new material arising in therapy fits into the existing personal system as a whole and what changes this new material implies for the total system. The counselor must, however, develop some understanding of what should be elaborated and when these elaborations should come and what form they should take. As mentioned earlier, a 'rough classification' or *structuration* of material should take place, followed by a refinement of this initial understanding into the more precise *constructions* of just what material should be chosen for elaboration.

Kelly provides at least an initial list of cues which the counselor can use for detecting what to elaborate and when to elaborate. Further elaboration is indicated: (1) When the client begins to produce strange or unexpected material. This tells the counselor he does not understand the client completely. (2) When the forthcoming material is indicative of the type of movement the therapist is expecting in the therapy plan. The client here is following through on a promising line of thought. (3) When the material is helping the client to sort out new relationships which could exist between existing constructs. For example the client may be starting to see that the construct *intelligence, per se*, may convey the quality *sharpness of thinking*, but this may not help the client to realize that one can be either kind or cruel in the way this sharpness is used in interpersonal relationships. Perhaps the client previously assumed that becoming brighter was all she needed to have a good relationship with others. (4) When the material is serving as a safe harbour for further experimental work. The client may begin to talk about her lunch group at school. This group may be serving as a 'safe group' for her to explore some larger life problems.

Although several other indicators are mentioned by Kelly (1955, pp.1008–1009) the reader has perhaps gained a general idea of this line of reasoning from the above four examples. In summary, it is important to understand enough about the client's construing to know when certain material should be elaborated. The counselor should always pause to consider whether the present elaboration and subsequent encounter are consistent with the person's further growth or whether the person is getting in too deep too fast and needs to delay elaborating the material for the time being.

Recapitulation

A specific technique for the encounter inside the therapy interview is to aid the client in elaborating the personal system by recapping what has been said over the past several sessions, weeks, months, etc. The therapist is attempting here to accurately capture what has been taking place in the therapy. This is an invitation for the client to encounter the very nature of the therapy itself, to clarify the central theme of the therapy and to further test out some of the implications of this central theme. Certain aids can be used such as reading over a therapy log of therapy events or playing back portions of the interview on video or audio tape. it is important to remember that recapitulation should never be used unless the counselor really is prepared to handle the problem in a 'summarized' form. This may prematurely precipitate the client into a line of action to which he might not want to commit himself, if he had more time to consider it (Kelly, 1955, p.1012).

Probing

Another very powerful technique for the encounter is the use of probes. Because this is a directive technique by the therapist it must be used very carefully, when the counselor is quite confident concerning who the client is and what is going on in the counseling at the time. In fact, a probing procedure should only be used when the counselor has a very good idea of what the client's reply to the probe is likely to be.

Kelly states that 'Probing is a way of controlling the client's participation in the interview. It can be used in two ways: to push the client into dealing with matters he might not otherwise mention, and to keep the client from talking about other matters he is not psychologically prepared to discuss at the moment' (Kelly, 1955, p.1012). The therapist should be sensitive to the fact that the clients can, upon occasion, say too much. They can get out of their depth at any time. When this happens a client may become overwhelmed with anxiety or become overly hostile in an attempt to control that anxiety. Direct probing should be done in an open and friendly manner, within an atmosphere of genuine concern and interest on the part of the counselor. It is not, in Kelly's words, to be 'a kind of inquisition which forces the client to incriminate himself' (Kelly, 1955, p.1012). The probe should always allow the client room to manoeuvre and express the complexities of his own position rather than pin him down. For Kelly the probe, 'should rarely be of the either-or type. (For example) A therapist may ask at a certain juncture in an interview, "Does this mean that you want to divorce your wife?" The client may say yes or he may say no, but the probing question is one to which he might also have given a qualified answer which might better have expressed his ambivalence. Contrast this formulation with the hostile type of question: "Either you want to divorce your wife or you don't—now which is it?" ' (Kelly, 1955, p.1013).

In general the use of probing questions is based on material that the client has mentioned earlier in the interview; therefore one can say that it is a *delayed probe* as opposed to the *immediate probe* which occurs just when the material is mentioned for the first time. In general the probe should be 'well-thought-out'. The immediate probe is generally restricted to minor points that the client may bring up and is used so that the therapist will have a richer context in which to understand the main idea. The immediate probe is the form of probe that involves the greatest danger of misuse.

Understanding Changes in the Construct System

In enabling the client to encounter (come to terms with) what is happening in the therapy, the counseling has to help the client understand the changes which are taking place in his or her system. This deals with the issue of how the client is experiencing the therapy itself. This is particularly important if this therapy indeed involves the client's going through some significant personal changes. Generally speaking these changes will not be first observed in the client's verbalizations to the counselor but rather will be observed in the kind of experientation the client starts to engage in with the therapist and with others outside the therapy room. This is to say change usually starts at the preverbal level and the client later becomes articulate in the therapy room—sometimes with the help of the therapist but sometimes not. Some clients get on very nicely with constructive therapeutic change if the counselor will just stay out of the way. There is frequently, however, a great deal of grappling with the material at a preverbal level before the client can fully grasp what is going on at the verbal level and thereby truly encounter the change that is taking place.

This brings us to a very important point in Personal Construct Psychology, that is, to face this question: *'Is the therapist ever more familiar with the client's construct system than the client is himself?'* (Kelly, 1955, p.1020). The answer is emphatically NO from a construct theory point of view. The therapist can at times verbally articulate the nature of the client's situation in a clearer fashion, but that is all. The client is always the expert on his own problems, for it is only the client who has access to the full meaning of what is happening at the moment. The therapist can only help the client: (1) gain a better verbalization which will fit the experience; (2) gain a better description of the experience: or (3) gain a better understanding of the unfolding nature of the experience. In some ways this technique is not really a specific technique at all but rather a general goal that is to be reached during the encounter phase of therapy. Kelly lists several techniques, such as citing detail, elaborating antecedents and consequences, summarizing events that are similar in nature, etc., but the importance of these specific techniques is to enable the client to encounter the main dimension along which he or she is starting to travel in order to understand the nature of what is happening in the therapy itself. For further elaboration of this point the reader could again profit from a detailed reading of Kelly (Kelly, 1955, pp.1015–1025).

Encounter through Enactment

One of the most effective techniques of encounter which enables the client to come to terms with what is going on in his or her life is for the therapist to invite the client to engage in a role enactment of a situation with the therapist. In this procedure the client is usually invited to play the part of some figure in his or her life, while the therapist plays the client. This role enactment usually centers around some situation involving a person the client is having difficulty in dealing with. Of course, any combination of parts to be played in the enactment is possible. The client might play himself, with the counselor assuming the role of, say, the client's brother. Generally it is a good idea for the client to play roles other than himself in order to have the opportunity to see how things are from someone else's point of view and to have the experience of being treated and perceived differently by the therapist in the counseling situation.

A very nice summary of the purpose of this technique, which is tightly bound to the personal construct definition of role, is provided by Kelly as follows:

> The function of enactment procedures is to provide for elaboration
> of the client's personal construct system, to provide for
> experimentation within the laboratory of the interview room, to

protect the client from involving core structures before he is ready to consider abandoning them, to free the client from preemptive constructions too tightly tied to actual events and to persons, and to enable the client to see himself and problems in perspective (Kelly, 1955, pp.1145–1146).

Enactment does not have to be very long, only 1 or 2 minutes, in order to be quite effective. Just to get the client and therapist to approximate an interaction in altered roles can provide a great deal of insight for the client and can often improve the nature of the relationship between client and therapist. The client gets to see the counselor struggle and fumble around with a role, make mistakes and become embarrassed just as the client might. It puts the client and therapist on an even footing and promotes the egalitarian quality of the counseling. It is very important in this regard for the client and therapists to exchange parts often, so that the client does not get the idea that the counselor is choosing the easier part for himself or choosing the part that has the upper hand. Because role enactment or role playing is experienced as risky for both client and therapist, often more resistance is encountered from the therapist than from the client. If the therapist has to maintain a perfectly calm and collected appearance at all times, role enactment is likely to be seen as particularly threatening. In training new therapists it is important to support them in the initial training using role enactment with clients. It is important for the therapist to avoid caricaturing the client or using the role playing to reveal the therapist's own hostility toward the client. If the encounter produces this result, the therapist can work with it as a way of finding out more about the therapy itself. The therapist can learn from it about what is going on in the relationship. It can be a very powerful tool for helping both the client and therapist to deal more effectively with the therapeutic enterprise.

There are various imaginative ways to use an enactment in therapy even when it does not go as the therapist has planned. The following example is taken from Robert Neimeyer's study of George Kelly's taped interview with a client.

K: If you were to . . . imagine yourself in my place, and I were asked to describe Cal Weston to someone, with some care, what do you imagine you would say? You're Dr. Kelly, describing Cal Weston to a close associate in whom you have confidence, and you wish to sketch accurately and with some depth, some sensitivity, the Cal Weston that has been seen for eleven interviews now . . . I'll be the friend; you're Dr. Kelly.

C: Outside of what I've said, I don't know if I could say anything; I can't think of anything.

K: 'I'm seeing a fellow by the name of Cal Weston.' This could be your first sentence. Now what sentence comes next?

C: (Long pause.)

K: What kind of a patient is this, Dr. Kelly?

C. I'm trying to think of something, but I'm not getting anywhere fast.

K: You mean you can't describe him, Dr. Kelly? (Long pause.) How well do you think you know your patient, Dr. Kelly?

C: I don't know how that would be answered. I'm just drawing a blank in my mind, that's all. Nothing.

Kelly's approach to this therapeutic exercise typifies his use of casual enactment techniques, informal role-playing procedures which can be used spontaneously in therapy with therapist and client enacting the parts. This specific scenario that Kelly suggested invites Cal not only to take perspective on his problems, but also to indicate his interpretation of Kelly's outlook (Kelly, 1955, p.1152). Cal, however, has considerable difficulty playing Kelly's part, a fact that is hardly surprising given the concretistic character of his interpersonal construing as evidenced on the Rep Test. Kelly attempts to control Cal's tendency to drop out of cast by staying in cast himself and interpreting even his silences as if they occurred in his role as 'Kelly' (1955, p.1154). Even this tactic is unsuccessful, however, and Kelly steps out of cast to discuss his client's uneasiness.

K: How do you feel about this kind of exercise? Is it disturbing?

C: No. I just get nothing.

K: Do you have some doubt about how I would really describe you?

C: I don't know how you would describe me . . . to make a description, I'd have to remember what I've talked to you about in the past . . . and I can't remember anything . . . the only thing that I've been able to construct so far is that I came in to see you, and, uh, felt I had a problem when I came in, logically enough. But the development beyond this is zero.

K: What did this fellow talk about, Dr. Kelly?

C: (Pause) Well, for one thing, whenever you mention me as Dr. Kelly, I get an uneasy feeling. I don't like it. But to carry on with the idea . . .

K: Well, we can change this. Go on . . .

C: I'd say one of the problems was the problem in school, not being able to achieve and maintain a standard which the individual feels he should.

K: Um-hm. This was his main, or his initial comment?

C: Yeah. The discussion was about the individual and his problems in school, and family background, educational background. (Pause.)

In resuming the enactment, Kelly formulates his question at a lower level of abstraction, merely asking Cal as 'Kelly' to recapitulate the material that had been discussed in the sessions. This tactic meets with some limited success, but Cal soon bogs down again, leading

Kelly to modify further the role play in order to make it less anxiety-provoking.

K: Well, let's say that you're Dr. Jones, who has been seeing Cal Weston. Does that make it a little easier? It takes some of the 'personal' out of it.

C: Yeah, but still there's an uneasiness in that you're asking me to make a judgment which I'm not qualified to make . . .

They then discuss Cal's concern that his emotional involvement in the therapy makes it impossible for him to present a 'true picture' of what has transpired from the therapist's point of view. Before dropping out of cast entirely, however, Kelly frames one last inquiry in enactment form.

K: May I ask one more question of you in your role as Dr. Jones? Dr. Jones, what kind of *person* do you think this man is?

C: What do you mean?

K: What motivates him? Or let me put it this way—what is it like to meet him? What kind of *feeling* do you get when you meet him?

C: I doubt that I could answer that.

K: Is it a little threatening to ask this question?

C: I don't think so (loudly): I just don't see how I can reflect on myself and describe myself from that sort of view.

Cal goes on to explain the difficulty he encounters in taking up Kelly's perspective.

C: I'd have to . . . guess at how someone else might see me. But I would have no idea, no basis for describing the person that was doing the seeing, or how he would see me.

K: Do you feel that you have no basis for knowing how I see you, or do you have a *sense* of how I see you?

C: I'd never thought of it. I think if anything, I tried to keep an idea like that out.

K: Why?

C: Well . . . what I expect of you is an objective, rational study of my problems, provided you can find them, the roots of them, and trying to help me sort them out through questions and discussions. At least that's what I assume . . . the role of the psychologist is. What was the question again? (Laughs.)

K: What kind of a *sense*, what kind of an *impression*, what kind of *feelings* do you think I have about you? Or did you have the feeling, or the conviction that I would have as few feelings as possible and be as analytic as possible?

C: *And* the development of any emotional friendship with you would tend to lead me to answer any questions . . . with a bias towards maintaining that friendship . . . I'm not in a position (to play your role.) I would be assuming some of the points of view you might have, and to develop those points of view I'd have to come to know you a little bit, and know how you think and how you feel. I've tried to prevent anything like that from happening, so that I wouldn't feel emotionally involved in our personal relationship. That's strictly—professional. You're the doctor. I'm going to keep this strictly on an 'M.D./guy with a cut throat' situation.

K: What kind of situation?

C: 'Cut throat.' I tried to come up with something rather radical.

In exploring in some depth the nature of Cal's resistance to the enactment, Kelly has arrived at a much clearer understanding of Cal's conception of therapy and the role he expects the therapist to play. As he frequently does, however, he validates his interpretation of the client's viewpoint before moving on.

K: This discussion we're having now is good. Now let me see if I understand. This is my examination now; you see if I can pass it. In a sense you are saying, 'I'm going to keep Kelly at arm's length, so that he'll be a kind of doctor, so that he can cut my throat if it's logically required. I'll keep him at a distance so that I can tell him the worst about me, so that I can bare myself to the worst that can happen. For if I get too close, I'll be afraid of losing him, and I'll start having a kind of personal relationship.'

Cal confirms that Kelly has captured his point of view, and adds that the distance he has interposed between himself and Kelly has made it difficult to put himself in the therapist's shoes (Neimeyer, 1980, pp.87–90).

Another suggestion for a creative use of enactment is to ask the client to play the hypothetical part of a close friend who has come to talk to the psychotherapist about the client. It gives the therapist a chance to ask some interesting questions which would not be feasible to ask in 'straight' counseling. For example, the therapist can ask, 'Do you know whether your friend Mary is secretly afraid that she will lose her husband's affections or has ever confided in you to that extent?' Or this same manoeuvre can be used to talk about the therapist. 'When I talk to your friend Mary are there any special attitudes or feelings that I should be particularly sensitive to? What is likely to be her response to me?' (Kelly, 1955, p.1152).

Summary

The encounter phase of personal construct psychotherapy is designed to bring the client into contact with personal material beyond a narrow problem area, so that the client can use more of his or her total personal strengths in reaching the goals set for the therapy. The techniques presented for this purpose were divided into two main groups: (1) Techniques which might be used outside the day-by-day, step-by-step processes of the psychotherapeutic interview. These might be thought of as special assignments, homework, or special tasks taken up as a part of the therapy. (2) Techniques which were designed to fit within the flow of the natural course of the interview sessions. The first group included the use of the Rep test, the use of several self-descriptive and autobiographical techniques, helping the person elaborate his life-role, aiding the client in confronting alternatives for action, and actually aiding the client in undertaking certain activities. The second group covered such techniques as recapitulation, probing, aiding the client in dealing with transitions, and using enactment or role playing for the purposes of encounter. It is important to remember that it is also an aim of this encounter phase in therapy that the client should come to understand, at some level, what is taking place in therapy so that the client is learning not only what is happening but also how it is happening. The aim of therapy is not only to solve problems but also give the client a general strategy for life problem-solving which can be used in the future.

Note

1. This is an unpublished technique, which Emily Stogdill employed in class-room teaching.

CHAPTER 6

Confirmation and Disconfirmation

As we consider this fourth phase of the cycle of experience as it applies to psychotherapy, our attention is drawn to ways in which the therapy operates to enable the client to test out the construct system so that some confirmation or disconfirmation can take place. In the earlier phases of this therapy, we have been mainly concerned with the ways the system operates, the characteristics of the system, and the extent of internal consistency which exists in the system. Here, however, in the confirmation and disconfirmation phase, our attention is drawn to the ways in which the new meanings that the client is beginning to grasp can be worked with in a creative fashion. This phase carries the use of the existing construct system up to the point where new meanings can enter the system. These new meanings emerge precisely as a result of the fact that some confirmation or disconfirmation can be found for what has been anticipated. This confirmation procedure is carried out in such a way that new modified meanings start to emerge. These new meanings come about by allowing the system to be tested.

Building on the commitments the client has made earlier, the client now begins to shape new meanings, and these new meanings have to be brought into focus clearly enough so that some progress can be realized in the therapy. It is here that the therapist focuses on what is perhaps the most important professional diagnostic dimension. This is the process of enabling the client both to loosen and tighten single construct dimensions and then tighten and loosen the construct system as a whole. It is the aim of the therapy, in this phase, for the client to learn how to alternate between tightening and loosening in order for his or her constructions to be confirmed or disconfirmed and thereby promote the continued growth and change of the system. It is seen as severely limiting if the client can only loosen or can only tighten without being able to move back and forth between tightening and loosening in a continuous process.

The reader, no doubt, recognizes this dimension of tightening and loosening as the creative process described earlier, in chapter 2, as the 'Creativity Cycle' — the process whereby new meanings are given to old constructions and entirely new constructions are created and tested out. This testing out often involves, in addition, the implementation of the C-P-C (Circumspection, Preemption and Control) cycle which we will describe shortly. For the most part, however, this chapter will be concerned with the process of loosening and tightening as a way of describing how an insight or idea of the client can be worked with in such a way that what might otherwise have been just a vague notion is turned into a clear statement which can be put to some sort of test. After all, one of the services offered in therapy is for the client to be able to see just what his or her ideas amount to—what they turn out to be. It is no service to keep the client in a fog. This process of clarification involves moving from a loosening to a tightening process so that predictions can be made and the person can then move into an appropriate C-P-C cycle where some action can take place. This tightening after loosening is a way for the client to let something (which can be either confirming or disconfirming) take place. If psychotherapy is to be successful, it is always implied that the client should start with loose construing and then move to a tightened construing, which can then be tested and either confirmed or disconfirmed. In this way new meanings and understandings are brought to bear for effective living. This means that, in opting for the exercise of a confirmation or disconfirmation, the client gains a sense of something happening. These new meanings are not just ideas, but meanings in action that one can do something with in such a way that some progress can be seen to have taken place. By first loosening an existing meaning one allows varying predictions to emerge. By then tightening one of these predictions the actual testing of the construction is accomplished. In such a way either a confirmation or a disconfirmation can take place.

In this respect it is important to note that loosening is like the circumspective phase of the C-P-C cycle (action cycle), but tightening does not commit one to action. It only creates the possibility for action, in that the construct is restricted to a set of unvarying predictions. Tightening makes it possible for the action resulting in a C-P-C cycle to take on a clear meaning for the person. The action is based on a precise prediction that can then be either confirmed or disconfirmed. It must be realized, however, that one can initiate an action (engage a C-P-C cycle) at any place in the creativity cycle—for example in the loosened part of the constructions. The consequence, however, is that the action will have a less clear meaning, in that it offers little evidence of exactly which prediction was being tested. Here true confirmation or disconfirmation is not being accomplished. If, however, the action (C-P-C) cycle is delayed until at least some tightening has taken place, then something more profitable is likely to take place—specific prediction can be either validated or invalidated. Following this process, at least, leaves open the possibility that something can be made of one's experiences. As was stated earlier, the aim of therapy is to enable the client to complete the experiential cycle in therapy to the point where some confirmation or disconfirmation of one's ideas, understandings, or meanings of the world can take place. Let us now examine carefully the particular parts of the tightening and loosening process, since both are necessary for true growth to take place.

Loosening

Kelly considered it very important to have the counselor understand that loosening and loose construction refer to a special kind of structure rather than indicating a lack of structure or a lack of order. For him it was important to recognize that loosening does not mean disorganization or chaos in thinking. On the contrary it indicates a way of thinking that has certain set characteristics. It is not that this type of thinking is disorganized, it is just that these thoughts are elastic and lead to varying predictions.

In construct theory terms, you will remember that the actual loss of structure manifest in chaotic thinking is experienced as anxiety. Looseness is not the same thing as anxiety, which means not having a construct system capable of handling events. In loose construing events are handled, but they are handled in such a way that the predictions based on these constructs lead to various ideas rather than precise expectations. It is interesting to note that in Bannister's (1960) work looseness has been seen as a way of reducing anxiety in schizophrenic patients. Bannister and his colleagues (Bannister and Fransella, 1971) postulate that schizophrenic patients maintain looser constructions than normals because they need to maintain a system that cannot be further damaged by continuing to receive invalidating information. The loosened construction allows them to maintain a system leading to varying predictions such that no one prediction can be tested and subsequently risk possible invalidation. This lack of risk would not be possible if the system were tight where precise predictions, in fact, could be made.

At this point it may be very helpful to give a detailed account of looseness and how it operates in psychotherapy. Kelly provides the following description:

> 'How does it feel to think loosely? One thinks loosely in dreams. There the shadowy figures loom large without losing their diminutive proportions; they are black yet they are white; they are alternately ominous and comforting, until the dreamer despairs of telling his tight-thinking therapist anything about them at all. To think loosely? One does it, despite oneself, in the daily appraisal of people and things. Today's joy is tomorrow's sadness and yesterday's regret; the failure of the moment is the success of a lifetime; and the inanimateness of stationary things turns into wilful intransigence whenever we stub our toe. Yet the wavering construction remains substantially the same: joy is still contrasted with sadness, failure blocks success, and inanimateness precludes wilfulness; it is only that they have unstable relationships with the object they are designed to keep in proper array' (Kelly, 1955, p.1030).

Again it is very important to take note of the fact that in this description there is a specification of a type of structure in the client's experience. This is not the absence of an ordered way of thinking. The client's thoughts make sense both to herself and to very close friends (if they are clever) in a loose kind of way. It is just that for those on the outside (outside the person and the friendship circle) this production of loose thinking by the client appears to be disorderly and chaotic. It is sometimes necessary for the counselor to purposefully loosen his or her own construct system in order to understand the loosened construction of the client. If the counselor remains perpetually tight, he or she will never understand such thinking in clients. There is no denying that there is a schizophrenic quality in the loose client's thinking but it must be remembered that this type of thinking represents a type of ordering or structuring of thought rather than just verbal garbage.

Usefulness of Loosening

Perhaps a good place to start our direct concern with loosening is to take into consideration what advantage might be gained by actively inviting the client to pursue the looser aspects of her system. Kelly notes four main implications. *First*, during loosening there is a general movement in the system as elements are shifted back and forth between the poles. For example, in loosening, that which was harsh and cruel may now become kind and welcoming. This kind of movement would elicit new responses from the client and from others with whom the client interacts. The client gets to explore different ways of responding and being responded to by others. *Second*, the loosening can serve to *dilate* the system so that the client considers a wider variety of material. In a tightened state the client may be ignoring some of the more interesting aspects of her world. This might serve also to help the client recall material that had not come to mind for some time. This broadened view offers the opportunity also for the client to reorganize some of her thinking in a more superordinate way or just to put together and compare in her thinking things that she had not put together before.

Third, the loosening can serve to extend the range of convenience of the client's existing constructs. Clients with loosened construction handled material with their present systems that they would not have previously thought their constructions could handle. This would make the client bolder by finding out that she could indeed use her construct system to make sense out of things that had just never occurred to her to try in the first place. *Fourth*, Kelly states that loosening carries the possibility of enabling the client to become open to new experiences of all types. The new experience can now fit into her system and make sense to the client. For example, this increased permeability might enable the client to make verbal thoughts that up to that time had remained preverbal. By loosening the verbal labels the client might be able to fit together experiences which were only dream-like and hazy before. This loosening might, in addition, serve to release the client from preemptive ways of thinking about things. For example, instead of a friend being thought of as nothing but a nice guy, the client might now see her friend as a person who might need to protect his own feelings from time to time, because the friendship is threatening in some respects.

The usefulness of loosening might be summarized in the following way, 'All of these functions (of loosening) may be preliminary to the reconstruction which therapy seeks to induce. They may set the stage for rotation of the personal-construct axes, for an eventual tightening of construction along new lines, for a more spontaneous elaboration, and for experimentation' (Kelly, 1955, p.1033).

Specific Techniques for Loosening

In therapy it is often very useful to have in mind certain ways to help the client loosen the construct system. As was mentioned previously there are times when it is to the client's advantage to be able to abandon a tightening way of conceptualizing a matter and move to a less precisely drawn conception. In fact at times, it is *very* important for a client who has tightened to loosen for a therapeutic advantage.

Kelly lists four main techniques for facilitating loosening: (1) using relaxation exercises; (2) inviting chain associations; (3) providing uncritical acceptance of the client; (4) recounting dreams. Each of these will be considered in turn. Because of the vast wealth of material contained in them, however, the main emphasis will be on dreams.

The *first* technique, relaxation, is perhaps the most familiar to many psychotherapists because it is used extensively in stress management programs and systematic desensitization programs, and has received detailed descriptions in studies of relaxation responses (e.g. Girdano and Everly, 1979). For promoting loosening, any of these established procedures for relaxation will serve the purpose. As Karst (1980) has pointed out, personal Construct Psychotherapy is eclectic in respect of the techniques employed in counseling. The aim of this technique for personal construct therapy is to get the client to, 'relax his thinking and his voice as well as his muscles' (Kelly, 1955, p.1034). The usual procedure is to ask the client to tense and relax each major muscle group, comment on the nature of this state and then begin to report on the thoughts occurring during this relaxed period.

The *second* technique, chain association, is familiar to many therapists, particularly those familiar with psychoanalytic procedures. This technique is an operationalization of the basic rule used in psychoanalysis, which is to invite the client to say everything and anything which comes to mind. The client is further instructed not to try to make sense out of the material at the moment and try not to leave out anything that comes to mind. The aim of this technique is to enable the client to produce a richer and more varied amount of information than he could normally produce in a therapy interview situation. This technique is often used with clients who are very 'uptight' and have structured their thinking in very narrow and carefully defined terms. For this reason some clients need even more guidance in the form of explicit instructions, such as asking the client the following types of questions which are designed to access feelings:

'But how does all of this *feel* to you? What is it reminiscent of?

What does all of this vaguely resemble? Does this feel like something you have told or experienced before and yet cannot quite put your finger on? You are telling me facts—let's not deal with facts just now, let's deal with deeper meanings, with pressures, with lurking anxieties, with vague uneasiness, with yearnings, with ideas that are hard to put into words' (Kelly, 1955, p.1036).

The *third* technique of uncritical acceptance is used frequently by Rogerian counselors. It is one in which the counselor is willing to accept the outlook of the client completely. In Personal Construct Theory terms this means adapting a truly *credulous* approach in counseling, as discussed in chapter 1. All questioning and probing by the counselor is suspended. The client is simply encouraged to keep unfolding the meaning of the issues she has come to work on in the counseling. The idea is to enable the client to be uncritical and not constricted in any way in expressing the way that she sees things. The therapist conveys the idea that the client is understood, even when that client is only barely understood.

The client is not asked to explain what she says nor is she asked to follow clear implications of her thinking. It might even be helpful for the counselor actively to reassure some clients with the message that, 'I understand that you are telling me how you feel about things and that you are not necessarily trying to tell me what is exactly *so* and what is *not so*' (Kelly, 1955, p.1049). Kelly points out that this may be particularly important for the client who fears misrepresenting others in conveying the nature of the problem.

The *fourth* technique, recalling dreams, is perhaps the most important means by which loosening can occur for clients. A dream is, in fact, a band of loosened constructions of the world which is often over-filled with all kinds of different meanings. In fact Kelly (1955, p.1037) states that, 'Dreams represent about the most loosened construction that one can put into words.'

In a construct theory approach to dreams it is the loosening that is of primary interest rather than the dream itself. It is the loosened quality of the client's conceptualization which is being generated by recalling the dream.

Because of this, our concern is not with the accuracy of the dream report. The focus is on the nature of the person in the present rather than on the analysis of the dream. It is then the analysis of the dream *recalled*, as a technique for dealing with loosened construction, that concerns us. The primary emphasis is on the meaning that is emerging in the recalled dream. As Kelly states it, 'His act of reporting the dream involves his (the client's) loosened constructions; that is what we want to see' (Kelly, 1955, p.1038).

Many clients who are overly tight in their constructions and are generally feeling very anxious about trying to relate dream material need some special instructions in order to produce the dream recall. This can be accomplished in a number of different ways. The following examples are offered as instructions to the client:

'Let's not worry about the dream. Just relax now and think about the dream for a few moments and then let your mind wander. After a little while you can start telling me what you are thinking about' (Kelly, 1955, p.1038). 'Was it a happy dream or a bad dream? Was it simple or complex? Were there many people? Who seemed to be the principal actor? Where were the break points—the points at which the setting seemed to change? . . . What other dreams or experiences have you had which seem *something like* this one? . . . What other dreams come to mind just now?' (Kelly, 1955, p.1040).

In working with dreams from a personal construct perspective, the counselor should be very careful about interpreting material too early in the process. Interpretation always starts a type of tightening process that may take place before sufficient loosening has occurred for productive material to come forth. It is usually a good idea to have interpretation as close to the client's own terms as possible without the counselor's meanings (personal or professional) entering into the picture. The idea is to stay as close to the client's own experiences as possible and to be as true to this personal phenomenon as possible.

Like many other systems developed for dealing with dream material, the construct approach also advises the client to place a pen and pad beside the bed so that the client can record the dream, if possible, without turning on the light. Bright lights will cause focusing and tightening of the construct system.

Mile-post dreams. From a construct theory viewpoint, it is important to be aware of the occurrence of what may be termed 'mile-post dreams'. These are dreams which, 'assume epic proportions' (Kelly, 1955, p.1044). These are dreams which appear to integrate a great deal of material even within their loosened structure, and are of extreme importance for the client. As a general rule these are dreams which stand on their own and do not need to, and should not, be interpreted. They represent real movement in therapy. Mile-post dreams illustrate the use of dreams as ends in themselves rather than a means to an end. The main themes of the client's life occur in the dream. Such dreams have implications for new behaviors and further insights. Kelly offers an example of such a dream from one of his clients.

> 'A certain client who had showed a great deal of hostility and constriction and had enacted her constructs in terms of somatic complaints such as anorexia was beginning to show some therapeutic progress. She dreamed vividly of preparing a meal for her family. It was one that she, her husband, and her son liked. In the dream her husband announced that he was going "off to the races", an expression which had been associated with his going to burlesque shows and with his extramarital adventures. She then threw the whole meal on the floor. This client had considerable difficulty with the role of housewife and mother. There had been vomiting and a great deal of hostility. There had been difficulties expressing aggression appropriately. The dream also represented admirably many other

features in her construction system. She spontaneously interpreted the dream as a summary of her whole predicament. The interview was soon followed by some changes in her behavior pattern, although, in this case, certain administrative complexities in the therapeutic plans made it impossible to exploit the advantages she had gained' (Kelly, 1955, pp.1044–45).

Preverbal dreams. There is another special category of dreams which is of particular interest to personal construct psychotherapists. These are dreams that are '. . . characterized by vagueness, visual imagery, absence of conversation in the dream, slow unfolding of the content during the interview, and the feeling of the client that it may have been his "imagination" rather than a dream' (Kelly, 1955, p.1045). These are preverbal dreams—dreams that contain constructs which truly are not yet able to be put into clear verbal symbols, nor able as yet to be represented clearly in any verbal form. There are often very crude constructions that existed before the person really had a verbal language to express this meaning. Kelly provides a good example of the preverbal dream in the following case:

'A client of the writer's . . . had shown a great deal of passive hostility and construction in certain areas of interpersonal relations. She reported a preverbal dream. The report followed upon a period in therapy when considerable loosening had been used. During the interview in which the dream was reported she had been asked to relax, and various loosening techniques were employed during the hour she was telling the dream. She was not sure she had dreamt at all. She had a vague feeling that she was lying in a crib, that she was feeling isolated from a man and a woman who were in the room. It seemed as though there were a netting between herself and the woman. The woman seemed like a certain aunt who was pretty and to whom she was much attracted when she was a very young child. The man seemed like an uncle whom she remembered as the first person in her life who had seemed to accept her. The most important feature of the setting appeared to be the netting, which seemed to excommunicate her from the persons with whom she had sought or had found a role relationship.

The dream was reported in fragments and the client had the feeling that some of it might have been a memory, a story that she had been told, an old fantasy, or even something which she might be making up on the spot. It was definitely associated with the feelings of unworthiness and guilt; indeed, the feeling of loss of role was the principal feature of the dream. This dream, together with other features of the case, established the deep-seated and preverbal nature of the client's guilt feelings as an important fact to be considered by the therapist. Moreover, it threw light upon one of the client's own aggressive techniques, that of excommunicating other people from her own society. This technique had been her principal second line of defense and accounted for many of the constricting measures which she employed. One measure, for example, was the often repeated childhood phantasy of believing herself dead. As a child she had frequently lain in her bed imagining herself comfortably dead' (Kelly, 1955, pp.1045–1046).

In general, the use of dreams deals with material that is ordinarily not available to the person. In another system this might be referred to as *repressed* material but in construct theory it is seen differently. With repression one gets the image of material buried in the unconscious. A construct theory approach views this matter in terms of meanings that are not available for a number of reasons, and views the 'repressed' material as an extension of an existing structure. There is a definite emphasis, here, on the extension and creation of meaning rather than an excavation of something buried in the unconscious which contains the meaning of the material.

In addition to preverbal material mentioned above, dreams are often seen to reflect a submerged pole of a bipolar construct. In dreaming the person will reveal just the opposite of that which is presently reflected in the waking life. For example, 'A client who has always insisted he loved everyone may dream that he is fighting someone' (Kelly, 1955, p.1047). Finally dreams may reflect the *suspended* part of a person's system. This is a part of the system that has had to be suspended because it is incompatible with the system as a whole, or has had to be suspended for some other reasons such as the lack of an opportunity to use the material in a meaningful way. In addition to preverbal dreams, submerged poles, and suspended material, there is an overall interest in examining the *level of cognitive awareness* at which the material rests rather than an interest in finding material supposedly contained in a psychological area or domain such as the unconscious.

Difficulties and Hazards in Loosening

The concern here is with the difficulties and hazards and therapist encounters when the therapist employs some of the techniques designed to facilitate loosening of the construct system. Let us first consider what are, as Kelly puts it, the 'resistances' to loosening that the therapist encounters from the client when the therapist has judged it to be therapeutically desirable for the client to move in the direction of loosening. As was mentioned earlier, resistance in personal construct theory terms is seen as a much more positive feature of therapy than when it is used in traditional psychodynamic therapy systems. Resistance is seen less as the client's thwarting or blocking the therapist's moves than as a potentially wise move on the part of the client to pursue a line of meaning that is simply different from what the therapist had in mind. A distinction must be drawn between the possibility that resistance to loosening is indicating something about the relationship with the therapist (such as perceiving the therapist as threatening) and the possibility that the resistance should best be seen in relationship to the actual therapeutic task that is being undertaken. From a Personal Construct Theory perspective, the resistance encountered in loosening is more likely to be involved with the client's actual content material than anything else. For the moment, the therapist has faded into the background as a significant person and the client is almost completely taken over by the content of his or her own system. This does not imply that the relationship with the therapist should be overlooked: that relationship is just as important as the meanings that the client is presently pursuing.

One of the first difficulties in this work is caused by the therapist's not recognizing just where the client is in a loosening to tightening sequence. This is due to the fact that the client may be talking about specific events or things, but may not really be using them in a concrete or literal manner. These specific events may simply be serving as makeshift symbols for a concept which is just now being formed in a very loose way. The therapist, therefore, must always approach the client with the idea that loosening may be taking place even though what the client has to say sounds very tight. At this moment the therapists may think the client has not loosened when, in fact, the client is quite advanced in loosening. On the other hand the client may be wisely moving toward tightening even though the therapist desires more loosening (Kelly, 1955, p.1052).

It is important for the therapist to stay out of the client's way, when it is beneficial for loosening to take place, by not offering interpretations prematurely. It cannot be overemphasized that interpretations promote tightening. In fact it is important to remember that in a loosened condition the client may take incidental or casual remarks to be interpretation. An example of the situation is as follows:

'A client who has been expressing loose constructions of sexual matters may find himself threatened when the therapist mentions the client's teenage daughter. The mere introduction of this new element serves to alarm the client. The loose construction threatens to undermine his parental role structure. In the resultant confusion he is brought to the brink of guilt as well as of anxiety. He may straighten up and start tightening his constructing processes. The therapist may view this tightening as a form of personal resistance, but he will do better if he sees it as a defense against anxiety, a defense that was made necessary by his own remark. If a therapist is to avoid resistance to loosening, he must be careful not only in expressing evaluations of what the client produces, but also in the introduction of contextual elements' (Kelly, 1955, pp.1053–1054).

Kelly suggests several ways in which resistances to loosening can be dealt with—with a good chance of some success. To begin with there is a situation in which a tightly construed area is specifically related to a loosened area and

128

the client seizes upon the tight area as a way of escaping from dealing with the more meaningful but loosened area. A tight area of construction *interferes* with the more meaningful, but loosened way of trying to deal with really important matters. The following example is provided:

> 'Suppose the loosely formed construction seems to be revolving around a construct something like that of a symbiotic realtionship to persons. In a loose, vague way he sees himself cultivating friends as if they were to be husbanded for their nurturant services. It is as if he saw his mother as a cow to be possessed for the milk she supplies and as if he dealt with society as with a swarm of bees which are to be systematically robbed of a portion of their honey. That strikes a clear note. Now he thinks of bees. He recalls a painful childhood experience with bees. He goes on to describe the incident in precise detail' (Kelly, 1955, p.1055).

It is important for the therapist to realize this has happened and not be misled by a line of meaning which is being developed as an interference or one that the client is using to deliberately side-track the therapy.

Another way to deal with resistance to loosening is to use enactment to reduce the threat that some loose constructions pose. The person can get caught up in the part and start to produce some spontaneous material which again can be handled as non-threatening in an 'as if' role-playing segment which the client can relate to as not really pertaining to the self. Another suggestion is to use context shifts to reduce the resistance to loosening. 'A person who does not dare to think loosely about sex or financial matters may be perfectly capable of thinking loosely about music or social organization' (Kelly, 1955, p.1056). In addition, the therapist can use the role relationship with the client to encourage loosening. The therapist gives the client the acceptance he or she needs in order to feel unashamed and secure in producing loose ideas in the therapist's presence.

Hazards. There are some particular things to be aware of, in order that loosening should not be carried too far. The first issue is the relation between loosening and anxiety. Loosening can be extended to the point at which the client truly does not have a structure to use to order events, thus producing anxiety. It must be remembered, however, that this is really not a complete breakdown but it can cause some severe disruptions for the client. On the other hand, loosening can help the client *deal* with anxiety by making 'elastic' the kind of predictions that can be made. These predictions then fit everything while nothing fits very well. In this way the client is not proven wrong but the client does not get to be right either. Disappointments are averted but then so are satisfactions. Nevertheless the client could become addicted to this style of dealing with anxiety, which is generally seen as a disservice to the client and not consistent with psychotherapeutic aims.

Finally there is a potential hazard in using loosening with the client *'who depends upon tight construction'* (Kelly, 1955, p.1059). This is a client who is very dependent upon a very tight and narrow conception of life where the client acts as if his life depends upon this tight construction (and perhaps it does). If loosening is employed with such a client then it may force the client to deal with more than he or she could possibly manage.

Tightening

Our concern now shifts to the other end of the creativity cycle, the tightening of a construction. Concentration on tightening brings the fourth phase of psychotherapy, disconfirmation and confirmation, into clearest focus. It is only by tightening one of our constructions that we can hope to bring either confirming or disconfirming evidence to bear on our conception of our life and the world around us. It is through tightening that we can hope to profit from the experiences we are having. Before we begin our more detailed examination of tightening, however, it is important to stress again that tightening is not synomomous with the C-P-C cycle. This, as will be recalled, is the sequence beginning with the circumspection (surveying a number of bipolar alternative dimensions), then moving to preemption (choosing one of the bipolar dimensions), and finally to control or choice, where the person precipitates herself into action by choosing one pole in preference to the other. The C-P-C cycle is a way of understanding the pattern of human action which we will have more to say about in connection with the final phase of the cycle of experience—constructive revision—to be discussed in chapter 7. Tightening simply refers to the process of formulating a construction in such a way that clear predictions can be made from that construction. The meaning of an idea is clarified in such a way that precise implications can be kept in mind. Certainly we can all see advantages in dealing with a number of fairly tight constructions in the circumspective phase of the C-P-C cycle, but one may at times be in a situation where the C-P-C cycle is found to operate on only loosened constructions. This is perhaps a long way round to simply stating again that the C-P-C cycle deals with *action* , while loosening and tightening only deal with the creation of meaning. While it is true that tightening also allows clear actions to take place, there is nothing inherent in tightening that forces an action, whereas embracing a C-P-C sequence always finds one taking action of some sort. One can take action on the basis of either tightened or loosened construction. It must be remembered, however, that only by taking action with a tightened construction can one hope to gain either validating or invalidating evidence from that action (Kelly, 1955, p.1061). It would seem that it is generally a good idea to have client choose a line of action from among a number of fairly tightened constructions for either validation or invalidation to take place. If this were not the case the client would be faced with not really knowing what had just taken place—when the client had, in fact, taken some action. Only through tightening can experimentation with life take place. Kelly, however, is careful to point out in discussing this matter that 'tightening (is) not always desirable' (Kelly, 1955, p.1063). If a client deals only with tightened forms of thinking, then much is sacrificed in truly creative thinking. This is why the client is better off if he is able to move swiftly back and forth from tight to loose and back to tight, rather than attaching himself to the notion that either tightening or loosening is a 'better' way to experience the world.

Usefulness of Tightening

In examining the reasons for helping a client to tighten her construct system, Kelly lists five major points that are worth consideration. These may be thought of as advantages of tightening.

First, in tightening the client gains the advantage of refining predictive power. The client has a clear idea of what has been predicted and what has come of this prediction. The client can in this way receive either validating or invalidating evidence for her way of living. This gives the client a sense of clarity, a sense of mastery and perhaps some sense of maturity in what otherwise would be a cloudy and bewildering world (Kelly, 1955, p.1064).

Second, the tightening of the constructs tends to stabilize the system. It gives the client a sense of personal integrity and dignity, coupled with a sense of wholeness and completeness of life that would not be possible with a looser construct system. The client has a sense of knowing exactly what she is like and where she is in the world.

Third, the tightening of a system of constructs aids in the client's being able to impose some order in her thinking issuing from 'ordinal relationships in the client's construction system' (Kelly, 1955, p.1065). Through tightening the client has the ability to deal in a very careful and precise way with the details of life. This provides the possibility that superordinate constructions can be imposed over these events. The client develops superordinate constructions (higher level values) which have clear implications for the details that make up the events of everyday living. In this way the system is better organized from top to bottom. Many of the techniques in the next section of this chapter and the new techniques to be presented in chapter 9 can be seen as aids in operationalizing this third advantage of tightening.

The *fourth* advantage in the use of tightening as a technique is one that may not be obvious from what has been said up to this point, and that is that tightening can aid in reducing a construct to a state of impermeability. This is a way in which a construction of the world which is not serving the client well can be made inoperative. One way of accomplishing this is to encourage the use of the construct in such a concrete way that it can only deal with a very specific and unusual set of events.

The *fifth* use of tightening brings us in a very specific way to the task of invalidation and validation. This is the fact that tightening aids the client in actually entering into active experiments when he subjects his ideas to some test, so that outcomes can be assessed. 'When he (the client) tightens up a construct it becomes more and more a brittle hypothesis and more and more he must be prepared to perceive it as expendable. He drops his hostility and leaves it up to nature, human or otherwise, to demonstrate whether his prediction was accurate or misleading' (Kelly, 1955, p.1067).

The support and positive therapeutic atmosphere in which this tightening takes place can enable the client to face the possibility of actually allowing an important construction to be tested. From a personal construct theory point of view, the frequent use of a hostile approach to life, where the client is unwilling to let his construction be subjected to testing, is a major cause of human misery. Of course the counselor needs to offer a great deal of encouragement and support to the client as this type of tightening takes place.

Case Illustration of Tightening

In the following example Kelly is conducting an interview with a client who has been having difficulty in dealing with vague feelings and disturbing impulses. It was Kelly's decision to try to help the client to tighten his system so that some clearer understanding could be reached. For the main part we will see in this passage the emergence of a tightened construction of 'black moods' versus 'white moods' which emerges from a preverbal to a verbal level and then gets further specified as 'rational hope versus irrational despair' (Kelly, 1958, p.238). Kelly reports the case as follows:

> 'The client introduces content in the following passage and immediately uses it to document a construction of his own behavior. He points out his own reaction to the breakthrough of impulsive behavior and then goes on quickly to anchor his construction in other events. Of course, at this stage he has neither the words nor the syntax to express his constructs effectively. He must therefore weave back and forth between efforts to say words that will delineate the constructions and the citation of selected events upon which the constructs are focused.
>
> *C7:* Ahh, one thing came up this week. I don't know. I suppose it has some importance. I don't know. Ahhh. (pause) Yesterday, ahh, I was killing some time, ahh, down on the pool table in the basement.
>
> *T8:* Umhuh.
>
> *C8:* And Mom came down and began to iron and began to chat a little and, ahh, there developed in me (pause) a desire to get up and go — run — get out — a, ahh, (pause) a feeling that, at the time, I described as 'hate' — hatred' towards my mother.
>
> *T9:* Ummhuh.
>
> *C9:* Now, this does not, what, this presents a problem immediately in that, ahh, in my picture this is not the feeling I should have.
>
> *T10:* No, of course not.
>
> *C10:* But, just the same, it was there.

T11: Yeah.

C11: And, ahh, I thought I'd bring that up. (pause) Another thing I, ahh, that came to mind and I suppose I have indicated already in my discussion—discussions *with* you, but, ahh, for some reason it didn't come through *clear* to me until just recently. And that is, ahh, when I have these explosions or blowups, they are triggered by an outside force—some *event* happening other than involving myself, and they *may* involve myself.

T12: Yeah.

C12: But, sometimes they don't. So I'm just using an outside force and, ahh, at least the most recent one which I happened, I think, since our last discussion, ahh, immediately or, frequently after the immediate—the first—explosion, the first feeling of anger—

T13: Yeah.

C13: —against some *external being—person—*, ahh, there was a, *(pause) you know, like a rubber ball bouncing off a wall, the feeling came back at myself*, a feeling of disgust, a feeling of anger at myself for having (laughs) the original *feeling*.

T14: Yeah.

C14: —for losing control, and it seemed to me, that of the two, this was the most severe.

T15: Ummhuh.

C15: And, ahh.

T16: (pause) The ball comes back harder even than you thought?

C16: Definitely! or, at least, this is the *impression* I get the most experience.

T17: Yeah.

C17: The one that's most clear in my mind. Now the others I, I don't remember seeing them in these two distinct categories.

T18: Ummhuh.

C18: But it, what, *seems*, it feels, like this is the way they've gone.

T19: Yeah, (pause) Did you feel this way after, after your recognition of your, of this impulse of this feeling toward your mother yesterday?

C19: Yes, and ahhh, I got out of the house and drove off. Now that was at 4:10 and I got back to the house at about five, ten minutes to five, about forty minutes.

T20: Yeah.

C20: And I'd say at least a *half* an hour of that time was spent in *anger* of varying degrees—

T21: Yeah.

C21: Against myself, (pause) primarily, for, what, having this feeling and trying to piece it out. Ahh, there was no, ahh, any, no progressive thought pattern or no constant progression of thought. It was just, ahh, (pause) I suppose, like a little kid with a hammer and stone, trying to break it up. He pounds at it any ol' way it happens to be turned up.

T22: Yeah.

C22: So that's just the way I was going at it.

T23: No logical sequences.

C23: No logical sequence, no pattern or anything, just, ahh, — oh, I'd drive for a while and then I'd think of something and then I'd pound at that, and then I'd, ahh, get nowhere, I suppose, is the only way to say. I *got* nowhere trying to figure the thing out, except that some of this is, was developed at that time. Ahhh, developed I won't say, ahhh, the ideas *emerged* at that time, but they become more crystallized, more, they fitted in more during that time. But I'd say half an hour of the time was spent blowing off steam. I don't know, I drove down Avon and up and around, and came out north of Barton Road across from the Calumet coming down Sixty-one and Digby Road, and it wasn't until about the time, well, are you familiar with that territory out there at all?

T24: More or less — yes.

The client has just confronted himself with the lack of logical sequence in what has happened. He turns to a recitation of times and places. It would be easy to call this resistance. But from the point of view of personal construct theory, resistance is a poorly drawn psychologist's construct and might better be abandoned. The client is groping his way through the experience here in the therapy room, just as he groped his way through it on the day he is describing. Like anyone who gropes he reaches out for tangible objects. And he asks others to verify their presence.

C24: There's a road that goes up parallel to Calumet. It's got quite a few houses, new development out there, relatively new, four or five years old.

T25: West side of the Calumet, isn't it?

C25: It's on the west side of Calumet, parallel to it and relatively close to it.

T26: Yes, I know that road.

C26: Well, I went up that road and crossed over, ahh, north of Barton Road, I don't know what road I was on, but it goes out to Eton on one — . If I'd turned left going west, going to Eton, and I turned right, came over to Sixty-one, and down Sixty-one, Ahhh, it comes out. You know that antique shop on Digby Road?

T27: I know there is something — .

C27: There is one. There's a filling station that's next to it.

Or something. There's two right there, and there's an antique shop on one side. Got some, oh, wagon wheels laying up against a fence there.

T28: That is a beautiful drive up on the west side there.

C28: Yeah, well, just as, I'd say about halfway up that drive this feeling of anger and so on completely left, well, completely— essentially— completely left me. There was some little stirrings of it but I began to notice (pause) my surroundings. That is, it wasn't a case of knowing that they were there and not being able to, ahh, think about them or anything, because of the break-ins of this anger or whatever.

T29: Yeah.

C29: And then I drove around, watched the skaters on the Calumet and drove home. (long pause) Now, that's one thing. There's something else that has come up in my mind and I don't know how you intended it . . . (pause) Ahh, last time I was in here, you began to ask me the why behind my idea of going into the ministry.

T30: Yeah.

C30: And there was a little question there, on one part, ahh, the decision, of this as a possibility has been coming more and more crystallized.

T31: Ummhuh.

C31: And there's a little possibility— little question there of whether or not you were questioning whether or not that's where I fitted. I didn't know whether you were or not.

T32: Pretty hard to, ahh, *not* to wonder, isn't it?

C32: Well, it is. Well, what, there are *two halves* of me.

T33: Yes.

The client now turns to an attempt to spell out a principal construct dimension. The therapist now has to decide how tightly this dimension ought to be drawn. If the client sees his alternatives in these terms only and if the implications gather up his whole life's pattern, will he not be endangered the next time he is caught up in impulsivity? This is a point of therapeutic risk. The decision is to go ahead and make the construct as explicit as possible.

There are, of course, many different kinds of comments that could be made about each passage— the kind of externalized control the client uses, his returns to anger and guilt, the fact that the full picture of hostility is not yet sketched in the interview series, the relation with the mother which is almost entirely construed preverbally at this time, the emphasis upon the notion of being 'triggered' together with its gunlike or sexual implications and its association with his mother, and many other matters.

C33: And when the black half is in command it makes absolutely no sense to even have this idea as—well, actually, there are two, *two* ways of looking at even *this* half. You can say, "no, this isn't it," and, on the other hand, you can say, "yes", because in the search for this perhaps I can help someone else. When I'm in my bright mood, like I feel like I am right now, it makes sense. (pause) Another thing, ahh, sometimes I have these dark moods: I get mad and then I get mad at myself in return, and I start mentally browbeating or whatever.

T34: Yeah:

C34: If there is something on the outside. But then, I can turn this off, like a radio. Now, ahh, and what, present an outside cheery appearance. Say, I'm down—usually, this is when I'm alone, I mean it's not when I'm in a group—but if I'm alone, something else will—becomes—more than, if one, unless it's my mother. I can still retain my anger when she's present—my father to some extent, but not so much—my brother, usually I turn it off.

T35: Ummhuh.

C35: But it's something like a radio. *You, I turn it off,* and assume a different attitude! And this, I don't know, whether it just is turned off and suppressed or just dies out of its own accord.

T36: There has to be something external or an occasion?

C36: External, ahh, *to turn it off!*

T37: Yes.

C37: But, ahh, I can let it die out in, I suppose, anywheres from twenty minutes to half an hour or so, based on a rough estimate of time from previous occasions and on the time it took this last, ahh—

T38: Yeah.

C38: —situation to cool off.

T39: (pause) What is the contrast between these two parts, the two main parts of yourself as you're describing them now?

C39: Well, I doubt, I doubt if, ahh, they're this extreme, but they're sort of like black and white. One side is—

T40: That's quite a contrast, isn't it?

C40: Well, yeah, ahh, well, as I say, I don't think they're quite as extreme, but they *seem to be*, ahh, *pretty close*. On one hand I feel good, cheery, ahh, present myself, ahh, fairly well to the outside—

T41: Yes.

C41: Ahh, get along fine with friends. (long pause) On the other hand, when I'm by myself and ahh, what, kick myself when I'm down ahh, (pause) this black feeling kinda snowballs.

T42: Yes.

C42: And down, and down, and *down*, and DOWN! And it's,

ahh, a steep curve going into and a gradual curve coming out.

T43: Yeah. Unless some event intervenes, where you just postpone it.

C43: Yeah, ahh, where, I don't know what you'd say. I do not desire the out—the other, the other people to see myself in this condition.

T44 Well, I can see where, in one case, you see *yourself* as seeing the world as bright. In the other case, it's—

C44: It's not so much the outside world, as it's, ahhh—

T45: "Me," huh?

C45: Me! My own feelings!

T46: Yeah:

C46: Because, ahh, I take this assumption simply from the fact that I can *switch*.

T47: Yeah.

C47: So that when I'm what . . .

T48: (pause) There's no question as to whether, as to where the mood arises, *actually* arises. It arises within you then?

C48: Though it's usually *triggered* by something, some event.

T49: It's triggered. Something outside?

C49: Something outside!

T50: Yeah. And you turn it off some—

C50: Now I got *very*, *very* upset, ahh, last Wednesday, New Year's. Ahh, I was best man in a wedding Saturday.

T51: Yeah.

C51: And we had the wedding gifts that had to be delivered. And, ahhh, Mom was making the suggestion that Dad take them over and then when she suggested Dad take them over she said, "Do you want to take my present at the same time?" Then she said, "Maybe you'd better not." "Yes." "No." It went—four distinct different movements—yes, no, yes, no. Ahh, and I *exploded!* More violently than I had in a long time! And it took me, ahh, two to three hours to cool off enough so that I came back up. I went down to my room and stretched out and read some comic books and ahh—there was another book, I don't know what it was—but cooled off.

T52: This was between your father and your mother.

C52: No, between my mother and myself.

T53: Oh, between your mother and yourself.

C53: Though, I can be triggered, for instance, when my mother and my brother were discussing something.

T54: Ummhuh.

C54: I mentioned that either last time or sometime recently in the past, I was *triggered*. And I can be triggered when my father and my mother are discussing. It's not as likely.

T55: Anything that involves haggling *could* trigger you.

C55: Yeah.

T56: Particularly, if you get involved *directly*.

C56: Well, not necessarily. It's not necessary for myself to become involved directly.

T57: Just even to sit on the sidelines gets you triggered sometimes?

C57: Yeah. And yet, other times, it doesn't bother me at all.

T58: Yeah. You can remain detached at other times.

C58: I can remain detached at other times. I imagine it's, ahh, just how I'm feeling at that particular moment, whether I'm susceptible or not.

T59: Yeah. Now there are two men by the name of Zeons, you then would say.

C59: Yeah.

T60: Looking at these two men from the outside, not just superficially, but I mean judging them as objectively as you can, or judging them whatever way you can, what is the difference between these two men? . . . On what dimension does it lie?

C60: (very long pause) I'm not too sure exactly what you want. I, I'm a little puzzled here.

T61: Well, let's look at these two men. Can you tell me what the difference is between them? (pause) The two men aren't here now. I'm pulling you out from them—

C61: Yeah, I'm trying to, trying to, ahh, what, find something to, ahh, to, to, first I'm trying ot find out what they are like and then trying to see where they differ, ahh, because, ahh, I haven't, what, looked at them from the outside, I've only described to you how I feel.

T62: How *you* felt.

C62: When, ahh, when I'm in these moods.

T63: Yeah.

C63: Ahhh, how I don't know that this is an adequate description. These are estimates, stabs in the dark. The one seems too cheery, outward looking, that is, I'm using "outward" as opposed to, what, I was going to describe the other one as "inward looking".

T64: Yeah.

C64: Then of course, the other one is moody, dark, that's what I use the two black and white terms, ahh, light and dark. Ahh, (very long pause) the one—Now, ahh, I'm also ascribing, what, absolutes to these, to these charac-, characters which may or may not fit. But, trends in this direction may fit.

T65: Yeah.

C65: Ahh, the light one would be ahh, cheery, outward looking, enjoys life—.

T66: Rational?

C66: (pause) That does not necessarily fit, I don't believe.

T67: That's another dimension.

C67: Ahhh, the *other* one, I definitely add "irrational" to the dark one.

T68: Yeah.

C68: And, if you—you want to put opposite in there, I suppose you'd add "rational" to the light one, but it doesn't necessarily fit, it seems to me. Ahhh, "puzzled", "disturbed", "confused", "irrational", in that this, nothing seems to make sense.

T69: Which one of them wants to go to the seminary?

C69: The light, the cheery one. Well, I think they both do.

T70: They both do.

C70: But for different reasons.

T71: O.K.

C71: The cheery one because of the, ahh, because of the ahh, of what this is a step towards, in that it is a service to people, helping people.

T72: Yeah.

C72: The other one in helping self, trying to find some pattern. This can all be sifted out and made to fit into some sort of relative pattern, some sort of, some sort of an outline or at least *something* so it isn't a confused jumble of emotion and irrationalities.

T73: Looking for some way to extricate one's self from this jumble.

C73: Yeah. (pause) And, when I'm in a dark mood, it seems to me this idea, ahh, of the light mood, of going through seminary and so on, may be a rationalization, a reason which I build up for myself so that this one makes sense, but that is, so that it doesn't seem like I'm doing this strictly for a purpose of self. Which also seems to fit.

T74: When in a dark mood you're skeptical of the bright mood, huh?

C74: Yeah! In other words, what reasons I can give when I'm feeling cheery, feeling good, ahh, when I'm in a dark mood. I wonder if I don't *make* these reasons.

T75: Of course.

C75: So that these don't *appear* as if I'm doing purely as a matter of self.

T76: So when you're in a dark mood you think *that* really is the real self; the other one is a superficial overlay, sometimes?

C76: Yeah. And, ahh, when I think about it, when I'm in a cheery mood, I can progress toward the darker mood because I'm thinking *towards myself*, which I do when I am in the dark mood. And, oh, I don't know, I just start edging over towards that way.

T77: So even when you're in a cheery mood, cheerful mood, and you wonder which of the two selves is real—

C77: Oh yeah.

T78: And you begin to wonder if it isn't the dark one.

C78: (pause) The dark one, in some ways, seems more real. It presents somewhat of a challenge to try and find out why I am the way I am. I think that's, ahh, I don't know. I don't know why the term "why" keeps coming up. But so many times, in fact, I think almost always—I could go so far as to say "always"—the term "why" comes into the question. Why am I the way I 'm? Why do I have these dark moods? Why? (sigh) Well, I suppose, by any approach to it, using the term "why" comes up.

T79: So "why" is always in this outcry.

C79: Yeah. What is behind it?

T80: (long pause) What do you think?

C80: (laughs) That's why I'm here, I don't know. (long pause) I suppose, somewhere it's background, the experiences I've had in life, both at home, school, work, play, what have you. And I imagine it's the fact that I have not allowed myself or forced myself, depending upon which viewpoint I take, to make very many friends. I am not particularly comfortable in a social atmosphere. (pause) But when I'm in my cheery mood I get along with people fine. When I'm in a dark mood I have to force myself.

T81: Ummhuh.

C81: Though I can force myself into a fairly acceptable cheery mood.

T82: That's this turning off that you mentioned awhile ago.

C82: Yeah. But it's, ahh, I tell you when I'm doing that, ahh, I'm tense. I definitely feel like I'm forcing myself.

T83: Ummhuh.

C83: Ahhh, I, I, I don't know how to say this. It's not—there are times when that's the case, and times when that's not the case. For instance, one time I was mad at myself, I was downstairs, my brother called that I had a phone call.

T84: Ummhuh.

C84: No problem. Just turn it off. Now, I think I was fairly well out of darkness. I was pretty well up towards, ahh, average between the two, or whatever you want to call it.

T85: Ummhuh.

C85: There are other times though, when I would be in a situation,

where I'd be continually tense. I think this is becoming . . .
less the pattern than it was in the past.

T86: Good.

C86: But it's still there! Particularly, it's there when I'm not prepared
for class—or any other circumstances where I am *uncertain
of the results.* I can build up a blacker picture than may be
the case.

T87: So whenever you're confronted with something of any
kind of importance, where you don't know what's going to
happen—

C87: Yeah. (pause) My imagination can get going, and, ahh, I don't
know, the impossible makes it seem pretty rugged. Whereas—
usually I'll say al—always—it's never *that* bad—as I paint it.

T88: But you do a good job of painting.

C88: Yeah.

T89: What *does* your imagination do at these moments of
uncertainty? What are some of the worst of things that can
happen?

C89: I don't know if I can describe any of them. When you ask for
a description of something, ahh, there is—

T90: Just a whole lot of—.

C90: Nothing comes to mind.

T91: Is that the worst that can happen to you? Sheer, utter
confusion? (pause) Not knowing?

C91: (sigh) I don't know as I can say that. I was merely describing
my feeling right now.

T92: Yeah. O.K., you might say it a little differently on other
occasions.

C92: Ahhh, (pause) Whenever I'm faced with a problem which
I don't know, I'm uncertain about the (pause) event.
(pause) Well, I'd say, ahh, I'm scared, which I assume to
be normal. I assume that, ahh, when approaching an
uncertainty or an unknown, most people are a little bit scared.
But, I'd say I build upon this. I present the barriers as
greater than they actually turn out to be. The problem is
greater. I don't know whether I would say it's more
serious, or more important than it was. Sometimes this
happens.

T93: Ummhuh.

C93: But I'd say usually. It's just that the difficulty of *doing it*
becomes greater in my mind. Although actually, when I arrive
at the doing of it, it is not any more difficult than it would
have been anyway. (pause) White-washed it instead of painting
it black!

T94: Yeah. But the feeling—.

C94: (pause) Fear that I'd fail, I think, is the simplest way of putting it.

T95: (pause) What would happen if you failed?

C95: I'd be in a black mood—kick myself.

T96: And then what?

C96: (pause) Well, after applying the club rather thoroughly, I imagine I'd (pause) get over with it—go on.

T97: But that isn't the way you feel at the moment. You're not thinking about getting over it. You're thinking of the worst that can happen, aren't you?

C97: Yeah.

T98: What is this worst than can happen?

C98: (Pause) Be in a shameful position.

T99: Yeah.

C99: (silence).

We are now in a position where the black–white construct has a certain amount of tightness to it and it has been wrapped up in verbal terms to some extent. We now move back in the direction of documentation, choosing this time to get further away from local events. As we do this we may expect the construct to be tested out against other memories and, as a result of examination in other context, to be altered somewhat. The alteration is not something we can expect to happen in this interview, but perhaps in later ones' (Kelly, 1958, pp.240–250).

Specific Techniques for Tightening

Given the advantages covered in the first section and the case example illustrating aiding a client to move in the direction of tightening, it is appropriate at this point to cover some rather specific techniques that the clinician can use for accomplishing this aim. Let us start with techniques which are designed to aid clients in imposing some superordinate meanings on material that they are attempting to deal with. Here the purpose is to help the client impose some order and overarching meaning on material which otherwise would be difficult to understand. To this aim Kelly suggests the following instructions that the counselor can use when dealing with a client.

'Now just what have you been saying today that you have not told me before?' . . . .

You have told me about a lot of incidents and feelings but it is not clear to me how you see these matters as fitting together. Are they simply illustrations of something?' . . . .

'You have told me about a number of feelings and ideas today. What should I know about you now that I did not know at the beginning of the interview?' . . . .

'Now could you go back over what you have been saying; I want to be sure I have it straight' . . . .

'Could you summarize again the last three dreams you have reported' (Kelly, 1955, pp.1068–1069).

Tightening can also be accomplished by attempting to provide some context for the tightening to take place in, either a time context or the context of another person. Some instructional examples are as follows:

'When did you first start having these thoughts?' 'Have you ever felt like this before?' 'What does this remind you of?' . . . . 'Do you know of anyone else who may feel this way?' 'Can you remember hearing anyone else express these kinds of thoughts?' 'When you feel this way who are you most like?' (Kelly, 1955, p.1070).

Another approach to tightening can be accomplished by the counselor's taking a very direct and confronting approach to the client as seen in the following comment:

'I don't understand; could you make it clearer to me just what you mean?' 'I follow you up to the part where you said . . . . Now what was it you said next?' 'Could you explain just how it is to feel this way?' 'What happens inside of you?' . . . 'I find this a little confusing. First you said . . . and now you say . . . can you help me understand?' (Kelly, 1955, p.1070–1071).

Yet another important approach to tightening is accomplished by the use of *enactment* or role playing. Enactment can be structured in such a way that the client is given practice in how to explicate his system in terms of what actions follow the nature of particular constructions. For example, the client might come to relate to the counselor during a role playing sequence:

'Now I know what it is that I have been trying to tell you about my mother. It was that . . . . Therefore, if you are going to play the part like her you will have to . . .' (Kelly, 1955, p.1073).

Another example is illustrated in the following excerpt:

'What I have been saying about my mother doesn't make too much sense. Now here is the way she would have to act. That puts her in an entirely new light, doesn't it?' (Kelly, 1955, p.1073).

Kelly comments that this latter type of remark indicates not only that there has been some tightening but that the axes have been rotated into a new position (Kelly, 1955, p.1073). By this he means that the relationships among existing constructs have been rearranged such that a new meaning appears. Here the client is aided in understanding what role he plays in certain situations and the roles that other people play. Kelly comments how, in general, this procedure is helpful, 'It helps the client to become explicit *within his own construct system rather than within a construct system superimposed upon him by the therapist* (Kelly, 1955, pp.1073–74).

Another frequently used technique is the Role Construct Repertory Test instructions which can be used in forming tightened, well developed, precise constructions during an ordinary therapy interview. The following comments are suggested:

> 'You have mentioned this, this, and this. Let's see if we can understand these three things better. Think about them. Are two of them alike in some way that seems to set them off from the third?' (Kelly, 1955, p.1074).

Along these same lines of formal instruction the client can be asked to supply validational evidence.

> 'How do you know that?' 'What has happened to make you see matters this way?' . . . 'What kind of evidence would it take to convince you that you were mistaken?' 'If this were not so how would you know it?' (Kelly, 1955, p.1074).

This procedure is also similar to techniques developed by Landfield (1971) in his pyramid procedure, which will be presented in chapter 9, and to some procedures outlined by Hinkle in Fransella and Bannister (1977), *A Manual for Repertory Grid Technique.*

The final technique to be mentioned here involves tightening in such a way as to bind the construction to a context or location. For example, in word binding, 'The client is asked to name each of his constructs and stick with the same name . . . . New ideas are quickly pigeon-holed into word-labeled categories' (Kelly, 1955, pp.1074–1075). In another example, a kind of time binding is used, where the client is encouraged to place his ideas in a specific time reference and keep them there. For example, using this technique the client might come to comment: 'This is a view which was applicable to what I experienced when I was in high school but it is no longer applicable.' . . . 'There *were* miracles (back then) but they don't happen anymore' (Kelly, 1955, p.1076). Binding can also be accomplished by using specific situations or confining the client's attention to particular persons. The object of the technique is to produce more or less impermeable constructions through tightening.

Difficulties and Hazards in Tightening

In talking about the difficulties and hazards in using the tightening techniques, Kelly outlines two broad areas of concern. The first deals with tightening the client's system before the client is ready. The tightening may bring the client 'face to face' with issues, feelings, thoughts, that the client is not prepared to deal with. The client feels as if moving explicitly into a certain matter is too much of a risk in terms of what it might oblige her to do, think, and feel; the risk of obtaining evidence which could either validate or invalidate a particular construction is too much to be ventured. In such a case it is best to keep constructions very loose and unformed for the moment. Tightening along these same lines may face the client with more internal contradiction than she may be prepared to handle. It would be best for the overall integrity of the system to leave the system a bit loose for the time being. Also involved here would be concern that the tightening could produce, in the client, a sort of hostility. Tightening may imply the possibility for testing a construction that could yield an invalidation in an area where it could not be tolerated. And the person here 'tries to extort validation in favor of his disconfirmed construction' (Kelly, 1955, p.1083). This is the construct theory definition of hostility.

The other main caution in using these tightening techniques is that they may promote '*loss of comprehensiveness, permeability, and propositionality*' (Kelly, 1955, p.1084). In tightening, the client could, in fact, make certain constructions extremely impermeable. That might not serve the client well if these tightened constructions then render the client insensitive to other important outside events. This also happens in terms of ruling out other constructions, where the person thinks very concretely and literally about matters (Landfield, 1980, 1982).

There is also a chance that the tightened constructs might produce a type of system where the comprehensiveness of the system would be reduced. This would result in the lack of an ability to produce superordinate constructs which were broad enough to have a sufficient amount of perspective so that a wide world view could be maintained. The client might get along from day to day, but then not hold up under life's larger issues. These concerns are summed up by Kelly as follows: 'When some clients attempt to formulate broad concepts precisely, they seem to have to sacrifice their comprehensiveness or their permeability. They find it impossible to state a broad principle in precise terms. They have to narrow it down to a collection of incidental cases in order to state it exactly. They may have to go even further. They may have to deal with the construct preemptively, once they have stated it precisely' (Kelly, 1955, p.1084).

In closing it must be noted the best way generally, in order to have a creative, alive, healthy system, is to weave back and forth between tightening and loosening. 'After a form of adjustment has been worked out at the tightened level for a time, the therapist may open up the construction again, perhaps dealing with the same contextual elements, perhaps in a new area. The client may then have to reconsider his last set of 'insights'. After a period of loosened construing, the therapist may move in the direction of tightening again and seek to establish a mode of adjustment at a new level. The cycle, which is essentially a Creativity Cycle, may be repeated many times in the course of protracted treatment' (Kelly, 1955, p.1085).

Summary

The main emphasis in this chapter was placed on how the dimension of loosening and tightening can be used productively in psychotherapy so that confirmation and disconfirmation can be accomplished. In general it is advised that the process should start with loosened constructions and then move to tightened constructions so that some definite predictions can be formulated and made available, to be either confirmed or disconfirmed by external evidence. Although the best advantage is gained by the client if she can move smoothly from loosening to tightening and then back again, some advantage is seen in explicitly employing techniques for loosening and techniques for tightening so that the client can accomplish either tightening or loosening at specified times. The advantages of both tightening and loosening were noted as well as the hazards and difficulties encountered with the use of either set of techniques. Special emphasis was placed on the use of dream recall as a technique for loosening. In total the client is guided through the creativity cycle starting with loosened, divergent constructions and then aided to tighten for precise predictions which can be either confirmed or disconfirmed. In this chapter we brought the total cycle of experience in psychotherapy up to the final phase, that of constructive revision, which will be discussed in the next chapter.

CHAPTER 7

Constructive Revision

This final phase of the experiential cycle as applied to psychotherapy finds both client and therapist trying to make something of what has gone on in the therapy, both moment by moment and for the whole psychotherapeutic enterprise. For the main part, this phase of the therapy centers on the client's being able to make sense out of and profit from what he or she has learned about the confirmation and disconfirmation that has taken place. It also centers on the revision of these constructions in such a way that further growth (elaboration) of the system can take place. In the most successful cases clients reach a place in their conceptualization where they can take stock of what their life is really about. The main focus is on the active elaboration, the overall movement in psychotherapy, and the integration of new meanings which were produced earlier in the therapy.

One of the first things to be mindful of in constructive revision (reconstruction) is that the therapist must show a great deal of tolerance for the different outlooks clients might come up with through their own construct revision work. This is another example of the application of the constructive alternativism principle. The client has the right — and perhaps the obligation — to try to make his own unique solutions work for his life problems. The test is in the living of the new construction by the client, not in the therapist's professional judgement of that solution. There is no one solution or way of living, nor any one way to revise a present way of living. The aim of personal construct psychotherapy is for the client to be able to make his system work for him. It is not necessary for the therapist to like the client's solution or to see it as one the therapist would choose for himself. What we have to do as professionals is to be open to the alternatives the client can use for optimal development.

In getting our presentation of reconstruction under way it is important to be mindful of what a construct is really all about: '. . . a construct is a psychological process of a live person. It is not an intangible essence that floats from one person to another on the wings of an uttered word' (Kelly, 1955, p.1088). This emphasizes the fact that constructs are real in a psychological sense and the construct is not ephemeral. It is something to be dealt with substantially; a thing of substance. The personal and substantive nature of the construct is further expressed by Kelly in the following way: 'Not only is a construct *personal*, but it is a *process* that goes on within a person. It thus invariably expresses anticipation . . . . When one attempts to communicate with a client, he is attempting to direct a process in the client's mind; he is attempting to generate certain anticipations' (Kelly, 1955, p.1089).

Interpretations

In aiding the client in the reconstructive process, one of the most important areas to pay attention to is the nature of the interpretations that the counselor offers the client and the interpretations that the client is able to come up with on his own. In this light Kelly advises: '*All interpretations understood by the client are perceived in terms of his* [the client's] *own system*' (Kelly, 1955, p.1090). It is, in fact, the client and not the therapist (who actually does the interpretation) when we focus on the interpretation as understood.

The basic question being asked when an interpretation is being employed is 'How does the therapist know the client is making progress in reconstruing life?' (Kelly, 1955, p.1092). Reflecting upon this question makes one realize that much of the work for this reconstructing takes place in settings other than the psychotherapeutic interview — for it is the living out of a life solution that provides this information.

Kelly suggests several clues that can be used to indicate that this kind of reconstructing is taking place or has just taken place. *First* is 'the surprise that the client shows when puzzling elements seem to fall into place. This is the "Aha!" phenomenon' (Kelly, 1955, p.1093). *Second* is when the client provides spontaneous documentation for some general new principle. The client supplies new elements which indicate that a more comprehensive view of the problem has now been grasped. *Third*, one sees signs of new construction or reconstruction to the extent to which fresh permeability of the construction can be detected. 'The therapist can be particularly reassured if the client indicates that he has used the construct to produce new responses in a social situation' (Kelly, 1955, p.1093). *Fourth* is when there is a change in the client's 'mood', whether or not there really is any other behavioral change. An example of this is given as follows: 'I seem to keep on doing about the same sort of things each day but now I *feel* less upset about them. The changes seem to be more of a change in *feeling* than a change in behavior . . . . As far as I can see, I am facing the same sorts of problems I always faced, only now they don't seem quite so overwhelming . . . . The only difference seems to be that *now I meet emergencies differently*.' (Kelly, 1955, p.1094). *Fifth* is the often surprising, 'tendency for the client to perceive his present behavior as contrasting in many ways to his earlier behavior' (Kelly, 1955, p.1094). In ths this way real change or movement during the therapy is clearly perceived. The client sees where he has moved from since the therapy began. *Sixth* is when the client begins, 'the dropping of certain complaints or even substituting of new complaints for old ones' (Kelly, 1955, p.1096). *Seventh*, reconstruction can be detected in the ways that the client summarizes what has been happening. The nature of the summary reveals the insight. *Eighth* is when the client produces a change in the loose, autistic material he is trying to deal with. In this type of reconstruction, dreams and free associations start to include new material, with this material becoming significantly more vivid (Kelly, 1955, p.1096).

At the same time that the therapist is aware of the new constructions which are serving as true therapeutic gains, the therapist needs to be aware of others that are not so adequate and not likely to serve the client well at all. The following are cues to inadequate constructions. *First* is the production of 'erratic or loose verbalization of the new construct'. 'Client keeps expressing new opposites' (Kelly, 1955, p.1097). *Second* is when the client produces bizarre documentation—the new documentation horrifies the therapist. *Third* is the production of gross oversimplifications which include grand new insights that will solve everything for the client. *Fourth* is when the client shows a very sudden change to the opposite end of present construing—a sudden slot change. 'Yesterday he was hostile; today he loves everybody' (Kelly, 1955, p.1097). *Fifth* is when the client makes 'rigid or legalistic applications of his new insights' (Kelly, 1955, p.1097).

These inadequacies in reconstruction may have occurred for a number of reasons. One is the client's excessive anxiety. 'A very anxious client may grasp at new interpretations in sheer desperation' (Kelly, 1955, p.1098). It would be better in this case just to help clients support what they have gained up to that point in the therapy rather than aid the client in maintaining an understanding he really does not yet have in a secure, well thought out way. In this case the counselor might have jumped on one of the client's really loose constructions and made it into something more than it really is. On the other hand the counselor may be 'betraying his own (the counselor's) anxiety and confusion' (Kelly, 1955, p.1098). The client might see this anxiety of the counselor and than accept the new interpretation for fear the therapist might be getting them both in trouble. The interpretation is accepted in order to help the counselor feel better.

Client's Readiness for Constructive Revision

The key question here is 'How does the therapist know when the client's role relationship with him will sustain a certain type of inquiry?' (Kelly, 1955, p.1105). First, Kelly mentions that an indication comes from the general manner of the client; is the client relaxed? Does she have spontaneous movement from one type of material to another and is she able to loosen construction at will and share dreams and free associations and generally become non-defensive? This is evidenced by the way in which contrasts are used in the therapy; for example, the client is ready for new movement when she can contrast the present with the immediate past even with evidence of a recent revision in her point of view, and she can contrast the present with future outlooks. Here the client is conscious of herself as 'a changing person'

(Kelly, 1955, p.1106). This is all done with an optimistic view. There is also evidence of general readiness for and presence of change when the client can freely and easily change her own construction. An example is as follows: ' "A few months ago I said that . . . I am not so sure that I really think that way." Or a client might say, "I seem to be making quite a point of this . . . I wonder if that means I am defensive about it." ' (Kelly, 1955, p.1107). Generally the client's readiness for reconstruction is evidenced by a lack of defensiveness and the client's ability to show the strength of being able to reject the interpretation of the therapist, and even by the client's being somewhat aggressive toward the therapist. The client must learn how to protect herself, and know when things are becoming too threatening. This is a healthy protection. Another attribute is the client's ability to gain real perspective on the therapy and gain an understanding of the role of the counselor as well as understanding the role that she is in as a client. This is evidenced by such statements as ' "Here is an attitude that I have which seems to be related to the fact that I am undergoing therapy" or, "I suppose all patients feel this way at times . . . ." "I think I expressed that idea last time more because I thought you wanted me to than because it was something I would have thought of myself" ' (Kelly, 1955, p.1108). Finally this readiness for new movement is expressed by a general lack of impulsivity. In this regard it is very important to detect whether one is dealing with a *secure spontaneity* and/or an *insecure impulsivity* in the client. In such incidences where insecure impulsivity is detected, the therapist must be prepared to pull back and be more conservative and cautious than the client might desire. The counselor could say, 'This is something that we shall want to consider thoughtfully before these sessions are finished. Just now, however, you do not know me well enough to talk about this without wishing afterward that you hadn't. Let's save it for a while' (Kelly, 1955, p.1109).

Role of Anxiety and Guilt in Reconstruction

In examining guilt and anxiety, both normally viewed as negative aspects of personal experiences, the emphasis is on the 'constructive' or positive aspects of these frequently encountered and necessarily unavoidable aspects of personality functioning during constructive revision. In fact, Personal Construct Theory takes the position that it 'concerns itself primarily with the affirmative processes in man's ongoing quest' (Kelly, 1955, p.1111).

Anxiety is the awareness of failure of structure in a situation. It is recognized that anxiety is a necessary part of adventure and change. When the client steps out into new territory she has little or no structure and the presence of anxiety is felt — particularly the pleasant and exciting part of anxiety. This anxiety, however, has to be controlled so that it does not serve to inhibit the adventure. The same thing goes for guilt. 'Guilt is the awareness of dislodgement from one's core role structure' (Kelly, 1955, p.1111). This can then be used in either productive or counterproductive ways. 'Guilt, representing as it does within our system the perception of loss of core role, may serve either to restore teamwork (let the person fit into a role relationship to others) or to stifle initiative (with all the pain and the dread, depression and suffering and immobility this implies)' (Kelly, 1955, p.1111). Our task here is to deal with these two (anxiety and guilt) in the psychotherapeutic interview so that constructive revision can take place. To accomplish this Kelly outlined the following techniques for dealing with them.

Techniques for Dealing with Anxiety

First, keep the interview structured and keep the person dealing with tight constructions which are at the same time comprehensive enough to enable the client to function adequately. *Second*, don't push on into new problem areas unless the present reconstruing is more or less complete. *Third*, use the various binding techniques (time binding, situation binding, etc.) which have been mentioned earlier. *Fourth*, use differentiation to break the problem into segments to be dealt with in manageable units. For example, the counselor might state: 'Let's be sure to keep this straight; this is *not* the particular kind of anxiety we were talking about a while ago; this is different; note that it is . . .' (Kelly, 1955, p.1119). *Fifth*, give the client a careful appraisal of the feelings involved. Give the client a careful description and understanding of just what feelings have been expressed in such a way that the client feels she knows what is happening. *Sixth*, use an active anticipation of hurdles that the person is going through or about to go through. Help the client anticipate how she will feel. *Seventh*, be specific about what is worrying the client. This forces the client to become concrete about the problem, and in this way the problem becomes more containable. *Eighth*, use a structured outline in the interviews so that problems are taken up in an orderly fashion. *Ninth*, control the tempo of the interview to the extent that long, self-reflective pauses by the client are kept to a minimum. The counselor can make direct inquiries about matters in a way that keeps the client at a regular, even tempo (Kelly, 1955, pp.1117–1121).

Techniques for Dealing with Guilt

First, keeping in mind that guilt is the awareness of the loss of core role, help the client expand his role in such a way that it includes what would ordinarily be dislodging. This might come in a line of thinking that is working out in such a way that it helps the client relate to other people in a different way. The client now sees other people meeting some of his needs and himself in turn meeting some of their needs. *Second*, help the client find alternative roles to replace the one he has lost. Help the client, for example, find a new occupation or new direction in life. *Third*, help the client to better understand the people that he has to deal with in developing role relationships. This is another way of helping the client to redefine his role. *Fourth*, help the client to broaden his base for the building of role relationships both inside and outside the therapy. Help the client build a new comprehensive role relationship, first with the therapist, and then help him expand his new role relationship to include other people in his life. (Kelly, 1955, pp.1121–1122).

Reconstruction Through Experimentation

At this point, it is appropriate to consider the nature of the basic process whereby reconstruction takes place. In this chapter the basic principles of what takes place in the normal course of psychotherapy will be laid down. The next chapter will take up specialized techniques based on these principles—in particular Fixed Role Therapy.

Kelly asserts that 'The relationship we see between psychotherapy and scientifc research is more than a mere analogy. We believe there is a fundamental similarity' (Kelly, 1955, p.1123). Here the importance of the nature of the relationship between scientific inquiry and psychotherapy is being pointed out. This relationship constitutes the basic principal for the development of the rest of the system. Of primary importance also is the fact that in experimentation the nature of the C-P-C cycle is illustrated. In experimentation we are dealing with action which is the end result of the C-P-C cycle. The person begins with circumspection (C) or alternative constructions, moves to a preemption (P) or a choice of one alternative, then to control or choice (C), which means taking some action based on the interpretation.

Aims of Experimentation

In undertaking an experimental approach in psychotherapy, it is necessary to be concerned with what is being accomplished by the experimentation. Kelly lists the following: *First*, it can 'give the client a framework for anticipating what would otherwise be incredible' (Kelly, 1955, p.1125). The client has some way of understanding what has happened to him. *Second*, it can help the client to deal better with reality and not be victimized by reality. When negative results come in and the client suffers an invalidation, it prepares the person to undertake the reconstruction work needed. *Third*, it helps the client to test out the system; to see what is implied by the system he has. There are many things we understand implicitly which we need to understand verbally so that we can make better use of them. *Fourth*, it can help the therapist to a better understanding of the nature of the case, even if it means that the therapist reveals his misunderstanding of the client's problems. In this way it serves as a check for both client and therapist. *Fifth*, it can 'open new vistas of experience'; it can raise as many questions as it settles. One question leads to another (Kelly, 1955, p.1126). *Sixth*, it can help put the client in contact with other significant people (or people who can become significant) in his life. In this regard it is important to note that explicitly paying attention to the way others construe life is of critical importance in therapy. This is thought to be more important than just being concerned with seeing oneself as other people see you. It makes for a much wider view. Kelly states it as follows:

> 'From our point of view it is more valuable for the client to learn to see how others see their worlds . . . . If the emphasis is placed upon being able to see the world as others see it, albeit from the vantage point of one's own system, the client sees ways open to him for adjusting his role to a more effective relationship to others. If his aim is only to see himself as othres see him, he becomes caught in their expectancies and must either adjust to them by conforming to their expectations or break out in hostile revolt against them. It seems far more healthy for all concerned for one to play out his part through a critical understanding of others' outlooks than by trying to conform to their expectations' (Kelly, 1955, p.1127).

Techniques for Experimentation

These are techniques that can be used to facilitate experimentation in psychotherapy within the therapy sessions and as homework assignments outside the therapy hour. As mentioned earlier, role playing or enactment is one of the main ways to get experimentation going. Here are some other things that will facilitate this kind of experimentation.

First, it is possible to give the client a kind of permission to enter into experimentations of various types. This helps the client to dilate the immediate situation. The instructions suggested by Kelly are as follows:

> 'This therapy room is to be an unusual kind of place. Here you will be able to say many things, express many feelings, think many thoughts which you might not ever consider on the outside. Here you will find that we can dispense with some of the rules for good manners in order to get down to your real feelings and attitudes. You can laugh, when otherwise you might not laugh; you can cry, pray, swear, and experiment in many ways in order to find out how you really feel about things, about yourself, about people, or about me' (Kelly, 1955, p.1129).

Other ideas that would help this kind of experimentation are the inclusion of responsive situations in which something different can happen; the client is encouraged to try things out in a new situation just to see what will happen. The same is true for novel situations or providing the client with special tools for experimentation, such as some kinds of social skills or a new approach in terms of dress or hair style (Kelly, 1955, pp.1130–1131).

Another effective way to facilitate experimentation is to encourage the client to set up specific hypotheses, ones that have specific predictions—for example, 'What would Mary do if . . . . What would she not do? What are some of the other alternatives?' (Kelly, 1955, p.1131). This has also been expanded by Epting and Suchman (1969) in enabling subjects to design their own experiments and by Mair (1970) in his procedures for setting up experimentation using a conversational model.

Yet another approach is to get the client to interpret the outlook of others and to portray and enact these interpretations. Get the client to see how another person views him and others. Get the client invested in seeing if his interpretations of others are right so that the client gets to test some of his interpretations out in particular situations (Kelly, 1955, p.1132).

Yet another avenue open to encourage experimentation is to make sure that negative predictions as well as positive predictions can be made. Here the client sets up something that he expects to be disconfirmed. For example the client might predict that he will be very anxious during a particular situation and then find out later that it was not as unpleasant as he was expecting. This gives a well-rounded picture of experimentation (Kelly, 1955, p.1133).

Experimentation of this type can also be extended to certain kinds of biographical hypotheses, where the client elaborates kinds of 'biographical' antecedents which would make certain kinds of things possible. For example, the client acts *as if* she had had the kind of support and encouragement that would give the self-confidence she now needs (Kelly, 1955, p.1133). In addition, the client could be encouraged to place himself in social situations where others are anticipating the same kinds of changes that she is expecting. For example, a client who likes plays, opera and the arts but who is presently in an engineering program and has mainly friends in engineering, might be involved in a therapy group where the other group members are trying out new experiences and pursuing interests which they find most fascinating.

Lastly, we might mention a direct appeal, which is only used with caution, since it could make for an overly dependent client. An example of this approach might be 'See here, why don't you do this and see what happens; we'll go over the results in our next interview and decide what ought to be dne done next' (Kelly, 1955, p.1134).

Obstacles and Hazards in Experimentation

There are various kinds of difficulties that are frequently encountered in attempting certain kinds of experimentation. For example, both hostility and anxiety can cause complications. With hostility the client cannot bring himself just to let 'nature take its course' and see what the evidence brings in terms of confirming and disconfirming information. The hostile client must have things come out the right way for him. This would mean the client may then constrict very severely and demand validation of his original ideas in an experimentation (Kelly, 1955, p.1135).

With anxiety the client may not really be prepared for the implications of his reconstruction. For example, the whole system may be shaken up considerably even though the experiment has been a success. Some clients are too anxious to undertake a certain experimental venture. For them the experiment would have too many far-reaching implications. In this case the counselor would be getting the client far beyond what his personal structure could handle by involving him in the experimental venture, so that a genuine threat is seen in the possible outcome of the experimentation. There is simply more at stake in the experiment than the client is prepared to risk (Kelly, 1955, p.1137).

Another difficulty may arise if the client is very dependent on the counselor and will only accept validation directly from him. The client takes the position that 'something is no good unless the therapist says that it is good for me'. This is one of the negative consequences of having an overly dependent relationship develop between the client and therapist (Kelly, 1955, p.1138).

Another very different situation which Kelly lists is that of trying to work with a client who is experiencing excessive guilt where he feels so dislodged from core role structure that he is paralyzed in terms of making choices or any movement. For example, a client says: "'I don't see any use in trying that. It really doesn't make any difference, no matter what the outcome." . . . (Kelly comments) What the client means is that he feels himself dislodged from his role and that nothing that he can do seems relevant to is re-establishment' (Kelly, 1955, p.1138). The key to helping the client here is for a secure and well developed role relationship to be built with the therapist before experimentation is undertaken.

A very severe difficulty in initiating experimentation is found in the perception of a non-elaborative choice by the client. The client has the belief 'that he will be trapped by the results of the experimentation' (Kelly, 1955, p.1138). Whatever way the experiment turns out, the client is left with no apparent further place to turn. The experiment provides irreversible and terminal outcomes. In order to deal with this type of difficulty the therapist tries to get the client to lighten up and see more alternatives. This perception of a non-elaborative choice is also closely tied to a situation in which the client may be operating with an excessively loose conceptual framework with no real place to fit the outcome into an otherwise very tight and meaningful structure.

Finally the client may choose to carry out the experiment in an inappropriate milieu, in which disastrous outcomes are likely or in which there are risks to the client. Here the therapist may be unprepred to help the client make anything positive out of the outcome of the experiment as such, and can only help the client to see, later, how poor his chances were for succeeding in the experiment with that choice of a setting for testing out his ideas. It is important to help a client deal with failures as well as success in experimentation (Kelly, 1955, p.1139).

Case Illustration

Having discussed many aspects of reconstruing, it may be helpful in closing to illustrate what reconstruing looks like in a particular case. The case chosen is one involving the therapy of a very disturbed woman who was successfully treated by Larry Leitner (1980) using a construct therapy approach for approximately one year. During this therapy Leitner employed many of the techniques that have been discussed up to this point. The aim of the therapy was to enable the client to understand herself more completely and deal more effectively with her world. The aim of the therapy was to provide the client with the kinds of skills that would serve her long after the formal therapy had ended.

The following is Leitner's account of the construct revisions which had taken place ten months after the therapy had formally ended.

'I called Sue to obtain some information regarding her current life situation. She reported that she has decided to divorce John. She elaborated this by discussing it in terms of a growing feeling of "independence". She stated that she and John were "good friends" but "were not meant to live together".

Related to this growing sense of independence, Sue is now attending college. She has set her sights on a career in nursing. She has an 'A' average, and is on the President's Honor Roll. She is justifiably proud of this accomplishments. Her financial support is a combination of scholarship, welfare support, and child support from John.

She reported an upsurge in chest pains immediately after my departure. However, these rapidly disappeared and have not returned. The terrifying dreams and fantasies are no more. She reported experiencing a "sadness" one day when she felt her dreams and fantasies were gone forever. When her mother became condemning about the impending divorce (even calling her a "slut"), Sue confronted her. Sue told her that she "should know better than to say things like that". A noticeable improvement in their relationship occurred following this confrontation. Sue even took some responsibilities for contributing to their problems.

As Sue talked to me, the notions of "taking responsibility for myself" and "being human" appeared to be very meaningful to her. This latter notion allows her to forgive herself and others for mistakes and shortcomings. Consequently, her resentments over her past are gone.

Perhaps the best way of concluding the story of Sue is to quote her view of herself and the therapy.

"I've grown up at long last thanks mainly to our visits. I went from a shaky kid ready to kill myself and take my kids with me, to an adult willing to take responsibility for my life. As I look back on it, I don't see how we came so far in so short a time. My basic self hasn't changed like I was afraid it would. Just my outlook has. I really can't describe it . . . I'm still the same person only I'm totally different"' (Leitner, 1980, pp.120–121; reproduced by permission of John Wiley & Sons, Inc.).

This is a most interesting case which deserves to be read in its entirety. It is a good illustration of the progression of events which can be seen from the initial anticipation phase all the way through to the reconstructive phase.

Summary

The first main theme in constructive revision discussed in this chapter pertained to the nature of interpretation. Reconstruction first takes place in the way in which interpretations are made by the client, with the counselor aiding in this process. The question raised is what does the client make out of what has happened to her. It is important in considering reconstruction to be mindful of the special role that anxiety and guilt play in this process. This is very important because anxiety and guilt can both facilitate or diminish the way in which constructive revision takes place. Special attention was given to the techniques that can be used for dealing with both anxiety and guilt.

One of the main vehicles used for reconstruction is the innovative use of experimentation in the therapy hour and in the outside world. The aims of experimentation were explored, as well as the techniques used for facilitating it. Because of the nature of the risks involved in experimentation, special attention was given to the difficulties, obstacles, and hazards which are invovled.

The last section provided an illustration from a case where this final stage of therapy had taken place and had begun to take form in the client's life. The aim of the therapy was to provide the client with useful tools for living which could be made use of after the formal therapy had ended.

PART III

Techniques and Evaluation

Now that the basic features of a Personal Construct Psychotherapy have been presented, this last section will be focused on the specific techniques that have been developed using this theoretical approach, and an evaluation of the total enterprise. As presented in chapter 8, the initial concern will be with fixed role therapy, the best known of the specific techniques. This is followed, in chapter 9, by a description of a number of other techniques such as group therapy, couples therapy, and family therapy, as well as techniques used in counselor training and supervision. In the last chapter, emphasis is placed on those features of Personal Construct Therapy that may be considered as the core features of this therapeutic approach — those that serve to compare and contrast it most clearly with other approaches.

CHAPTER 8

Fixed Role Therapy

The best known of the specific techniques which have been developed in Personal Construct Psychotherapy is the fixed role therapy. This procedure was originally developed by Kelly and was presented in some detail in the first volume of his two-volume work (Kelly, 1955). Since that time both Kelly (1973) and others (Adams-Webber 1979, 1981; Bonarius, 1967, 1970, 1980; Bannister and Fransella, 1971; Pervin, 1980) have provided descriptions of this procedure. Bonarius, however, has, without doubt, provided the most extensive and detailed examination of the total enterprise.

Briefly stated, fixed role therapy is a procedure whereby the client is invited to assume an identity other than his or her own for approximately a 2-week period of time in order to have a chance to experience the world differently for this brief period. Working closely with the therapist, the client is asked to become someone else for a short period of time. Instead of just continuing to be themselves, the clients are asked to approach the world as if they were a different type of person just to see what that altered perspective may provide. The client is asked to be in the world in a very different way for a brief period of time.

Following Kelly's lead of often describing therapy as a voyage or journey, Bannister (1975) describes much of the work undertaken in Personal Construct Psychotherapy as analogous to the task of rebuilding a ship while it is under full sail. The client is like a ship that cannot be put in dry dock for repairs but must continue to sail in some pretty rough waters from time to time. The therapist is like a fellow workman who helps the client rip up one board (personal construction) at a time, then slap another one down in order to keep going. With this image in mind, fixed role therapy can be seen as a technique whereby the counselor assists the client in 'jumping ship' for a brief time, just to see what it would feel like sailing in a different vessel. The idea here is that the client must eventually come back to the original vessel, but this brief interlude may just turn out to be a grand adventure, one that the client may find useful in eventually deciding to redesign the original vessel. It is important to note that in taking this approach the client is not asked to give up his former perspective; he is only encouraged to actively explore a new perspective.

This technique of fixed role therapy is an excellent illustration of what Kelly called an 'epistemology of creative action'. 'Man understands his world by finding out what he can do with it. And he understands himself in the same way, by finding out what he can make of himself. Man is what he becomes. What he becomes is a product of what he undertakes—expected or by surprise' (Kelly, 1973, p.398).

Design

At this point let us sketch in the broad outlines of this technique. It begins with the counselor's requesting that the client prepare and bring to the next counseling session a self-description in the form of the self-characterization presented in chapter three. This can be explained to the client as the first step in a new technique which has the potential for therapeutic gain. In fact some therapists describe the whole project in detail to the client in order to avoid any mystification of the therapy enterprise. It is important to note that some therapists do not use a formal self-characterization but instead rely on more informal procedures. If, however, the more structured procedure is used, it will be recalled (see chapter 3) that Kelly suggested the following instructions:

> 'I want you to write a character sketch of Harry Brown (client's name), just as if he were the principal character in a play. Write it as it might be written by a friend who knew him very *intimately* and very *sympathetically*, perhaps better than anyone even really could know him. Be sure to write it in the third person. For example, start out by saying, "Harry Brown is . . ." ' (Kelly, 1955, p.323).

It is generally left up to the client just how much material to produce, but it is sometimes wise to indicate that at least two paragraphs are necessary for this therapeutic procedure. In receiving this material from the client the counselor adopts the *credulous approach*. As explained earlier (chapter 1) this means that the counselor tries to see things from the client's own viewpoint and accepts things the client says as the client's way of representing what he sees. The main job for the counselor is to find within the sketch the main construct dimensions the client is using in describing his world view. There are many ways to analyze the self-characterization, which Kelly describes in considerable detail in his original work (Kelly, 1955). It may be noted here that many counselors feel they know the main dimensions of the client from earlier therapy interviews and skip, altogether, the formal procedure of eliciting a self-characterization. Others use not only a self-characterization but a Rep test as well. There are a number of ways of obtaining an adequate description of the way the client sees his world at present. That is, after all, the main purpose of the self-characterization.

After the client has returned the self-characterization or the therapist has obtained a view of the present outlook by some of the other means mentioned above, the therapist prepares an *enactment sketch* for the client. The enactment sketch is a briefly written description of the new role the client will be enacting for the next couple of weeks. This new role is given a name—such as 'Sally' or 'Kirk'—which makes it more feasible for the client and counselor to think about the new 'fixed role' as a real person. Upon presenting the client with the enactment sketch for the first time, the counselor must be sure to obtain from the client two important pieces of information. First, the counselor must be assured that the client sees the new role as a real person. The fixed role must be like a real person, rather than some ideal, or fantasy figure, or caricature of a real person. Second, the counselor must make sure that the client finds the new role interesting. The new role is one that holds some fascination or interest at least to the extent that it seems like someone the client would like to know better. There may be some threat in the way the present enactment sketch is written, and this should be attended to and dealt with if it arises. It is sometimes necessary to modify the enactment sketch so that it better suits the client and the objectives of the therapy.

The fixed role sketch or enactment sketch is usually based upon the understanding of the client that has been gained from the material in the self-characterization. As mentioned earlier, this knowledge of the person's system can be gained through the use of Rep techniques as well as interview material. In any case, the enactment sketch is designed to include or encompass several different features. First, the enactment sketch is designed to test out at least one major hypothesis about how the client might be different which could be of some benefit for the client. This hypothesis comes about in the form of a major construct dimension which is put into the enactment sketch and is different from a construction the client is presently using. Kelly (1973, p.405) gives the example of a client who describes himself as 'meticulous' as opposed to being 'casual.' Rather than aiding the person in becoming casual, which he probably knows a lot about, and has tried already and rejected, it may be better to introduce a new dimension such as 'generous' versus 'grasping.' Bonarius (1970) reports the development of a fixed role sketch for a client, Peter, whose main construct was 'being free' versus 'being tied down.' For Peter, Bonarius initiated the therapy using a construction where the main dimension was that of 'understanding people' versus 'not understanding' as the main and regnant construct which served as the fundamental prescription for an enactment sketch named 'Goert Douwe.' Under this, several other constructions of Goert were organized as follows: (1) listening versus persuasion; (2) feeling versus discussion; (3) forgiving versus compulsion. These other constructs were used further to define and clarify just what was involved in either understanding or not understanding people.

The purpose of introducing these new dimensions in the enactment sketch is that you as a counselor believe that this sketch may provide some promise for the client without implying that this is a way the client should change in order to be necessarily 'cured.' The whole venture is meant to be an experiment and an adventure for the client. The fixed role procedure must not be allowed to deteriorate into just a roundabout way to get the client to change certain behaviors. In a construct theory approach the aim of the counseling is *not* to try to get the client to adopt the new behaviors. The purpose is just to get the client to try the new constructions on for a possible fit. In this way fixed role therapy contrasts with a behavior therapy approach. The whole plan of the therapy is explicitly explained to the client. If the client asks if this is what you, the counselor, think she should be like, the counselor answers that no one really knows what the client really should be like, but that this particular perspective contained in the sketch just might contain something that the client could learn to use and then later come to value, but on the other hand it might be something she would clearly want to reject. The only way to tell is to try it out for a while to see what does happen.

It is the job of the client to get on with assessing the new role by getting into the fixed role in order to see if there is something worthwhile in it for her. From the outset it is better for the client to see the fixed role as just a way to be different from what she is right now. After all, the whole thing should be seen as just a game; something to be experimented with and to learn from, not something to stake one's future life on necessarily, nor something to be taken deadly seriously.

Another important point is that the integrity of the client's own personality must be preserved (Kelly, 1973, p.411). This is accomplished by ensuring, in introducing the new role, that it is not put forth as a rejection of, or a way of making fun of, what the person is like at present. One way in which this can be accomplished is for the role sketch not to contain just the polar opposite of the present personality qualities. The fixed role descriptions should contain some of the same core role constructions that the client has at the moment. In the new role, many of the dimensions written in are quite different from the present self but some of the material should be the same as the present self. In this way a deep respect is shown for the integrity of the present self.

Another element in the enactment sketch is the presence of true *role constructs*, the nature of which is explicitly stated. This is expressed by having something in the sketch that states that the client in the new role must practice taking the role of the other as part of the new character. The new role is always described as a person who tries to have her actions and reactions based on what she understands the outlook of the other person in the interaction to be. As the reader will recall, in construct theory a role relationship is defined as construing the construction processes of the other.

Examples

The following is a self-characterization (uncorrected) which a client turned in, followed by the enactment sketch which was prepared for the client, based on this material.

Self-Characterization

'In my opinion C. N. is not a shy girl by no means. She mixes well with both sexes but is frequently moody and therefore is irritable to those surrounding her. Carrie lies quite often knowing she is doing wrong, but continues to do so. She exaggerates about things concerning herself which she feels would like to be true but are not. I find she becomes dissatisfied with herself and the things she is doing quite often. For example, she gets disgusted with school and wants to quit and has no desire to study. Also she feels as if she wants to go to a new environment to meet new people. I also feel she possess a selfish character at times and other times quite generous depending upon her so-called mood. She has a strong desire to be happy and satisfied with the things she has and therefore have peace of mind. She sometimes has the feeling that she wants everything to come her way without working for it and she would like to possess a feeling of wanting to give as much as receive. She would like very much to fall in love and not only looks for what he could give her, now but first look for how ambitious he is and what he will have in the future. She is dead set against marrying a doctor because of that life a doctor's wife leads. She feels she requires constant attention and love in order not to have that sense of insecurity she so frequently feels' (Kelly, 1973, p.408).

Enactment Sketch

Julie Dornay is a good person to have for a friend. She is spontaneously and sympathetically interested in people. She is a good listener. She is sensitive to the ways other people feel. People value her friendship, not only because of the things she can give them or the favours she can do, but more because of the encouragement and strength her friendship gives them. Having had problems of her own, she is well equipped to play a sympathetically supporting role to the people who confide in her. While she does not feel that all her own problems are solved, when others come to her she lays her own problems aside in order to be of help. Basically she believes that all people are worthwhile in their own right, regardless of their accomplishments or wordly successes. Because of this fundamental belief in people her own worthwhileness is simply and naturally taken for granted.

There is an undercurrent of impatience in Julie's way of life. She is quick to express her liking for her friends. She is always ready to speak up on their behalf. When she sees someone pushed around she really stands up and lets her voice be heard. But this impatience never seems to come into conflict with her underlying feeling of kindliness and sensitivity for others. Indeed, one might almost say that her impatience is a result of this feeling.

Julie's capacity to be a good friend leads her into many new and interesting adventures. While some people pick and choose the friends who conform to their own narrow specifications, Julie selects a tremendous variety of friends, no two of whom fit precisely the same set of specifications. Thus her own life is enriched and widened and new horizons are continually opening up before her.

When you talk to Julie you soon become aware of the fact that she is interested in you because, first of all, she fundamentally accepts you as you are and whole-heartedly believes that you are genuinely a worthwhile person. She responds to you spontaneously and takes your acceptance of her for granted. But most of all you discover that she is ready and eager to know you as a unique and different personality among her many and varied friends (Kelly, 1973, pp.408-409; reproduced by permission of University of Miami Press).

Kelly comments that generally the development of role relationships with others is emphasized. Specifically this sketch is designed to involve the client in commitments to others which are spontaneous and open. It also includes her search for a friend mentioned in the self-characterization. This fixed role sketch also allows the client to extend her social relationship to include other people at the same time as she continues her search for a boyfriend. Her concern for others is respected in the sketch but it is expanded into an open and spontaneous way of reacting to others.

Procedure of Enactment

In this section the whole procedure for enactment is presented in essentially an outline form. Kelly (1955), in his original two chapters in volume one of his two-volume work, provides much more detail, both in analyzing the self-characterization and in describing the enactment procedure. The reader is encouraged to consult this material for further information.

In introducing the enactment sketch to the client, Kelly suggests a set of directions which may be used with a client, as follows:

> 'During the next two weeks, instead of dealing directly with your problems, I would like to suggest that we do something altogether different. Let us suppose that Q. M. (client's name) is going to have a two-week vacation in the mountains, and, in his place, you are going to be "E. S." (the fixed role). You will act like "E. S.", talk like him, think like him, do the things you think he might do, eat the way you think he would eat, and if you can, even have the dreams you think he might have.
>
> 'Here is another copy of "E. S's" character sketch. Keep one copy with you all the time and read it at least four times a day— particularly at night when you go to bed, and again in the morning. Read it also whenever you have difficulty playing the part' (Kelly, 1973, p.410).

It is important to try to get the client to immediately start the procedure by getting into the part with the therapist rather than spend time talking *about* the character. The idea here is that one can learn best by doing rather than sitting around analyzing the situation. It is believed that just a few minutes in actual role-playing and active in-role dialogue with the therapist has a tremendous advantage over just understanding and analyzing the part.

This is usually a very difficult time for the therapy because the client feels awkward and foolish. Because of this it is a good idea for the counselor immediately to take on playing the part of the fixed role and allow the client to play some other life figure, such as the boss or a clerk, with whom the fixed role character is supposed to be interacting. This takes the pressure off the client and enables the client to see the therapist feeling awkward and struggling to stay in the role. This puts client and therapist on a more equal footing and promotes the cooperative spirit of two people working together on a joint project. The efforts of both the counselor and the client are directed toward spending as much time as possible in the actual role-playing—stopping from time to time to comment on how each can help the other maintain the role—but otherwise maintaining the interaction 'in role.' Some time is, of course, spent in talking about what just happened in terms of the experience of being in a new role, but this is kept to a minimum during the early stages of the fixed role therapy.

As Kelly (1973, pp.414-421) originally structured the sequence of sessions, it was recommended that three meetings a week should be scheduled for the client in a 2-week period of time, resulting in a total of six sessions. The recommended content of these six sessions is as follows:

(1) In the first session, after the enactment role is introduced, the therapist immediately starts into a role-playing interaction involving the client's teacher, supervisor, or boss. This is a role-playing encounter with a non-emotionally involving figure who has some authority relationship to the client. It is initiated, usually, with the client enacting the fixed role and the counselor playing the authority figure; roles are then switched. After this some discussion is devoted to how the client can play out this role in an actual situation. After each session the client is invited to carry the role forward into an actual situation before the next session. It is important to let the client be the judge of how extensive the 'outside' role-playing should become. The client is advised not to push on into the role if she believes, at the time, that she should not go any farther.

(2) The second session is centered on interaction with a good friend or a peer group member. Here the emotional involvement for the client is deeper and more difficulty in maintaining the role is usually encountered. With each step an attempt is being made to increase the personal involvement of the client.

(3) In the third session the main concern is with a truly emotionally charged situation, with the spouse or an affectionate friend. It must be emphasized here that the client is not to tell the spouse or friend that a role enactment is being tried out. It is thought that the situation would become very artificial if the other knew that it was all just a game. Also, if the friend knows about the enactment, the client will not gain the benefit of truly being in a new kind of a relationship with the other person.

(4) The fourth session has its main concern with parental interactions. The client is to have some kind of contact with her parent in her new role. This can be on the phone, in a letter, or in an actual face-to-face meeting. It is believed that particular difficulty may be encountered at this point, due to the fact that the client has had such a long-standing relationship with parents that being different in their presence is quite a challenge.

(5) The fifth and last role-playing session involves the client's ultimate values in some way. This is usually done by inviting the client to stay in role during some type of religious experience—perhaps by asking the person to pray or address in some fashion what for the enactment sketch character would be ultimate in life; that for the sake of which life itself has meaning. It is best in this step to stay away from particular religious creeds and concentrate attention on purely personal concerns about these issues. Although this fifth stage is often skipped by counselors who are unfamiliar with dealing with ultimate values in counseling, it is thought that this session can be particularly important for the client by enabling her to see exactly what all the role enactment sketch implies and how she may come to choose different ultimate values.

(6) The final session involves no role-playing inside or outside the session. Instead the client is invited to look back over the two weeks of work in order to evaluate, in general terms, what has been taking place. At this point the client can decide what this experience has meant and perhaps choose to keep some things that were beneficial and definitely discard some that were of little or no benefit. This is the time for an integration of the experience. It is a time for constructive revision and is the terminal stage of the therapy. The therapy may end at this point, or it may go on to other issues, but the structured fixed role therapy is stopped.

Throughout the fixed role therapy procedure the counselor is attempting to be very supportive of the client. It may be remembered that support, in construct theory, means enabling the client to experiment widely and creatively with life in a specific situation. One way in which this is done is for the therapist to help the client anticipate the reaction of others to the role being enacted and to rehearse extensively with the client during the role-playing sessions. It must be realized, however, that the sequence, as just outlined, is a set procedure which can be modified considerably. For example, many therapists feel that the step dealing with religious issues should be omitted, while others feel that an extensive amount of time should be devoted to this step. The most important aspect of the sequencing, however, is that the client should be taken through a progression of experience which start with relatively superficial role relationships and progress to more intimate levels of interaction.

Some counselors prefer that the final session, devoted to the client's taking stock of the whole experience, should not be a single session but, instead, a series of two or three meetings. The idea here is for the client to be able to thoroughly evaluate what has taken place. The client is asked to differentiate between what she may now want to incorporate into her own personality and what has been only an interesting adventure and now holds no further interest for her. It is a common outcome for the client to comment that she felt that in many ways the fixed role was very much like what she considered herself to be ordinarily, but had not yet been able to enjoy or develop in herself. Kelly reports that the wife of a client commented that, to her, her husband (a fixed role client) had been more himself in the last two weeks than at any time in the recent past. In total, the client will, it is hoped, be left with the impression that if she has now changed in one respect, then other changes are possible. In discussing the objectives of this procedure, Kelly stated that it is for the client, 'to realize here and now that his innermost personality is something he creates as he goes along rather than something he discovers lurking in his insides or has imposed upon him from without' (Kelly, 1973, p.418).

Developments in Fixed Role Therapy

There have been several innovative applications of fixed role therapy which demonstrate modifications in the original procedure. Fransella (1972) reports the use of fixed role sketches for clients whom she was treating for speech disorders. The clients were persons who stuttered quite severely and the fixed role concerned what they would be like if they were fluent speakers. Her clients maintained a whole life view or world view of themselves as stutterers. After using the *implication form* of the role construct repertory test (see chapter 3), in order to aid the client in construing fluent speaking, Fransella helped her clients to construct a brief fixed role sketch designed specifically for the area of the personal implications of fluency. Clients then enacted fixed roles of persons who were fluent speakers. Although speaking behavior itself was not a part of the role, Fransella reported that the enactment of the personality portrait of a fluent speaker enabled her clients to significantly improve their speech and avoid stuttering. The fixed role in her procedure was designed in such a way that it did not include a sketch of the whole personality structure, but instead was centered around the implications connected to fluent speaking. It was a specific and delimited fixed role sketch.

Epting and Amerikaner (1980) reported another modification in fixed role therapy employed by Epting and Suchman entitled *variable role therapy*. In this procedure the client was invited to construct a mini fixed role for dealing with types of difficulty the client was experiencing. For example, if the client was having difficulty dealing with authority figures she was guided in constructing a brief character who could deal with authority in a different fashion — just to try out the new approach to see if it had any advantages. The same was true of other problem areas, so that the therapy was filled with four or five mini fixed roles, each with its own name and brief description. The client was then invited to use any one of these when experiencing a particular problem.

Skene (1973) described a fixed role therapy that was designed to aid a young 19-year-old patient who was encountering legal difficulties resulting from his overt homosexual activities. Rather than using the self-characterization procedure, Skene used a Rep test for eliciting the constructs upon which the enactment sketch was based. The enactment sketch was not focused on the young man's homosexuality; instead, other personality dimensions were developed. Nevertheless, at the conclusion of the therapy the client was no longer interested in pursuing his homosexual activity and began heterosexual contacts and activities.

There have, in addition, been at least two research studies in which fixed role therapy has been assessed; one by Karst and Trexler (1970) treating anxiety while speaking, and the other by Lira, Nay, McCullough and Etkin (1975) dealing with the treatment of ophidiophobic subjects (afraid of snakes). Both studies revealed strong evidence for the effectiveness of this treatment procedure when compared with control conditions and other treatment procedures.

Advantages

Adams-Webber (1981) makes special note of the fact that one of the main advantages of this technique is its flexibility. Using this technique, there is no reason to rule out any particular category of patient. It can be used in the middle of therapy when the client is not making progress. It can be used to begin therapy when there is an indication that this would be a way of getting the client started. It gives the client something to do which is tangible. It can be used as a way of terminating therapy. The Fixed Role procedure can be used as a way of integrating material in the therapy by having the main dimension of the therapy, developed up to that point, woven into the enactment sketch.

Adams-Webber (1981) further notes the advantage that the counselor employing fixed role therapy does not have to worry as much about the type of the transference that involves excessive dependency. In Fixed Role Therapy the client is placed in a very independent position by going out into the world and trying things out. In the same way it can be used with a very defensive client, since the counselor is not asking probing personal questions. Instead the counselor is constantly engaging the client in enactment sketches. In addition fixed role therapy can be used to avoid over-intellectualization in the therapy and the tendency to dwell on past events. It is more concerned with everyday events in a very down-to-earth manner. Bonarius (1970) further notes that fixed role therapy is an efficient way to validate or invalidate constructions. It is a way of providing clear evidence for the constructions the client is asked to deal with. Finally, the whole sequence of the therapy can be planned out in advance.

Summary

The general aims and objectives of fixed role therapy have been described in this chapter. It is a type of brief (two-week) psychotherapy where the client assumes an alternative in living in order to explore possibilities for further personal development. The design of this therapy was described in some detail, beginning with the self-characterization, which is then followed by the fixed role enactment sketch, which is originally formulated by the therapist and then modified to fit the client's further specifications. The actual enactment contains six steps, beginning with interactions with low intimacy figures, such as a teacher or supervisor, and progressing to more involved relationships. The final session is reserved for evaluation and interpretation of the two-week experience. In closing, more recent developments in fixed role therapy were noted along with some of the advantages gained in employing this type of therapy.

CHAPTER 9

Other Techniques

In this chapter a variety of topics will be covered. These topics have been selected so as to give the reader an understanding of the scope of Personal Construct Theory as it has been applied to the field of counseling and psychotherapy. The first topic to be covered concerns some of the different group therapies which have been developed using this framework. Next will be an examination of the model of training and supervision of counselors that is recommended, and finally we will concern ourselves briefly with various new developments in personal construct psychotherapy.

Group Therapies

Because a number of group therapies will be covered in this section, it is important that we start with a description of the basic principles which Kelly used in his original work (Kelly, 1955, p.1155–1178). As might be anticipated, the approach taken to group therapy is structured around the same principles encountered in the individual therapy described in chapters 3–7. For example, the emphasis remains on enactment, and the active involvement of the therapist in the structure and process of the counseling sessions. Kelly divides the group therapy into six stages or steps. These six stages no doubt, overlap, but they do describe a progression of events that helps to provide an order and structure for the therapist so that she can maintain her sense of direction and purpose during the very complex interactional patterns involved in a group therapy. In fact, these stages exist more often in the mind of the counselor than they do in a form that could be precisely detected in the group interaction on any given day.

Initiation of mutual support. This initial step in the process is essential for providing a foundation upon which the further work of the group can be based. This first step involves there being both *acceptance* and *support* shown for the clients by the counselor, and by the clients for each other.

It will be recalled that *acceptance* was defined by Kelly as 'the readiness to see the world through another person's eyes—that is, readiness for commonality. *Support*, in turn, was defined as a broad response pattern in relation to which the client successfully experiments with a variety of constructs and behaviors' (Kelly, 1955, pp.1160–1161). It is largely through the active acceptance of the group members by each other that the group finds the support it needs for productive therapeutic work. Kelly felt that every member of the group must feel support from somewhere in the group before anything beneficial could happen. As a therapist, one must work to see that everyone in the group is receiving support from someone in the group, either from another group member or directly from the leader. There are, in fact, specific techniques recommended in this initial stage in order to develop this acceptance and support—namely the use of structured enactment sketches with role descriptions for the participants. It is advisable during these enactment sketches that the participants exchange parts from time to time and that the counselor tries her hand in acting a part with the group members. In this way the enactment of a part will be sustained long enough for new spontaneous material to start to be produced by the group members as they get into their parts and start to be inventive in producing fresh material (Kelly, 1955, p.1148).

This procedure is usually initiated with only two people playing the parts and the other group members observing. It cannot be overemphasized that the counselor should take part in this process, because it is beneficial for the group members to see the leader struggling to develop her part and generally stumbling around trying to find a way to get into the part. The counselor using this procedure has to produce an enactment sketch that centers around some problem area that may be of some interest for the group members. The group members who are observing are encouraged to jump in and help support the role-players, and to help facilitate the role-playing in any other ways that occur to them. In this way the therapist is able at an early point to step out of role as the primary support provider in the group. This structured enactment task gives the group members a way to interact with each other from the beginning and does not require excessive self-disclosure in this initial phase. It provides a way for trust to build and for the members to come to know each other as a by-product of a mutual task.

The following is a description which Kelly provided for this procedure, which he believes to be somewhat intense. He advises that in some groups a less conflicting and less emotionally arousing sketch should perhaps be used. The content of the sketch is determined by the nature of the group and the aims of the group therapy.

> 'Two participants are involved. The scene is the living room of the person played by the first participant. This person is the parent of a 10-year-old son. The time is 9 p.m. The participant playing the part of the second person knocks on the door of the house. The enactment starts at this point. After the therapist has structured the situation, as described above, each participant is asked, in turn, to leave the room until the other participant has been briefed before

the group as to the background of his part. Thus, when the enactment starts, neither participant knows the background of the part being played opposite him, but the non-participant members of the group all know the background of both parts. Following is the background structure given the first participant: Your 10-year-old son is generally considered to be a "problem child". He has been in trouble with the police, and the neighbors have complained to you about his impudent behavior. This evening the two of you had a quarrel and he became quite angry over your refusal to give him some money. He stamped out of the house, slamming the door behind him. You have not seen him for several hours.

Following is the background structure given to the second participant: About four hours ago you unexpectedly ran across an old companion whom you had not seen for several years. You have spent the early part of the evening together having a good time. While drivng home your car struck a child who was crossing the street in the dark between intersections. You stopped, an ambulance was summoned, and the child was taken to the hospital in an unconscious state. A bystander identified the child and gave you his home address. You are about to knock on the door of his home to inform his parents of what has happened . . . . It is important for all members of the non-participant group to know what the background information is and for each participant to know that they know the background for his own part. This is the reason for briefing each participant in front of the group. In this manner the participant may feel supported from the outset. He will need the support and will be inclined to accept it. As we have emphasized before, the parts should be exchanged, even though the re-enactment does not involve the element of surprise that the first enactment does. The re-enactment provides some protection for the second participants and it tends to emphasize the impersonal nature of the experiment' (Kelly, 1955, pp.1163–1165).

Initiation of primary role relationships. Again in this second step in the group therapy process, the focus is on the nature of the relationship of the group members with each other rather than being concerned with relationships outside the group. The initiation of primary role relationships involves having each group member express how she felt about what was happening during the role-playing sequence. Attention is focused on what the group members felt about what was going on in the enactment, and to express how they thought the participants in the role-playing were feeling at the time. This experience is designed to accomplish a number of things, among which is an assessment of shared meaning. In Kelly's words, 'The contrast that a client sees between the way another person appears to feel and the way he thinks he would feel in the same situation is a measure of the commonality the client perceives between himself and others' (Kelly, 1955, p.1168). It is also helpful at this point to have some group members play the enactment sketch out in an alternative version to the way it was played the first time. The counselor must be aware of both the amount of threat this might cause and the amount of hostility which might arise in this undertaking. It is important for the parts to be exchanged frequently so that different portrayals of what is happening gets demonstrated and discussed.

Initiation of mutual primary enterprise. In this third step the group members are beginning to develop a feeling for who each of the group members are as persons and something about how they are dealing with things in their own lives. At this point the group is ready to introduce its own content for enactment sketches based on problem areas and areas of interest in their own lives. Group members now suggest what kinds of issues they would like to explore. These then form the bases for the enactment enterprise taken on by the group. The sketches are much more informal and often briefer. If possible these enactments are limited to what goes on in the group and do not have important implications for life outside the group.

Explorations of personal problems. This fourth step is the point in the developing group process at which the members bring in problems from the outside — ones that are grounded in circumstances in their own lives. The other group members are invited to enact how they would handle a given client's problem situation in a manner different from that originally portrayed or described. Generally this all goes by at a very brisk pace. Usually the client does not play herself in the enactment sketches.

Exploration of secondary roles. In this fifth step clients in the group begin to reach outside the group in an important way. The client begins to role-play new insights outside the group and then brings this material back into the group. At this stage the 'task of the therapist is, then, to help the client extend the lessons he has learned about role relationships with a particular group of persons and apply them to other persons outside the group and to humanity in general' (Kelly, 1955, p.1175). Some caution is expressed here because of the jealousy expressed towards the client as he moves out to other groups and away from the therapy group.

Explorations of secondary enterprises. This sixth and final stage in the process of group therapy takes place when the client has primarily involved himself with issues outside the group — issues in life that he deeply cares about. At this point the particular member keeps coming to the group primarily for the benefit of the other members in order to help them reach that point themselves. The group here, however, still serves to help the member to protect himself against failures which he might be experiencing in these external ventures. Throughout these six stages of the group counseling much has been made of role enactment. In considering this type of group therapy it is important to understand what function enactment serves. The nature of this is very well expressed by Kelly in the following passage: '. . . it (the enactment) provides a transparent mask behind which the actor portrays, not a false self, but the true self which is so often hidden by daily conventions and manners. The mask is therefore not a disguise, but a screen behind which the person can divest himself of his customary pretenses' (Kelly, 1955, p.1178). In looking back over these six steps it must be remembered that it is the therapist, not the group members, who keeps the steps in order. As was mentioned earlier, these six steps are ways to keep things straight for the therapist. It should not serve as an ironclad structure for the group process itself. At any one time any number of these steps can be taking place at the same time. What is important is that the process should be complete at some point for all or most of the group members.

It is thought that group therapy has certain advantages over individual therapy. For example, group therapy can serve as an extended source of validation for the client's experimentation that a lone therapist could never accomplish, and the client gets an immediate impression of the diversity of constructions which are possible for any given situation.

The reader will no doubt be most interested in the work of J. Brenda Morris, reported in an appendix of Fransella and Bannister's (1977) *A Manual for Repertory Grid Technique.* Morris reports a group using the six-step procedure. The group, composed of eight psychiatric outpatients and two therapists, met weekly for about a year. Group members and leader took the Rep test periodically in order to monitor the movement during the therapy. It was found that the therapists were able to predict change fairly accurately, with the members moving generally in the direction of optimal functioning. In total, a positive effect of the therapy was reported. Particularly interesting was the report of therapist change as well as client change.

Group Fixed Role Therapy

Another form of group therapy that Kelly developed was based on the procedures in Fixed Role Therapy which can be used in very small groups of perhaps three to five clients. Based on self-characterization obtained from each participant, clients are presented with fixed role enactment sketches at the first meeting of the group. In this way each client hears the role description that each other client is assigned to play during the group meetings. The clients are instructed to maintain the enactment role during all the sessions except the last, which is devoted to an evaluation of the enterprise. During the regular sessions an attempt is made to prevent the clients from bringing their 'old role' (the way they are in everyday life) into the discussion too extensively. The participants are asked not to reveal very much about themselves in their 'old roles'. The counselor also attempts to respond to the client in the client's new role and not the old one. The group members are encouraged to support each other in playing the roles and to help each other understand the role they have been assigned. On the one hand, the group members take turns in playing out supporting roles for each other. For example, a group member might play the role of the job supervisor for the fixed role practice of a fellow group member. On the other hand, group members help others by taking on each other's assigned fixed role in order to help them portray a certain feature of it and show them how others might play this same role. The counselor is very active in the first part of this process, helping the group members to get into their roles. As the group progresses, however, the counselor takes less and less of the lead. The sequence of role-playing events is the same as that described in relation to individual fixed role therapy. The following is an example of the instructions given in order to introduce this procedure. These instructions are attached to each fixed role sketch distributed.

'This role has been prepared as a kind of venture for the person who is to play it. It is by no means to be construed as psychologically "correct or ideally suited for the role player". Solely as a two weeks' adventure, it may provide a vehicle for the role player to transport himself to new and interesting experience.

It is suggested that the role be played out as completely as circumstances will permit during a two-week period. The role player should read it three times a day, eat it, sleep it, think of himself by the new name, feel as the new character would feel, and generally commit himself wholly to the role. It is hoped that the role player will keep daily notes on his experiences.

It is suggested that group rehearsal periods of approximately one hour each, three times a week, be scheduled by the three people who are experimenting with new roles. The role players should represent themselves in their new roles in this situation as well as in others. Particular care should be taken not to discuss the original characterizations of themselves which were prepared by the role players. The role players should accept each other wholly in terms of the new roles and never let expectations based upon revelations of the old roles creep into the picture. In the rehearsals, each person should review his experience with his role during the preceding days, ask for suggestions and interpretations from others, and rehearse situations likely to occur in the coming days' (Kelly, pp.434–435).

Interpersonal Transaction Group

The interpersonal transaction group is a group technique that has been developed within the framework of Personal Construct Psychology by Landfield (1979) and his colleagues. This procedure is designed to allow a group of persons to gain experience in construing the construction processes of others. After an initial large group interaction session, usually centered around some specific topic, assignment is made to a system of rotating dyads. Each member is asked to interact with each other member for a brief 10 to 15 minute period of time. Each member has an opportunity to interact with each other person on a specific topic. This dyadic interaction can be done any number of times, with changes of topic. The group then meets together for a group interaction on that topic. In this way the group members understand and experience each other in pairs as well as in the large group. An exact rotation system is planned out and structured so that each person spends an equal amount of time with each other person in the group. Participants also assess their current moods and write them on 'mood tags' which are then pinned to their clothing so that others can tell what they are feeling as well as what they are talking about. As a way to get conversation started on a feeling level, this technique has been used with different groups, for example in alcohol counseling, group death education classes, and many other types of groups.

Couples and Family Therapy

Although there have been a number of studies using the Rep test in various forms to study couples during counseling (Ryle, 1975; Ryle and Breen, 1972; Wijesinghe and Wood, 1976) there have been fewer attempts devoted to actually constructing a procedure for conducting couples counseling from the Personal Construct Theory point of view. There have been, however, some recent developments which are well illustrated in the work of Greg Neimeyer (1983). This procedure is begun by helping the couple and the counselor to gain an enlarged perspective concerning the nature of the conversation or argument which is taking place during the couple's interaction. In the first step, *assessment*, it is a common practice for each partner to take a Rep test in order for the counselor to get an understanding of the couple's construct systems and for the couple to gain an understanding of the constructions, used by each other. In the second step, *clarification*, the two participants are asked to try to understand the other by both stating clearly what they want to be understood, and by listening carefully to the other in order to get a feeling for the perspective of the other. In the third step, *elaboration*, some effort is put into attempting to trace out the implications of the couple's systems. What are the issues couples are trying to deal with? Perhaps the husband does not put out the garbage on pickup days or the wife leaves her underclothes to dry in the bathroom. The couple is invited to express the implications that these things have for each other. Perhaps the wife feels that not putting the garbage out conveys a disregard for her or the husband feels that the laundry situation shows a dislike for the home. Obtaining these implications and tracing them further and further is similar to what Hinkle (1965) had in mind with his laddering technique, which will be described later in this chapter. By tracing these implications out, couples often find that they are trying to get at the same basic *values* (superordinate constructions), but are going about things in such a way that quite conflicting messages are being sent. Perhaps a basic superordinate dimension such as *trust* versus *distrust* is the main theme to the marriage partners, therefore, it turns out they are trying to get the same things out of their marriage. This technique can also reveal basic value conflicts. By using this technique, the couple can come to know that they are fighting over real issues of difference that need to be faced and dealt with in some constructive way, even if a decision is reached to dissolve the marriage. The fourth stage is one of *sociality*, where the couple starts to develop a system of mutual construing. This is a system which is adequate for the job of construing the other person. This is the start of a meta-construct system. They now have a way of stepping back and looking at the situation from the point of view of a third person who could be observing the couple in their difficulty. The purpose here is to try to teach the one partner the superordinate constructions of the other. At this point often the couple have begun to get an idea of what has to be avoided, what can't be talked about, as well as where the flash points are that produce the hottest fights. The couple are often invited to bring a tape recording of one of their arguments and to sit down with the counselor and start to analyze it. Here the couple are really working on the problem as a team. They work on the nature of the problem knowing what the super-ordinate constructs of the other are like, and they are able to communicate these insights. Finally, a role reversal is set up where the one partner plays the other. In this way the participants are able to step outside the confines of the nature of their relationship and see what is happening to them rather than just being caught up in it.

Along somewhat similar lines Harry Proctor (1981) has undertaken a personal construct formulation of family counseling. He has become interested in family constructions in a way similar to Neimeyer's (1983) interest in the couple's constructs. In the same way that each individual has a construct system, family members have a shared meaning system which constitutes a *family construct system*. Proctor sees the operation of a family construct system as a shared meaning generated within the family that governs how the family operates. Just as individuals are seen as structuring their lives around their own personal constructs, the family interaction pattern is structured around the way they see reality represented by a family construct system. The family construct system is seen as hierarchically organized and serves to make the family work as a unit. These characteristics also make the family resistant to change and capable of generating certain anxieties and threats when change is needed. For the family in trouble, the situation is seen as one in which the family has developed *disorders of negotiation*, where the family has avoided dealing with something it needs to deal with, or is rigidly dealing with certain problems in a dysfunctional way. In order to deal with the disorder, Proctor employs repertory grids specifically designed for the family, whereby an attempt is made to explicate some of the family constructs used to make sense out of existing interpersonal relationships. It is important to note that these family constructs are used both to order things within the family and to govern the way family members deal with people outside the family. As regards bringing about change in the family, Proctor takes the position that one must first change the way members of the family are interacting with one another in order to bring about a new reality reflected in a change in the family construct system. This tactic is very similar to that used by Kelly in designing *Fixed Role Therapy*, described in the last chapter. The construct system is changed by inviting the persons to act differently in order to help them change the way they see things. The emphasis is on changing the pattern of relationships within the family rather than working directly on the revision of a single person's construct system. Starting by providing the family with *acceptance*, *reassurance*, and *support*, as these terms were defined in chapter 3, the therapist is attempting to help the family to *'reframe'* their family constructions—which means helping the family consider alternative ways of construing present events, thereby consolidating changes in interactions with other family members over a particular issue. The therapist's job is to help the family to consider alternative ways of approaching things. This is largely accomplished through helping the family to have an opportunity to see clearly the validation and invalidation of their present system. This is done not in a didactic fashion by intellectually explaining the process, but by actually involving the family in responding to material that the therapist provides. The therapist spends a lot of time in confronting the family members with alternatives for them to try out and deal with, rather than in asking the family members to become introspective and spend their time reporting on the nature of things. Proctor takes the position that the family construct system for the most part is not available in conscious awareness; the counselor therefore spends his energy in creating situations for the family to deal with. These are situations that can offer family members new, creative ways of living together.

Training and Supervision

In this section we shall be concerned with the personal construct approach to developing psychotherapy skills in the clinical supervisory situation. Kelly's first concern is with the nature of the person who becomes a psychotherapist. It is a concern both with the way that person operates in professional relationships with clients and with the way he operates in purely personal matters. It is a concern with the total person in terms both of how well developed are the student therapist's preverbal constructs that can be used for 'emotional insight' and of how well developed are the verbal constructions that are used for 'intellectual insight' (Kelly, 1955, p.1179). This will govern how well the student therapist can understand a client by subsuming that client's own construct system. As might be anticipated from what was covered earlier in this book, the development of the verbal construct system should follow the scientific model in terms of keeping it 'psychologically informed, systematically intact, scientifically (empirically) supported, amenable to searching inquiry, and in the process of continuing revision' (Kelly, 1955, p.1180). In this way a professional construct system is developed that is grounded in the science of psychology. In the development of the preverbal constructs which deal with more private and personal matters, the aim is to make these explicit enough so that they can be prevented from interfering with the growth of the student therapist's client and can actually be used to promote better understandings. This means that during training the student therapist and the supervisor should get to know each other very well.

Along these same lines Kelly emphatically states that a personal psychotherapy can be very helpful for the future therapist and might best be carried out by a therapist who has a theoretical orientation similar to that which the student therapist will be adopting. This is a personal therapy which is specifically designed for the student therapist. In this special type of therapy several important things can take place. First, it provides an opportunity for the supervisor to illustrate techniques. This can happen at the time these techniques are being employed in the therapy or can be commented on at some later time by the supervisor's recalling to the student that a certain technique was used. The student therapist is learning at first hand. A second important function of this procedure is to give the student therapist a good way to identify with how it feels to be a client and so help the student therapist to a better understanding of his own clients. Third, it gives the student therapist a way of seeing parallels between herself and the client. This is most beneficial when the therapist can see that the client is now passing through a problem area that the student therapist also passed through and solved. This, however, can also be seen as detracting from the therapy when the student therapist has not solved the problem that the client is approaching. Some difficulty can also be encountered when the student therapist sees a superficial parallel between what the client is presenting and his own difficulties in the past. Fourth, the student therapist's therapy can provide a way for the young therapist to get an idea of how his own clients might be seeing him, and the ways they may need to depend on him for certain things. This special therapy may provide the student therapist with a way of seeing what role relationship his clients are likely to form with him. Fifth, this type of therapy helps the student therapist to sort out his own life in a better fashion. It is designed to help the student therapist both personally and to become a better therapist (Kelly, 1955, pp.1181–1184).

These functions of the special therapy for student therapists are augmented by some procedures that Kelly felt were of particular benefit. First, the student therapist is encouraged to write a summary of the therapy interview which includes his feelings as well as the events that transpired in the interview. The student should also specify his own reactions and the experiences he has between the interviews. Kelly comments that recordings of the sessions can be made and passed on, but that these are not as valuable as the comments. Particularly important to note here is what the student therapist has decided *not* to discuss with the supervisor. This will also give the student some insight later into his own client's reluctance to confront certain issues with him.

Another technique that Kelly felt was helpful to use was for the client and therapist to step out of their roles momentarily and comment on what has been taking place. As the relationship matures the supervising therapist can comment on the tactics being employed — what has been moved away from and come back to later. The supervisor may also go so far as even to comment on the client's own feeling at a certain point, but he does this in an open and accepting way, as illustrated below:

'During the discussion of . . . it seemed to me that I observed in the client some indication of mounting anxiety, though of course I could not be sure. I decided to deal with it, for the time being, if indeed it was anxiety, by the use of tightening procedures. I therefore asked for a more explicit statement about . . . . If what I observed was a mounting anxiety associated with some aspect of the topic we were discussing, I am inclined to believe that it will come up again before long, perhaps in a context which will give me a better frame for dealing with it. Do you, as a psychologist, agree that this was an appropriate decision on my part, or do you believe that I should have handled the matter somewhat differently?' (Kelly, 1955, pp.1185–1186).

It is this level of responding and interacting which is aimed at in this type of therapy.

One problem that Kelly notes is that the student client–therapist will not be able to deal with his own problems spontaneously in this type of therapy, so that it calls for an aggressive move on the part of the supervisor. The supervisor has to move in on the student in an aggressive way. This is a problem because the supervisor will not want the student necessarily to take this type of aggression as a model for his own therapy.

Finally, one has to examine the way the student therapist becomes dependent on the supervisor. It is a complex affair. 'This means that the client-psychotherapist must not only depend upon him [the supervisor] for personal clarification, but that he must also win and hold the therapist's approval as a professional man' (Kelly, 1955, p.1186). The student and supervisor must constantly work with this complex situation in order for a mature helpful outcome to be achieved.

A Model of Supervision

Leaving now the topic of the special therapy that should be provided for student therapists, Kelly next specifies a model for supervision. Kelly has a preference for a group of three or four student therapists with an experienced teacher. Once the interviews with clients have been recorded, the group members are paired up, having each partner listen to all the other person's interviews with a particular client. A group session follows, in which the supervisor asks for reports of the student therapists' interviews. It is also helpful if the supervisor can observe some instances of the student conducting the interview. For the group presentation the student therapist prepares a report made up of four sections: enumerated by Kelly (1955, p.1193) as follows: '(1) The student's plan for the interview'. This should also include how the student took into account comments made by the group on previous presentations. '(2) A factual account of what he considers to be his more important observations'. Here the student is urged to be as concrete and specific as possible in saying why he chose these things to be the most important. If this material is presented at a high level of abstraction it is difficult for other group members to contribute to the understanding of the case. '(3) His [the student therapist's] interpretations of the interview at a professional level of abstraction'. This is very difficult and usually is finally drawn up as a consequence of the group discussion. This leads to specific hypotheses being set up for further therapeutic gain. '(4) His prediction as to what the client will do between interviews'. This is perhaps the most difficult task of all but provides a good way for the student to check his interpretations.

Some additional points are worth noting. It is generally a good idea for the student therapist to enact some parts of his case with the monitor or with the supervisor. Another point is that the student should face 'his overwhelming desire to compel the client to get well . . . Often the teacher has to remind the student therapist that the client has a full set of human rights, including the right to remain ill' (Kelly, 1955, p.1194). The supervisor must leave the initiative in the hands of the student therapist. It is his own decision what to do and what not to do in a session. The student therapist should not follow the instructions of the supervisor in a static fashion. The student therapist must be able to face the jealousy he feels when the client begins to show signs of independence. And lastly, 'just because a client loosens up a little, is hard to understand, and shows a little hostility, there is no reason to believe his construct system has fallen apart. It may be that the therapist's construction is confused—in othe words, that he is *anxious*' (Kelly, 1955, p.1196).

Other Recent Developments

A number of other techniques worthy of mention were reviewed by Fransella and Bannister (1977) in their repertory grid manual. The first is the laddering technique developed by Hinkle (1965) in order to aid people in generating superordinal high level constructs. In this procedure the person is asked why he prefers one pole of a particular construct over another. The question '*why*' when applied to constructs leads the person to higher level values. A very nice example of this technique is found in Fransella's work with clients seeking help with their stuttering behavior.

'For each construct elicited, the person is asked which pole of that construct he would prefer to be described by, for example, *verbally fluent* or a *muddled speaker.* If he answers that he would prefer to be *verbally fluent,* he is asked to give his reason for making that choice. If he were to say, that people who are *verbally fluent* are *able to get their ideas across* whereas *muddled speakers* only *confuse people,* then *get ideas across-confuse people* is another construct superordinate to the first. He would then be asked why he wanted to *get his ideas across* rather than *to confuse* and he might reply that he would prefer to *get his ideas across* so as *to be admired.* This same process goes on until there is no further answer to the question "why"—an overarching principle is reached' (Bannister and Fransella, 1971, pp.73–74).

This technique can be very helpful for therapy where the nature of overarching values are important, as was the case in Neimeyer's (1983) couples counseling mentioned earlier.

Another important development related to this procedure is Landfield's (1971) Pyramid technique where the same type of procedure is used. The client is asked to consider a single construct dimension. Here, however, the client is asked to think of a person who would possess this characteristic and then say what kind of person this would be. For example, in considering the *shy* versus *outgoing* dimension, the client might say that a shy person runs away from you whereas an outgoing person will stand and talk. In this way one ladders down to more subordinate meanings. This technique would be of particular help to use with clients who are dealing in generalizations and need to have specific concrete implications to talk about in the counseling. The reader is also recommended to consult Fransella and Bannister's (1977) manual for other related procedures such as the implications grid, the resistance to change grid, and the bi-polar implication grid, which aid the client in specifying what construction is implied by knowing a given dimension. For example, if you know the person is shy what else would you also know about him? This enables the counselor to get an idea of the constellation of constructs that exist and some notion of the hierarchical arrangement of these constructs. Much has been done in the use of the Rep grid as a vehicle for therapy. In some instances the Rep grid procedure has become the therapy. When this happens it may or may not be particularly closely related to the rest of what is meant by a construct approach to psychotherapy.

There have been a number of other types of development in the construct theory approach to therapy. For example, the work of Dorothy Rowe (1978) was mentioned earlier, in her therapy for depressed persons where she attempts to look at the ways in which people trap themselves into certain kinds of construct content which, in turn, keeps them stuck and depressed and unable to move. More recently she has adapted this approach to dealing with constructions of life and death (Rowe, 1982). She takes the position that the way the person is construing her own death has a lot to do with the kind of life she is free to build for herself. Again the concern is with the nature of the content of the construction. Related to this work Warren (1982) has shown how the Death Threat Index developed by Krieger, Epting and Leitner (1972) can be analyzed for clinical use by employing Slater's (1977) principal component analysis. The Death Threat Index is designed to enable the person to construe the nature of her own personal death. The Index enables the counselor to obtain a sample of the different constructions that the client uses in understanding her own death. This material can quite easily become a part of a counseling interview when life and death issues are being grappled with. At the time of writing, a special issue of the *Journal of Death Education* dealing with these issues (Epting and Neimeyer, 1984) is in preparation.

Also working directly with the content of construction has been the work of Uriel Meshoulam (1977, 1981) on stuttering. Building on early work by Fransella (1971), Meshoulam has taken the work in the direction of using existential theory and techniques to help the client to explore his construct system more extensively in order to find new pathways of movement.

Fin Tschudi (1977), with his colleague Sigrid Sandsberg, has developed, in construct theory, an interesting approach to therapy which is based on some aspect of Greenwald's (1973) Direct Decision Therapy. In this approach Tschudi and Sandsberg make use of what they term 'loaded and honest' questions in developing a directive therapy using personal constructs. Ravenette (1977) is one of the few workers in this field who has been directly concerned with children and young people in working with them to aid them in their personal development. Ravenette demonstrates his ability to get at the constructions of young people by discovering the kind of questions to ask the children so they can tell what their world view is like. 'He (the client) is then invited to say what he considers from his own point of view the trouble with different people might be' (Ravenette, 1977, p.270). In using this question, for example, he elicits from a client the comment 'the trouble with most fathers is they favor the girls more than the boys' (Ravenette, 1977, p.271). This leads to other material which proves to be a key in developing a therapeutic relationship with the child. In addition, Mancuso (1978) has been concerned with outlining a counseling related to children and adults. It includes some interesting ideas of how to use *teasing* in a constructive way and the role of the *reprimand* in examining what happens to the way children construe events. Lastly, Morrison and Cometa (1977) present what they call an emotive-reconstruction therapy where much use is made of imagery and hyperventilation in work with construct revision for therapeutic gains.

Summary

In this chapter a number of topics were covered in order to demonstrate the breadth of the application of personal constructs in the field of psychotherapy. In addition to the basic six steps involved in group therapy, special attention was given to fixed role group therapy, a therapy for couples and families, as well as a technique developed for a group therapy using rotating dyads.

Training and supervision was also described which involved both a special therapy for student therapists and a model for the supervision itself. The last section was devoted to various new techniques which have been developed and applied to aspects of the counseling process. These covered a range of topics and a variety of target populations.

CHAPTER 10

Conclusions and Evaluation

In this closing chapter it may be helpful to examine some of the larger issues involved in describing this theoretical orientation and evaluating this position as it relates to other theories. In some ways this chapter is designed to explicate some of the issues that may have been only implied in the step-by-step description of the theory of therapy contained in the earlier chapters.

First it should be stated that Personal Construct Psychotherapy is a humanistic approach to therapy, as opposed to either a psychoanalytic or a behavioral approach. There are many reasons for believing this to be the case. To begin with, a personal construct approach is mainly concerned with the study of human experience as opposed to being interested in behavior exclusively. From this point of view, psychology is the study of both behavior and experience, where experience is understood to refer to the meaning the world has for a person as that person goes about living. It is a study of personal experience and in this way is very similar to the traditional humanistic positions taken by Rogers (1959) and Gendlin (1962). Rogers (1971, p.315), recognizes this when he describes the personal construct approach in this way: 'He (Kelly) is attempting to hold persons as processes, not objects.' In addition, however, to this hearty emphasis on experience, Kelly has a very practical side and is as concerned as Adler (1969) was with a psychology of use. That is to say, Kelly is as concerned with behavior as he is with experience, rather than being as exclusively concerned with experience as the Rogerians appear to be.

Another reason for classifying this approach as essentially humanistic is the similarity that exists between the personal construct position—that clients move in the direction of making elaborative choices, as defined in the choice corollary presented in Chapter 2—and the general principle of self-actualization found in the work of Maslow (1971) and Rogers (1959). Although meaningful distinctions may be made, both elaborative choice and self-actualization indicate that the client is reaching forward to a completion of a yet unfinished project. This same principle is found in Combs and Snygg's (1959) concept of the maintenance and enhancement of the phenomenal self. In all of these theories, there is a basic process whereby the client moves to a higher level of completion.

Yet another reason for considering this position as humanistic is pointed out by Joseph Rychlak (1973): Kelly, like Rogers and other humanistic psychologists, conceives of a person as coming to know the world by actively inventing some meaning for the world to have rather than assuming, like the behaviorist, that the world imposes its meaning on the person. The person must frame a meaning using active higher mental processes rather than having meaning stamped in from mere exposure to the raw events of an external world. Although he realizes that meaning is created by a rich interchange between the person and the world, Kelly takes the position that the only meaning the world has for the person is the meaning that the person gives it. 'Man looks at his world through transparent patterns or templates which he creates and then attempts to fit over the realities of which the world is composed' (Kelly, 1955, pp.8-9).

The reasons listed above are just some of the issues which could be cited in order to classify a personal construct approach as humanistic. It is not designed to be a complete list.

Personal Approach

In concluding this book it is important to note that the *person* is central in Personal Construct Therapy. It is the client's own values, feelings, behaviors and beliefs that are of primary concern, rather than any preconception (theoretical or otherwise) the therapist might have about them. Making the client the central concern in the theory means that any theoretical model building that goes on is tied to each specific person where affect, cognition, and behavior are seen as a single unit called the Personal Construct. This is a holistic position which asserts that mind and body should not be separated but remain united in what Kelly (1955, p.17) ontologically classified as a *substantival monism*. This person-centeredness is perhaps most importantly manifested in this therapy by the way psychological explanations of life events are offered. They are consistently offered from the point of view of the person who is experiencing the event rather than from the viewpoint of an external observer. It is from the client's point of view that the therapist begins her understanding.

Because this therapy is person-centered it makes it useful for a wide variety of clinical populations and clinical situations. It is the counselor's job to meet the client on his or her own level of intellectual functioning and in his or her own ethnic background. It is the counselor's job to learn to speak the language of the client and to let the client know that this is what the counselor is trying to do. The counselor is trying to see the client in the client's own terms. The emphasis is not on the counselor's own language and background but on how well the counselor can come to the client on the client's own terms. In this way the counselor follows the client and lets the client know to what extent she (the counselor) has been able to understand him (the client). The counselor does not have to strain to be a superhuman therapist, or to be overly sophisticated about the client. She only has to let the client know that she is trying to understand, so that she can be of some help.

Concerning this person-centered issue, one might go so far as to say that Personal Construct Therapy should be described as a special kind of phenomenology even though Kelly declared many times that he was no phenomenologist. Construct theory goes to the person without preconceptions in the same way that a phenomenologist would, but construct theory takes a very tough and pragmatic stand. It brings its phenomenological view of the person into the realm of natural science. It takes subjective understandings of the person in the direction of making them explicit and measurable in the form of the assessed personal construct system. Personal Construct Therapy makes the subjective explicit both to the client and to others who care to take the time to study carefully the interlocking meanings of the client's world.

At the same time as construct theory is at work making the subjective explicit, it does not go so far as to become obsessed with *objective* reality. Like the phenomenologist, the construct theorist assumes that reality should be viewed as soft rather than hard; a reality that may be changed if we become imaginative in dealing with it. In construct theory, the fear is that the client will trap herself in what she takes to be an absolutely hard assessment of the 'realistic' circumstances of her life and not try for alternative possibilities. Clients habitually take reality to be harder than it really is and never test to see how soft it really could be. Construct therapy is particularly concerned with clients becoming stuck in reality and never testing it for possibilities. There is a respect for reality, but not a reverence for it.

One might say that a personal construct approach is a tough phenomenology, or what Joseph Rychlak (1977) has termed a rigorous humanism. Personal construct psychology supports a natural science research approach and at the same time maintains a central concern for and compassion for the client. This is to say construct theory has both a heart and a head. All too often this position has been mistaken for a cognitive–behavioral position in theory and therapy. In fact some textbooks (e.g., Pervin, 1980) have classified it as such. This may be due to the fact that this theory is laid out as a structural approach concerned with the natural of personal construct systems. In this respect it would appear to be very similar to the way a cognitive–behavioral approach portrays a person. For construct theory, however, one of the purposes for assuming a structural position is to provide a way for personal content to be left open to be handled in a phenomenological fashion. This, in fact, is a way of making the theory very personal and compassionate. It leaves the content of the theory open to be filled by the personal realities of each client.

It is unfortunate that all too often the structural properties of the theory are discussed extensively, while the content (personal) issues get much less emphasis. The whole enterprise often looks much more cognitive than it should. In this connection it is interesting to note that in some of the more recent formulations of Rogers' 'person-centered approach' the structural-cognitive aspects of experience are emphasized. This is partially true in respect of the person-centered therapy of Holdstock and Rogers (1977) and in the work of D. A. Wexler (1974).

Active versus Passive Approach

Another important aspect of Personal Construct Therapy is the extent to which the therapist takes an active position in the counseling. In addition to the more passive listening and reflecting material back to the client that would typify the Rogerian therapist, the construct therapist will often take a much more active role in the therapy. One might describe parts of this therapy as directive, but it is certainly not designed to be truly intrusive or manipulative. An example of this more directive approach is found in the use of the Rep test in therapy. It is used to elicit from the client a sample of the client's constructs so that it can be discussed and brought to bear on the initial complaint.

Patterson (1980, p.384) mentions this active stance taken by the construct therapist: 'In therapy . . . the therapist is active, responding to the client in a variety of ways.' This active approach is designed to get the client to engage with the therapist in the *task* of the therapy. For the counselor it is a way of actively testing out what the counselor presently understands about the client and the nature of his difficulties. In addition this active approach provides a way for the counselor and client to test out their best understanding of what is going on in the client's life.

In construct therapy there is a more or less active evaluation process under way, with the counselor trying to assess where the client is, where she is going and what the nature of the therapeutic relationship is at the moment. This is an active examination, but it is not necessarily intrusive. This can be, and should be done in its own time perspective, carried out in an interested but relaxed manner by the therapist. This feature of the therapy has led Rogers (1971, p.316) to conclude that 'One has the impression of an incredibly "busy" therapist.' This however, is only an external impression, and is not a true description of actual practice. It is active but not 'busy'.

In the construct approach there is, in addition, often an active creation of material for the client's consideration and reaction. As mentioned before, a project is created which engages the creative imaginations of the client and the therapist. In this way Personal Construct Therapy stands in contrast to the Rogerian client-centered approach, and much closer to what one might expect to find in a much more explicit existential approach where considerable attention is focused on the nature of the client's existential tasks. Some of these same features can be found in cognitive–behavioral approaches; however, the purposes and aims for using the tasks would be different.

In discussing this issue of activity it is sometimes assumed that the client is being taken over by the therapist and robbed of his or her own responsibility. This is certainly not the case here. The initiative for the therapy must never leave the client's control, and the client comes to understand that her constructions are her own responsibility. The therapist of course has his own set of professional responsibilities for the well-being of the client and of society, but this is true of any informed therapeutic approach.

New Approach

Personal Construct Theory is often appreciated as essentially a new approach to clinical work. It approaches clinical problems and the task of clinical work from a perspective different from that of most other positions. This is reflected in Patterson's (1980, p.385) comment that 'There is a fresh, new way of looking at things, divorced from the usual clinical terminology or jargon. The approach is not diagnostically or externally oriented.' As mentioned in Chapter 1, this theory takes a growth position rather than a deficiency or repair approach, such as is taken in much of traditional clinical theory.

Because it does approach clinical problems from a new angle, Personal Construct Theory has been perceived as useful by a wide range of clinicians. It has been used by both behaviorists and psychoanalytically oriented workers, even though it is theoretically grounded in the humanistic tradition. It is the kind of humanistic approach that leaves itself open to be picked up and used by people of a number of persuasions. Evidence of this kind of usefulness can be found in the work of Anthony Ryle (1975), who uses the repertory grid technique to assess properties of construct systems which are then interpreted within a psychoanalytic framework. This kind of undertaking has, at least, the possibility of providing new insights concerning the meaning of particular terms in both theories and provides the foundation for a true theoretical synthesis. Much the same has happened with cognitive behavior theory, because cognitive therapists are often attracted to aspects of fixed role therapy and see it as a powerful therapeutic tool (Huber and Altmaier, 1983). Cognitive therapists also appreciate the structural aspects of construct theory (Meichenbaum, 1977; Mischel, 1973).

Other Characteristics of the Approach

In addition to the issues covered thus far, it is important to touch briefly on a number of other issues by way of summary and conclusion. These are issues that are either unique to this position or serve to describe further the very core of this approach.

Transcendence

The first of these issues concerns the position Personal Construct Theory takes on the topic of transcendence. This is a central quality of a construct and of constructive revision, because in construing one must reach out beyond what exists at present to that which is emerging and becoming. In construing, the client is asked to transcend the present life circumstances, the present time, the present way of living, and to entertain new alternatives that may serve the client in a better way. It is a movement toward fulfilment, growth, and the development of potentials.

Approaching the client in terms of his system of personal constructs is a valuable tool in aiding the client to leave himself open to an emerging world with new possibilities for his life. Construct theory is a way of dealing with the unknown; a world not presently known but which is emerging (Kelly, 1977). Offering a construction is a way of making something out of nothing — nothing that existed before. It is a statement about the creative abilities of persons.

Understanding

Another important aspect of this therapy concerns the cooperative relationship that exists between the client and the therapist, who constitute a research team whose job it is to make headway in understanding the client's difficulties. As part of this work it is very desirable for the client to be able to build overarching constructions which make her present life circumstances manageable. The client is aided and encouraged to build overarching super-ordinate constructions which can contain the main themes of her life. These superordinate constructions do not all have to be highly verbalizable, but they should serve nonetheless to integrate a wide range of life experiences.

It is important, in Personal Construct Psychotherapy, for the client to understand himself as a person in the process of change. It is important for the client to see where life has been, and where it is going as it stretches out in front of him. Purpose, direction, and perspective are gained through this therapeutic process. The client even needs to understand something of the nature of the therapeutic process itself, so that the essential qualities of this process can be used long after the client–therapist relationship has ended. A client certainly *can* be helped without understanding just how that help was given and received, but it is thought to be even more beneficial if she can understand this aspect of the counseling.

Dichotomy

Without doubt Personal Construct Therapy places more emphasis on the use of dichotomy, contrast, and opposition than any other single therapeutic orientation. Other positions, such as Jungian psychology, certainly emphasize dichotomy, but it is not as thoroughly woven into the fabric of the therapy as it is in construct therapy. In construct therapy one cannot understand the content of any psychological quality, such as kindness, without understanding what the person takes the opposite of kindness to be. Since dichotomy is a property of every construct, and a person is seen as a system of constructs, any understanding of the person has to involve an understanding of that person's contrasting meanings (which are often implied and hidden), as well as what the person manifests in his assertions of personal qualities. Working with a client's contrasting meanings often provides a way for therapeutic movement to take place.

Choice and Commitment

Again in very close alignment with the existentialists, construct theory emphasizes the client's being able to make choices and to commit himself to those choices. Only by committing himself to a particular choice, for at least a brief period of time, can the person gain information about what he is like and what he can do. This is a therapy that requires action both inside and outside the therapy hour in order for change to take place. The therapist spends a great deal of time in structuring ways for the client to be able to make choices and commitments that do not require a monumental amount of risk. The use of role-play and playing 'as if' in Fixed Role Therapy are specific examples of this quality.

Hope

The final special issue we would like to draw attention to concerns the theme of hope. The emphasis here is on the client's expectations and excitement over the creative possibilities which now appear to her. The client is brought face to face with the truly creative aspects of her personhood. Hope is held out for further growth, and encouragement is given to the client to entertain her fondest dreams and wishes. Reason, reality, and good sense are, of course, brought to bear here so that the person does not just go floating off into an unreal 'wish world'. Related to this hope on a personal level, the therapy clearly takes a position opposing social and political oppression. It is a theory of alternatives; a theory of change and the emergence of new meaning. It is not a very good theory of therapy for those who wish to adjust people to a fixed social reality for the purpose of social control.

Progress and Future Developments

A great deal of work has been done on elaborating this theory since the publication of Kelly's (1955) two-volume work. Up to this time there are over 30 books and hundreds of theoretical and research publications, many of which are indexed by the Clearinghouse for Personal Construct Psychology co-coordinated by the author and Professor A. W. Landfield at the University of Nebraska–Lincoln. There have been five international congresses on Personal Construct Psychology held in the U.S.A., Great Britain, and The Netherlands, with a regular sequence of meetings of the congress scheduled for every other year. In addition to several therapy training programs in university academic programs in the U.S.A. and in Europe, there is now an independent training institute located in London founded by Dr. Fay Fransella, named The Centre for Personal Construct Psychology.

Although one can see from the above list that a great deal of elaboration of the basic theory and therapy has taken place, it is important, nevertheless, to make note of areas where further development is needed.

Perhaps the first area that needs to be mentioned is the use of therapy with children. In this area Kelly made some commitment and headway with his paper entitled, 'Behavior as an Experiment' (Kelly, 1970). In addition to the research studies mentioned in chapter 9 under the topic of development, Bannister and Agnew (1977) have discussed the nature of the self in children. Even when this work is surveyed, however, one realizes that a complete therapy for children has not been spelled out and is very much needed. The same might be said for marriage counseling and family counseling, although there is more active work in this area currently under way than there is with children. This area will no doubt develop as clinically minded developmental personal construct psychologists move into this area. Perhaps most progress has been made, up to this time, in the area of adolescent psychology (Ravenette, 1977; Williams, 1981).

Another area that needs this kind of basic development is in the use of dreams in therapy. Even though a beginning has been made in dream therapy, as described in an earlier chapter, much remains to be done. This is an area which can be easily developed for immediate use by both clinicians and researchers.

This is, without doubt, an incomplete list of areas in construct theory that need further development. I am sure that every reader will have his own list of critical needs. It is appropriate, I think, to conclude this account of personal construct therapy on this note of completion needed. It is hoped that this theory of therapy will always be in need of further development rather than being seen as the final answer to the therapeutic enterprise. Construct theory is very much an open system needing to stay in the process of constant development and change. This general theme is found in George Kelly's reflections about the nature of his own life in his article, *The Autobiography of a Theory*: 'But, still, if I had to end my life on some final note I think I would like it to be a question, preferably a basic one, well poised and challenging, and beckoning me to where only others after me may go, rather than a terminal conclusion — no matter how well documented. There is something exciting about a question, even one you have no reasonable expectation of answering. But a final conclusion, why that is like the stroke of doom; after it — nothing, just nothing at all!' (Kelly, 1963, pp.51–52).

References

Adams-Webber, J. (1969). Cognitive complexity and sociality. *British Journal of Social and Clinical Psychology*, **8**, 211–216.

Adams-Webber, J. (1979). *Personal Construct Theory: Concepts and Applications.* Chichester and New York: John Wiley & Sons.

Adams-Webber, J. (1981). Fixed role therapy. In R. J. Corsini (Ed.), *Handbook of Innovative Psychotherapies*. New York: Wiley-Interscience.

Adler, A. (1969). *The Science of Living.* Garden City, N.Y.: Doubleday Anchor Books.

Allport, G. W. (1962). The general and the unique in psychological science. *Journal of Personality*, **30**, 405–422.

Bannister, D. (1960). Conceptual structure in thought disordered schizophrenics. *Journal of Mental Science*, **106**, 1230–1249.

Bannister, D. (1975). Personal construct theory psychotherapy. In D. Bannister (Ed.), *Issues and Approaches in the Psychological Therapies*. London: John Wiley & Sons.

Bannister, D. (1977). The logic of passion. In D. Bannister (Ed.), *New Perspectives in Personal Construct Theory*. London: Academic Press.

Bannister, D., and Agnew, J. (1977). The child's construing of self. In J. K. Cole and A. W. Landfield (Eds.), *1976 Nebraska Symposium on Motivation*. Lincoln, Nebraska: University of Nebraska Press.

Bannister, D., and Fransella, F. (1965). A repertory grid test of schizophrenic thought disorder. *British Journal of Social and Clinical Psychology*, **2**, 95–102.

Bannister, D., and Fransella, F. (1971). *Inquiring Man: The Theory of Personal Constructs*. Middlesex, England: Penguin Books Ltd.

Bannister, D., Fransella, F., and Agnew, J. (1971). Characteristics and validity of the grid test of thought disorder. *British Journal of Social and Clinical Psychology*, **10**, 144–151.

Bannister, D., and Mair, J. M. M. (1968). *The Evaluation of Personal Constructs*. New York and London: Academic Press.

Bieri, J., Atkins, A. L., Briar, S., Leaman, R. L., Miller, H., and Tripodi, T. (1966). *Clinical and Social Judgement: The Discrimination of Behavioral Information*. New York: John Wiley & Sons.

Bonarius, J. C. J. (1967). De Fixed Role Therapy van George A. Kelly. *Ned. Tijdschr. Psychol.*, **22**, 482–520.

Bonarius, J. C. J. (1970). Fixed role therapy: A double paradox. *British Journal of Medical Psychology*, **43**, 213–219.

Bonarius, J. C. J. (1980). *Persoonlijke Psychologie*. Amsterdam: Van Loghum Slaterus.

Bugental, J. F. T. (1978). *Psychotherapy and Process: The Fundamentals of an Existential-Humanistic Approach*. Reading, Massachusetts: Addison-Wesley Publishing Co.

193

Bugental, J. F. T., and Zelen, S. L. (1950). Investigations into the 'self-concept'. 1. The W-A-Y technique. *Journal of Personality*, **18**, 483–498.

Combs, A. W., and Snygg, D. (1959). *Individual Behavior: A Perceptual Approach to Human Behavior* (Revised edn). New York: Harper & Row.

Duck, S. W. (1973). *Personal Relationships and Personal Constructs*. London: John Wiley & Sons.

Epting, F. R. (1972). The stability of cognitive complexity in construing social issues. *British Journal of Social and Clinical Psychology*, **11**, 122–125.

Epting, F. R. (1977). The loving experience and the creation of love. Paper presented at the Southeastern Psychological Association, Hollywood, Florida.

Epting, F. R. (1981). An appraisal of personal construct psychotherapy. In H. Bonarius, R. Holland, and S. Rosenberg (Eds.), *Personal Construct Psychology: Recent Advances in Theory and Practice*. London: Macmillan.

Epting, F. R., and Amerikaner, M. (1980). Optimal functioning: A personal construct approach. In A. W. Landfield and L. M. Leitner (Eds.), *Personal Construct Psychology: Psychotherapy and Personality*. New York: Wiley-Interscience.

Epting, F. R., and Boger, P. A. (1981). Personal construct psychotherapy. In R. J. Corsini (Ed.), *Handbook of Innovative Psychotherapies*. New York: John Wiley & Sons.

Epting, F. R., and Neimeyer, R. A. (1984). *Personal Meanings of Death*. New York: Hemisphere Publishing Corporation.

Epting, F. R., and Suchman, D. I. (1969). *Psychology: The study of experience*. Unpublished manuscript, University of Florida.

Fransella, F. (1972). *Personal Change and Reconstruction: Research and Treatment of Stuttering*. London and New York: Academic Press.

Fransella, F. (1981). Nature babbling to herself: The self characterisation as a therapeutic tool. In H. Bonarius, R. Holland, and S. Rosenberg (Eds.), *Personal Construct Psychology: Recent Advances in Theory and Practice*. London: Macmillan.

Fransella, F., and Bannister, D. (1977). *A Manual for Repertory Grid Technique*. London and New York: Academic Press.

Gendlin, E. T. (1962). *Experiencing and the Creation of Meaning*. New York: Macmillan.

Gendlin, E. T. (1977). Experiential focusing and the problem of getting movement in psychotherapy. In D. Nevill (Ed.), *Humanistic Psychology: New Frontiers*. New York: Gardner Press.

Girdano, D., and Everly, G. (1979). *Controlling Stress and Tension: A Holistic Approach*. New Jersey: Prentice-Hall.

Greenwald, H. (1973). *Decision Therapy*. New York: Wyden.

Hinkle, D. N. (1965). *The change of personal constructs from the viewpoint of a theory of implications*. Unpublished Ph.D. Thesis, Ohio State University.

Holdstock, T. L., and Rogers, C. R. (1977). Person-Centered theory. In R. J. Corsini (Ed.), *Current Personality Theories*. Itasca, Illinois: F. E. Peacock Publishers.

Huber, J. W., and Altmaier, E. M. (1983). An investigation of the self-statement systems of phobic and non-phobic individuals. *Cognitive Therapy and Research*, **7**.

Ivey, A. E. (1980). A person–environment view of counseling and psychotherapy: implications for social policy. In T. Marsella and P. Pedersen (Eds.), *Cross-Cultural Counseling and Psychotherapy*. New York: Pergamon.

Karst, T. O. (1980). The relationship between personal construct theory and psychotherapeutic techniques. In A. W. Landfield and L. M. Leitner (Eds.), *Personal Construct Psychology: Psychotherapy and Personality*. New York: Wiley.

Karst, T. O., and Trexler, L. D. (1970). Initial study using fixed role and rational-emotive therapy in treating speaking anxiety. *Journal of Consulting and Clinical Psychology*, **34**, 360–366.

Kelly, G. A. (1955). *The Psychology of Personal Constructs, Vols. I and II.* New York: W. W. Norton.

Kelly, G. A. (1958). Personal construct theory and the psychotherapeutic interview. In B. Maher (Ed.), *Clinical Psychology and Personality: The Selected Papers of George Kelly.* Huntington, NY: Robert E. Krieger, 1979.

Kelly, G. A. (1961). Suicide: The personal construct point of view. In N. Farberow and E. Schneidman (Eds.), *The Cry for Help.* New York: McGraw-Hill.

Kelly, G. A. (1962). In whom confide: On whom depend for what. In B. Maher (Ed.), *Clinical Psychology and Personality: The Selected Papers of George Kelly.* Huntington, NY: Robert E. Krieger, 1979.

Kelly, G. A. (1963). The autobiography of a theory. In B. Maher (Ed.), *Clinical Psychology and Personality: The Selected Papers of George Kelly.* Huntington, NY: Robert E. Krieger, 1979.

Kelly, G. A. (1964). The language of hypothesis: Man's psychological instrument. *Journal of Individual Psychology*, **20**, 137-152.

Kelly, G. A. (1965). The psychotherapeutic relationship. In B. Maher (Ed.), *Clinical Psychology and Personality: The Selected Papers of George Kelly.* Huntington, NY: Robert E. Krieger, 1979.

Kelly, G. A. (1966a). Ontological acceleration. In B. Maher (Ed.), *Clinical Psychology and Personality: The Selected Papers of George Kelly.* Huntington, NY: Robert E. Krieger, 1979.

Kelly, G. A. (1966b). A brief introduction to personal construct theory. In D. Bannister (Ed.), *Perspectives in Personal Construct Theory.* London and New York: Academic Press, 1970.

Kelly, G. A. (1970). Behaviour as an experiment. In D. Bannister (Ed.), *Perspectives in Personal Construct Theory.* London and New York: Academic Press.

Kelly, G. A. (1973). Fixed role therapy. In R. M. Jurjevich (Ed.), *Direct Psychotherapy: 28 American Originals.* Coral Gables: University of Miami Press.

Kelly, G. A. (1977). The psychology of the unknown. In D. Bannister (Ed.), *New Perspectives in Personal Construct Theory.* London and New York: Academic Press.

Kelly, G. A. (1980). A psychology of the optimal man. In A. W. Landfield and L. M. Leitner (Eds.), *Personal Construct Psychology: Psychotherapy and Personality.* New York: John Wiley & Sons.

Krieger, S. R., Epting, F. R., and Leitner, L. M. (1974). Personal constructs, threat and attitudes toward death. *Omega*, **5**, 299-310.

Landfield, A. W. (1971). *Personal Construct Systems in Psychotherapy.* Chicago: Rand McNally.

Landfield, A. W. (1975). The complaint: A confrontation of personal urgency and professional construction. In D. Bannister (Ed.), *Issues and Approaches in the Psychological Therapies.* London: John Wiley & Sons.

Landfield, A. W. (1977). Interpretive man: The enlarged self-image. In J. K. Cole and A. W. Landfield (Eds.), *1976 Nebraska Symposium on Motivation: Personal Construct Psychology.* Lincoln, Nebraska: University of Nebraska Press.

Landfield, A. W. (1978). Personal construct psychology: A theory to be elaborated. In M. Mahoney (Ed.), *Cognition and Clinical Science.* New York: Plenum Press.

Landfield, A. W. (1979). Exploring socialization through the interpersonal transaction group. In P. Stringer and D. Bannister (Eds.), *Constructs of Sociality and Individuality.* London and New York: Academic Press.

Landfield, A. W. (1980). The person as perspectivist, literalist, and chaotic fragmentalist. In A. W. Landfield and L. M. Leitner (Eds.), *Personal Construct Psychology: Psychotherapy and Personality.* New York: John Wiley & Sons.

Landfield, A. W. (1982). A construction of fragmentation and unity: The fragmentation corollary. In J. C. Mancuso and J. R. Adams-Webber (Eds.), *The Construing Person.* New York: Praeger Publishers.

196

Leitner, L. M. (1980). Personal construct treatment of a severely disturbed woman: The case of Sue. In A. W. Landfield and L. M. Leitner (Eds.), *Personal Construct Psychology: Psychotherapy and Personality*. New York: John Wiley & Sons.

Lira, F. T., Nay, W. R., McCullough, J. P., and Etkin, W. (1975). Relative effects of modeling and role playing in the treatment of avoidance behaviors. *Journal of Consulting and Clinical Psychology*, **43**, 608–618.

Livesley, W. J., and Bromley, D. B. (1973). *Person Perception in Childhood and Adolescence*. London: John Wiley & Sons.

Mahoney, M. J. (1977). Reflections on the cognitive-learning trend in psychotherapy. *American Psychologist*, **32**, 5–13.

Mair, J. M. M. (1970). Psychologists are human too. In D. Bannister (Ed.), *Perspectives in Personal Construct Theory*. London: Academic Press.

Mair, J. M. M. (1977). The community of self. In D. Bannister (Ed.), *New Perspectives in Personal Construct Theory*. London and New York: Academic Press.

Mair, M. (1976). Metaphors for living. In J. K. Cole and A. W. Landfield (Eds.), *1976 Nebraska Symposium on Motivation: Personal Construct Psychology*. Lincoln, Nebraska: University of Nebraska Press.

Mancuso, J. C. (1978). Counseling from a personal construct perspective. *International Journal for the Advancement of Counseling*, **1**, 303–313.

Mancuso, J. C. (1976). Current motivational models in the elaboration of personal construct theory. In J. K. Cole and A. W. Landfield (Eds.), *1976 Nebraska Symposium on Motivation: Personal Construct Psychology*. Lincoln, Nebraska: University of Nebraska Press.

Maslow, A. H. (1971). *The Farther Reaches of Human Nature*. New York: Viking Press.

McCoy, M. M. (1977). A reconstruction of emotion. In D. Bannister (Ed.), *New Perspectives in Personal Construct Theory*. London: Academic Press.

Meichenbaum, D. (1977). *Cognitive-Behavior Modification: An Integrative Approach*. New York: Plenum Press.

Meshoulam, U. (1977). *Stutterers' construing of speaking situations and non-speaking situations*. Unpublished Ph.D. Thesis, State University of New York at Albany.

Meshoulam, U. (1981). Reconstruing fluency: A constructivist approach to the treatment of stuttering. Presented at the Fourth International Congress on Personal Construct Psychology, Brock University, St. Catharines, Ontario, Canada.

Mischel, W. (1973). Toward a cognitive social learning reconceptualization of personality. *Psychological Review*, **80**, 252–283.

Morrison, J. K., and Cometa, M. S. (1971). Emotive-reconstruction psychotherapy: A short term cognitive approach. *American Journal of Psychotherapy*, **31**, 294–301.

Neimeyer, G. J. (1983). Couples' constructs: Personal systems and marital satisfaction. In D. Bannister (Ed.), *Perspectives in Personal Construct Theory Number Three*. London: Academic Press.

Neimeyer, G. J. and Neimeyer, R. A. (1981). Personal construct perspectives on cognitive assessment. In T. V. Merluzzi, C. Glass, and M. Genest (Eds.), *Cognitive Assessment*. New York: Guilford.

Neimeyer, R. A. (1980). George Kelly as therapist: A review of his tapes. In A. W. Landfield and L. M. Leitner (Eds.), *Personal Construct Psychology: Psychotherapy and Personality*. New York: John Wiley & Sons.

Oliver, D. W., and Landfield, A. W. (1962). Reflexivity: An unfaced issue in psychology. *Journal of Individual Psychology*, **18**, 114–124.

Patterson, C. H. (1980). *Theories of Counseling and Psychotherapy* (Third Edn). New York: Harper and Row.

Pervin, L. A. (1980). *Personality: Theory, Assessment, and Research*. New York: John Wiley & Sons.

Proctor, H. (1981). Family construct psychology: An approach to understanding and treating families. In S. Walrond-Skinner (Ed.), *Developments in Family Therapy: Theories and Applications Since 1948*. London: Routledge and Kegan Paul.

Ravenette, A. T. (1977). Personal construct theory: An approach to the psychological investigation of children and young people. In D. Bannister (Ed.), *New Perspectives in Personal Construct Theory*. London and New York: Academic Press.

Rigdon, M. A., and Epting, F. R. (1983). A personal construct perspective on an obsessive client. In J. R. Adams-Webber and J. C. Mancuso (Eds.), *Applications of Personal Construct Theory*. New York: Academic Press.

Rogers, C. R. (1959). A theory of therapy, personality, and interpersonal relationships as developed in the client centered framework. In S. Koch (Ed.), *Psychology: A Study of a Science. Vol. 3*. New York: McGraw-Hill.

Rogers, C. R. (1971). Intellectualized psychotherapy. In E. A. Southwell and M. Merbaum (Eds.), *Personality: Readings in Theory and Research. Second Edition*. Belmont, California: Brooks/Cole.

Rowe, D. (1978). *The Experience of Depression*. Chichester and New York: John Wiley & Sons.

Rowe, D. (1982). *The Construction of Life and Death*. Chichester: John Wiley & Sons.

Rychlak, J. F. (1973). *Introduction to Personality and Psychotherapy: A Theory-Construction Approach*. Boston: Houghton Mifflin.

Rychlak, J. F. (1977). *The Psychology of Rigorous Humanism*. New York: Wiley-Interscience.

Ryle, A. (1975). *Frames and Cages: The Repertory Grid Approach to Human Understanding*. London: University of Sussex Press.

Ryle, A. and Breen, D. (1972). A comparison of adjusted and maladjusted couples using the double dyad grid. *British Journal of Medical Psychology*, **45**, 375–382.

Simon, S. B., Howe, L. W., and Kirschenbaum, H. (1978). *Values Clarification: A Handbook of Practical Studies for Teachers and Students* (Revised Edn). New York: A. & W. Visual Library.

Skene, R. A. (1973). Construct shift in the treatment of a case of homosexuality. *British Journal of Medical Psychology*, **46**, 287–292.

Slater, P. (Ed.) (1976). *The Measurement of Intrapersonal Space by Grid Technique: Vol. 1. Explorations of Intrapersonal Space*. London and New York: John Wiley & Sons.

Slater, P. (Ed.) (1977). *The Measurement of Intrapersonal Space by Grid Technique: Vol. 2. Dimensions of Intrapersonal Space*. London and New York: John Wiley & Sons.

Spence, K. W. (1956). *Behavior Theory and Conditioning*. New Haven: Yale University Press.

Tschudi, F. (1977). Loaded and honest questions: A construct theory view of symptoms and therapy. In D. Bannister (Ed.), *New Perspectives in Personal Construct Theory*. London: Academic Press.

Warren, W. G. (1982). Personal construction of death and death education. *Death Education*, **6**, 17–28.

Wexler, D. A. (1974). A cognitive theory of experience, self-actualization, and therapeutic process. In D. A. Wexler and L. N. Rice (Eds.), *Innovations in Client Centered Therapy*. New York: John Wiley & Sons.

Wijesinghe, O. B. A., and Wood, R. R. (1976). A repertory grid study of interpersonal perception within a married couples psychotherapy group. *British Journal of Medical Psychology*, **49**, 287–293.

Williams, P. (1981). Outlining the relationship between attentional focusing, role model identification, and social-cognitive development: A personal construct analysis. Presented at the Fourth International Congress on Personal Construct Psychology, Brock University, St. Catharines, Ontario, Canada.

Wright, K. J. T. (1970). Exploring the uniqueness of common complaints. *British Journal of Medical Psychology*, **43**, 221–232.

Author Index

198

Subject Index